LEVERAGE OF THE WEAK

Social Movements, Protest, and Contention

Series Editor: Bert Klandermans, Free University, Amsterdam

Associate Editors: Ron R. Aminzade, University of Minnesota
David S. Meyer, University of California, Irvine
Verta A. Taylor, University of California, Santa Barbara

(continued on page 228)

LEVERAGE OF THE WEAK

Labor and Environmental Movements in Taiwan and South Korea

Hwa-Jen Liu

Social Movements, Protest, and Contention
Volume 42

University of Minnesota Press
Minneapolis • London

Portions of chapter 3 were published in "When Labor and Nature Strike Back: A Double Movement Saga in Taiwan," *Capitalism Nature Socialism* 22, no. 1 (2011): 22–39. Portions of chapter 5 were published in "Chongsin sikao yundongguiji: Taiwan yu nanhan de laogong yu huanjing yundong" [Rethinking movement trajectories: Labor and environmental movements in Taiwan and South Korea], *Taiwan shehueixue* [Taiwanese sociology] 16, no. 1 (2008): 1–47.

Published by the University of Minnesota Press
111 Third Avenue South, Suite 290
Minneapolis, MN 55401-2520
http://www.upress.umn.edu

Library of Congress Cataloging-in-Publication Data
Liu, Hwa-Jen.
Leverage of the weak: labor and environmental movements in
Taiwan and South Korea / Hwa-Jen Liu.
(Social movements, protest, and contention ; v. 42)
Includes bibliographical references and index.
ISBN 978-0-8166-8951-4 (hc)—ISBN 978-0-8166-8952-1 (pb : alk. paper)
1. Labor movement—Korea (South)—History. 2. Labor movement—Taiwan—
History. 3. Environmentalism—Korea (South)—History. 4. Environmentalism—
Taiwan—History. I. Title.
HD8730.5.Z8L58 2015
331.880951249—dc23   2014032697

Printed in the United States of America on acid-free paper

The University of Minnesota is an equal-opportunity educator and employer.

21 20 19 18 17 16 15   10 9 8 7 6 5 4 3 2 1

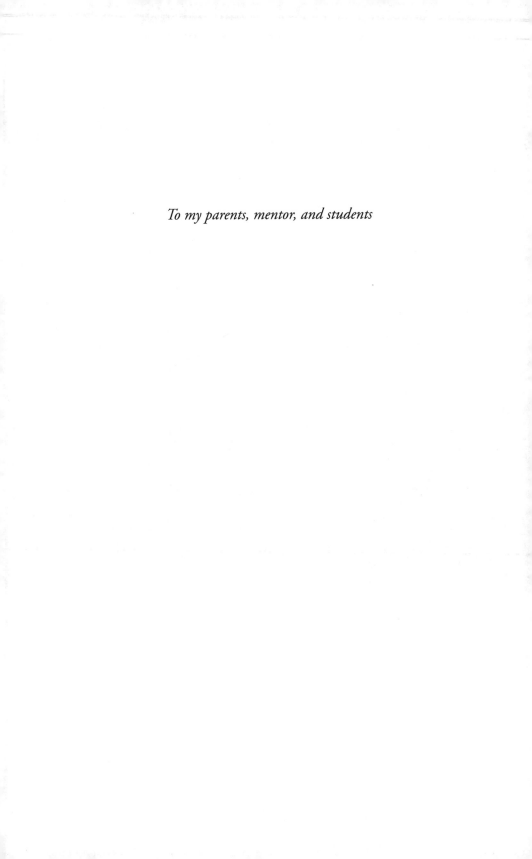

To my parents, mentor, and students

Contents

Acknowledgments

Completing this book convinces me that research and writing of any sort, no matter how lonely one may feel in the process, can never be an individual project. Every word I have written here is either a public salute to the many intellectual giants who came before me or a warm echo of brainy exchanges, cutting critiques, and margins full of densely written comments that inspired sleepless nights and bad headaches. Every word is an invitation to, as well as a product of, dialogue, repudiation, and transcendence.

The research for this book received financial support from public and private institutions. Foremost among them was the University of California at Berkeley, including the Graduate Division, the Institute of International Studies, and the Department of Sociology; and National Taiwan University, including the College of Social Sciences and the Department of Sociology. The Social Science Research Council, Academia Sinica, the Chiang Ching-Kuo Foundation, and the Fairbank Center for East Asian Research at Harvard University all supported the early data collection and fieldwork. The National Science Council provided research grants (NSC 97-2410-H-002-006-MY2, NSC 98-2410-H-002-128, NSC 99-2410-H-002-174-MY2, NSC 101-2410-H-002-102-MY3) for the collection of a comparable, time series protest data set on this book's four movements. If such generous financial support had been lacking, I would have been mired in economic necessity and toil, and this book would have remained a figment of my imagination.

This book owes a great debt of gratitude to those who provided intellectual guidance, logistic support, and encouragement at all stages. Michael Burawoy read and commented on earlier drafts of this project multiple times and maintained a level of enthusiasm and confidence in my project with which I could barely keep up. Peter B. Evans, Kim Voss, and Michael Watts offered expert advice and encouragement. Many friends provided valuable comments, including Carolyn Chen, Jennifer Chun, Matthew Garrett, Christel Kesler, Isaac Martin, Greggor Mattson, Gretchen Purser, Jeff Sallaz, Ofer Sharone, Cinzia Solari, Michelle Williams, and Kerry Woodward. Special thanks go to Elizabeth Popp Berman, Teresa Sharpe, Lisa Stampnitzky, and Youyenn Teo: they provided both witty conversations to cure writer's block and superb strategies to handle nasty comments from reviewers, and they are the best intellectual lifeline that one could ever hope to get.

I often reflect that it would have been difficult to enhance my understanding of Taiwan if it were not for Korea serving as a mirror, and vice versa. Many activists in labor and environmental circles spent hours talking to me, introduced me to their friends, guided me through the complex matrix of rapidly changing social life, and corrected my understanding of history and current affairs. In this regard, I am particularly grateful to Hee-Yeon Choi, Yeyong Choi, Jong-Hwan Kim, Yeojeong Kim, Dowan Ku, Song-Mau Ku, Weichieh Lai, Namju Lee, Yoonkyung Lee, Keon-Ho Ok, Chol-Soon Rhie, Kwang-Yeong Shin, Chih-Chieh Tsai, Jaeyoun Won, and Tung-Jye Wu.

Revisions of parts of this manuscript were helped by brilliant comments from audiences at the International Sociological Association, the Association for Asian Studies, the American Sociological Association, the Watson Institute at Brown University, the Fairbank Center at Harvard University, the Department of Sociology at Chung-Ang University, the Institute of Sociology at Academia Sinica, the Institute of Sociology at National Tsing-Hua University, and the Department of Sociology at National Sun Yat-sen University.

My past and current research assistants—Sheng-Han Chang, Yunchin Chiu, Han-Yu Fan, Hui-Tsen Hsiao, Chung-Hsuan Huang, Bo-Hsiun Hung, Yaching Hung, Helen Ko, Cheng-Cheng Wu, and Chia-Ying Wu—offered the most reliable support on data collection and analysis. They even brought food to feed me and nagged me about keeping to deadlines, and I thank them all. I am also grateful to Liam D'Arcy Brown, who provided invaluable editing help with humor and patience, and to those who prevented me from sinking in the strange ocean that is academic publishing, including Carolyn Chen, Dung-Sheng Chen, Peter Evans, Pei-Chia Lan, and Yenfeng Tseng. Talking to my brilliant friend Matthew Garrett is the best way to activate unused brain cells, no matter whether the subject matter is *Das Kapital* or a half-finished, crappy paper of mine. Thanks go to him for more than a decade of comradeship.

My parents, Mei-O Chen and Yang-han Liu, put up with my quirkiness and with love and trust let me do whatever I wanted to do. Michael Burawoy fundamentally reshaped my intellectual landscapes and inspired me to become a teacher. My students taught me, in and out of the classroom, how to enjoy life and stride toward a brighter future. This book is dedicated to them.

Note to Readers

Korean and Taiwanese personal names are written with the family name first, followed by the given name. I use the Revised Romanization (Ministry of Culture and Tourism, 2000) for Korean and the Pinyin system for Taiwanese (Mandarin Chinese), except for words and names that have their own commonly used orthography.

All translations of Korean and Taiwanese sources, including titles, are my own unless otherwise indicated.

All interviews were conducted in confidentiality, and the names of interviewees have been withheld by mutual agreement.

Abbreviations

DPP   Democratic Progressive Party (Taiwan)

EPA   Environmental Protection Agency (Taiwan)

FECF   Far Eastern Chemical Fibers (Taiwan)

FKTU   Federation of Korean Trade Unions

GCAA   Green Citizens' Action Alliance (Taiwan)

GFF   Green Formosa Front (Taiwan)

JOC   Jeunesse Ouvrière Chrétienne (Young Catholic Workers) (Korea)

KAPMA Korean Anti-Pollution Movement Association

KCIA   Korean Central Intelligence Agency

KCTU   Korean Confederation of Trade Unions

KFEM   Korean Federation of Environmental Movements

KMT   Kuomintang, the Nationalist Party (Taiwan)

PRI   Korean Pollution Research Institute

TCTU   Taiwan Confederation of Trade Unions

TEPU   Taiwanese Environmental Protection Union

UIM   Urban Industrial Mission (Korea)

Introduction: Strategic Comparison of Two Movements and Two Late Industrializers

Given the voluminous writings on social movements, both popular and academic, it is surprising how little we know about *movement sequences*—the temporal order of different movements coming into being. The stories of social movements, in most cases, have been delivered in such a way as to suggest that a lone warrior fights for justice and dignity in a sea of injustices and obstacles.[1] Yet from the perspective of movement sequences, warriors are never really alone. Each of them grows up amid the legends of elder warriors who have left either tearful memories or hope of triumph. This book is devoted to understanding how those early sagas come about and their impacts on subsequent warriors. I compare two distinct movement sequences in the context of rapidly industrializing Taiwan and South Korea (hereinafter Korea). In the Taiwanese case, environmental struggles precede the labor movement, whereas in the Korean case, labor activism leads and the environmental movement follows.

Comparing labor and environmental movements may seem like comparing apples and oranges, given their different constituencies and relations with the state and private capital. This pairing, however, is by no means a random choice. Labor and environmental movements tackle two key elements—labor power and nature—in capitalist production and are what Polanyi calls "social protectionist movements," emerging as a response to the assaults of market expansion and seeking to protect humans and nature from the negative effects of commercialization. "For a century the dynamics of modern society was governed by a double movement: the market expanded continuously but this movement was met by a countermovement checking the expansion in definite directions" (Polanyi 2001, 136). The basic plot of Polanyi's tale is that the self-regulating market, discursively supported by economic liberals, turned humans and nature into fictitious commodities. Rather than making everyone better off, the market created disasters for early industrializers on both sides of the Atlantic. The agricultural population was involuntarily released from the land and forced into the labor market; nature/land was put up for sale; the subsistence economy was smashed; social organizations— kinship, neighborhoods, guilds—were liquidated; and poverty, hunger, and all kinds of sufferings ensued (Polanyi 2001, 136–37, 171). However, for the sake of societal survival, protectionist movements struck back. Various social classes affected by the trend of market expansion and commercialization, including the landed classes, peasantry, and labor, came together to defend themselves and society as a whole.[2]

This Polanyian story holds contemporary relevance. Decades later, newly industrializing countries experienced their own double movement. Only this time around, the length of time a country took to revolutionize its production infrastructure and commodify its labor force and nature was greatly shortened, and as a consequence, the speed that labor discontent and environmental degradation knocked on the door was as swift as lightning.

A Reverse Sequencing Puzzle

On November 13, 1970, Chun Tae-Il, a Korean textile worker, led a ten-man demonstration in front of the Peace Market, protesting the dire working conditions common in the labor-intensive manufacturing sector for exports and demanding "a nine-hour workday with four days off a month" (*Korea Times* 1970). As the confrontation came to an end, Chun set himself on fire and shouted, "We are not machines! Enforce the labor code" (Cho 2003). Four months before Chun's self-immolation, a less dramatic action had been planned. Ninety-five Taiwanese farmers, led by their county heads and representatives, had petitioned the local government against a nearby food-processing facility that had discharged liquid toxins directly into the neighboring irrigation system, leading to tobacco and crop damage two years in a row. They had demanded financial compensation and relocation of this questionable facility (*China Times* 1970).

Neither Chun's nor the Taiwanese farmers' protest was an isolated incident. Chun's self-immolation and the struggles it inspired, led by female garment workers throughout the 1970s, heralded a budding democratic union movement and revealed acute capital-labor conflicts under the development scheme masterminded by the military junta. The farmers' episode, along with the sixty-four similar petitions, picketing, and confrontational action that took place in the same year, marked the first peak of Taiwan's antipollution mobilization, which aimed to curb unlimited industrial expansion under the auspices of the developmental state.

These two examples from Taiwan and Korea demonstrate contrasting patterns of protest. Using protest events reported in the *China Times* and the *Korea Times*, figures for both labor and environmental protests as percentages of the total number of all such protests in Taiwan and Korea can be calculated (for the methodology of protest data, please see the appendix). Fifty percent, then, indicates the equal presence of both types of protest in either country. On the labor side, Korea's labor protests were consistently beyond the 50 percent benchmark throughout the 1970s and the greater part of the 1980s, in contrast to the weak presence of Taiwan's labor from 1970 onward (Figure 1). On the environmental side, Taiwan's environmental protests dominated the scene starting from the early 1970s, while the weak presence of Korea's environmental protests is noted (Figure 2). This is further confirmed by a recent study that found that, among 4,553 protest events taking place in Korea between 1970 and 1992, labor issues accounted for 16.43 percent, whereas environmental issues did not even make it onto the list (Shin et al. 2007, 50–51; 2011, 30–31, Tables 2–4).

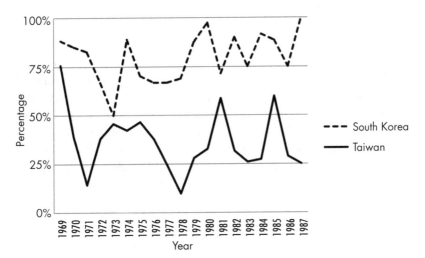

Figure 1. Percentage of labor protests in South Korea and Taiwan. Data for both countries were compiled by the author: Taiwan's data from the China Times *Fifty-Year Images Databank (http://140.112.152.45/ttsweb/) and Korea's data from the* Korea Times *and the* Korea Herald *microfilms archived in Harvard-Yenching Library, National Assembly Library of Korea, and National Taiwan University Library.*

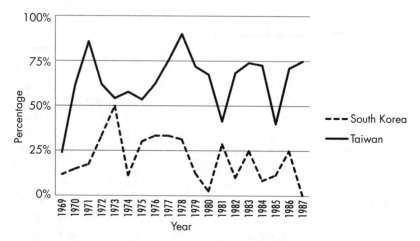

*Figure 2. Percentage of environmental protests in South Korea and Taiwan.
Data for both countries were compiled by the author: Taiwan's data from the*
China Times *Fifty-Year Images Databank (http://140.112.152.45/ttsweb/)
and Korea's data from the* Korea Times *and the* Korea Herald *microfilms
archived in Harvard-Yenching Library, National Assembly Library of Korea,
and National Taiwan University Library.*

Besides Korea's strong labor presence and Taiwan's strong environmental
presence in the wake of industrialization, the fluctuating year-by-year distribution of labor and environmental protests in each country reveals something even more. Looking at the period between 1961 and 1987 (Figure 3),
Taiwan's environmental protests rose to an initial peak in 1970, then fell
back, before they experienced a surge up to 1977, before finally reaching
the level of one environmental protest per day in 1984; throughout the
same period, Taiwan's labor remained relatively dormant. Not until 1984 did
Taiwan's labor go through a first surge of protest action, slowly building up
to a surge of labor strikes in 1988.

Korea's labor and environmental protests show opposite patterns (Figure
4). Looking at the period between 1969 and 1990, Korea's labor protests saw
their first wave in the early 1970s, around the time of Chun's self-immolation,
then a second surge in the late 1970s, finally peaking in 1987, when the
famous Great Workers' Offensive began. In contrast, Korea's environmental
protests during the same period of time showed neither great fluctuations nor
any great wave.

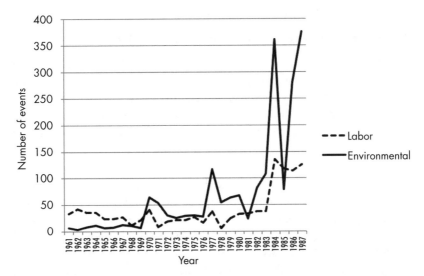

Figure 3. Frequency of Taiwan's labor and environmental protests. From the China Times *Fifty-Year Images Databank.*

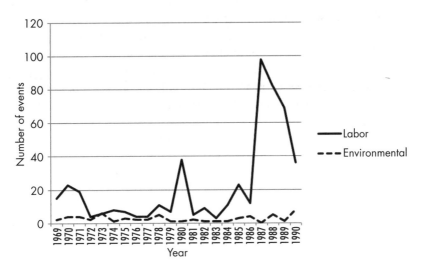

Figure 4. Frequency of Korea's labor and environmental protests. From Korea Times *and* Korea Herald *microfilms.*

If it can be ascertained that, first, Taiwan and Korea show different protest patterns and, second, Taiwan's labor protests lagged behind environmental protests, whereas in Korea, the opposite was true, the question remains, *Why?*

A Strategic Comparison across Movements and Countries

This book uses data from newspapers, government archives, interviews, and field observation to compare post–World War II labor and environmental movements in Taiwan and Korea, two countries that I would call "perfect twins" in the imperfect world of cross-national comparisons. Both were Japanese colonies[3] during the first half of the twentieth century, experienced divided statehood after World War II, and, from the perspective of international politics, became U.S. protégés under the geopolitical framework of the Cold War. On the domestic front, both countries were under the rule of decades-long authoritarian dictatorships in the second half of the twentieth century, experienced some sort of regime crisis in the early 1970s, and joined in the "third-wave democratization" to restructure their domestic political landscapes in the late 1980s.

As far as other social and economic indicators are concerned (numeric data are presented in Table 1), they also show striking similarities. Both countries are densely populated, are resource poor, and have had a comparable rate of population growth in the past three decades. They underwent the process of industrialization at roughly the same time and at similar speeds, as indicated through the change of sectoral shares in gross domestic product (GDP) and the shifting composition of the labor force over time. They were incorporated into the world economy after World War II and adopted an explicitly export-oriented industrialization strategy, given their comparable growth rates of manufactured exports. Considering the growth rates in GDP and the increase in per capita gross national income/gross national product (GNP), the overall national wealth of both countries was accumulated at such a rapid speed that both induced wonderment in international development agencies (World Bank 1993) and envy in other late-industrializing countries.

So despite all the structural similarities, it is curious that we can observe two such distinct sequences—in reverse order, in fact—in the rise of labor and environmental movements in these two countries. Through this paired comparison, a few things immediately catch our attention. First, there is nearly a decadelong hiatus between the appearances of early risers and latecomer movements. Second, there is plenty of evidence attesting to the coexistence of labor and environmental grievances in the 1970s; but whereas Korea's labor and Taiwan's environmental movements began to take shape, Korea's environmental degradation and Taiwan's labor plight did not arouse a comparable

Table 1. Macro-socioeconomic indicators of Taiwan and Korea

	Taiwan[a]	Korea[b]
Area (km^2)	36,188	99,538
Population (million)/density (person/km^2)		
1970 (Taiwan: 1972)	15.27/425	32.24/328
1980	17.81/495	38.12/385
1990	20.40/564	42.87/432
2000	22.28/616	47.00/473
Distribution of GDP by sector (agriculture/industry/services in %)		
1970	15.5/36.8/47.7	—/—/—
1980[c]	7.7/45.7/46.6	14.9/41.3/43.7
1990[c]	4.2/41.2/54.6	8.5/43.1/48.4
2000[c]	1.9/30.9/67.2	4.4/41.4/54.1
Distribution of labor force by sector (agriculture/industry/services in %)		
1970 (Taiwan: 1972)	33.0/31.9/35.2	50.3/14.3/35.3
1980	19.5/42.5/38.0	34.0/22.5/43.5
1990	12.9/40.8/46.3	17.9/27.6/54.5
2000[c]	7.8/37.2/55.0	10.6/20.3/69.0
EAP[d] by gender (female/male %)		
1980[c]	39/77	48/76
1990[c]	45/74	48/75
2000[c]	46/69	53/76
Average annual growth rate in GDP (%)		
1960–1970[e]	9.2	8.6
1971–1980	9.8	7.3
1981–1990	8.0	8.7
1991–2000	6.4	6.2
Per capital GNI[f] (U.S. dollars)		
1970 (Taiwan: 1971)	443	254
1980	2,155	1,645
1990	7,413	6.147
2000	12,916	10,841
Average growth rate of manufactured exports (%)		
1971–1980	—	39.9[g]
1981–1990	13.9	15.1[g]
1991–2000	8.9	10.3[g]

[a] Data from *Statistical Yearbook of Republic of China*, 2002 and 2003, Republic of China National Statistics at http://www.stat.gov.tw/, and online databases of Directorate-General of Budget, Accounting, and Statistics at http://ebas1.ebas.gov.tw/. [b]Data from *Statistical Handbook of Korea*, 2002, and online databases at Korea National Statistical Office at http://kostat.go.kr/. [c]Asian Development Bank, Key Indicators, 1999–2004, at http://www.adb.org/. [d]Economic active population (percentage of working-age population). [e]Data from Barrett and Chin (1987, 26). [f]Formerly per capita GNP. [g]World Bank, World Development Indicators, http://www.worldbank.org/.

level of public passion until much later. Third, the latecomer movements—
Korea's environmental and Taiwan's labor movements—did not become a
potent force challenging the state and market until after the democratic transition of each country in the late 1980s.

These being two settings with such similarities only makes the variations
over movement sequence even more conspicuous and unexpected, and Mill's
"method of difference"[4] finds two wonderful test cases. Or, in Ragin's language, the logic of inquiry in this case is that "two cases may appear to be
very similar and yet experience different outcomes . . . the goal is to identify
the difference that is responsible for contradictory outcomes" (Ragin 1987,
47). Furthermore, being in the same "development cohort" in the post–
World War II era, with a geographic proximity that was supposed to exert
stronger mutual influences, and given that the objective of inquiry is to
explain "difference" instead of "agreement," the comparison of Taiwan and
Korea may withstand regular critiques of cross-national comparisons such as
"freezing the history" (Burawoy 1989) or cross-case contamination[5] (Lieberson 1985).

Why and how did the two movement sequences come about, and furthermore, what were the long-term consequences of each of them? These
are the leading questions for this book. Why does the order of movement
sequences matter? From a path-dependent point of view, different starting
points narrow possible choices of action in the subsequent periods and may
very likely exert decisive effects in shaping either the following events or the
environment in which these events take place (Nelson 1995; Pierson 2000).
Labor and environmental movements provide two sets of devastating critiques against capitalism and the most fully articulated alternative visions for
a future society. Labor and environmental movements, distinct from other
social movements, are the most likely courses of action successfully to transcend full-blown capitalism. To understand how labor and environmental
movements evolve and mutually influence each other will help us envisage a
better society to come.

In addition, outlining distinct sequences challenges the implicit conviction that labor movements universally arise earlier than environmental
movements, regardless of the contexts of early industrializing and newly
industrializing countries. On one hand, though this conviction is by and
large confirmed by historical facts among the early industrializers, it simply
misses a good portion of other possibilities. Bramwell asserts that ecological ideas have arisen on the European continent since the mid-nineteenth
century (Bramwell 1989, chapter 1); but in contrast to the working-class
resonance with revolutionary ideas in 1848 and 1871, ecological thought was

confined to the European educated classes—we did not witness a genuine green movement backed by popular mobilization until the 1960s and 1970s. Why did it take so long for ecological ideas to congeal into social forms among early industrializers? In other words, the latecomer status of green movements in contrast to labor movements is a historical question to be explained, not a textbook fact to be assumed. On the other hand, among the newly industrializing countries, we observe either the simultaneous appearance of labor and environmental struggles—as in India and Brazil— or a case like Taiwan, with an environment-then-labor sequence that defies normal expectations. The paired comparison—both cross-national and cross-movement—represents a conscious endeavor to problematize the assumed universal sequence of labor and environmental movements and urges students of social movements to pay close attention to the social mechanisms through which different movement sequences are produced in the first place.

What Is to Come

The reverse sequencing of labor and environmental movements leads to three areas of empirical inquiry. First, I analyze the origins of the movement sequences to explain why one particular movement became the early riser. Next, I probe into the consequences of the sequencing. With different early-riser movements paving the way ahead, I highlight the differential impact on the succeeding movements. Finally, I examine the life "trajectory" of each movement. By observing how each of the four movements experienced setbacks, reoriented itself, and overcame obstacles, I address why the two labor movements shared a very similar trajectory in stark contrast to that of their environmental counterparts.

I use *movement power* as the organizing concept of this book and throughout all three areas of inquiry. Different types of movement power exercised by labor and environmental movements are key to explaining the reverse sequencing and contrasting movement trajectories. Seeing movement formation as a process in which each social movement breaks out of institutional confines through the exercise of its power, I argue that each early-riser movement takes advantage of a relative lack of structural constraint in the location that corresponds to its specific and respective form of movement power. This early-riser movement would then leave an organizational and cultural legacy (a product of the early riser's need to expand its power base) to the latecomer movement, which would selectively appropriate that legacy according to its own needs in exercising its unique movement power. The contrasting trajectories that labor and environmental movements have undergone in the past three decades have also resulted from their respective endeavors to maximize different types of movement power and to transcend the limits imposed by their own power-maximizing practices.

Chapter 1 provides an overview of the existing literature on social movements and argues that social movements as collective actors rooted in human associations derive their power from different sources. A movement may either derive power from the structural position its constituency occupies or gain power from ideas and ideology that it commands to solicit cross-sectional, popular consent. Labor and environmental movements exemplify these two sources of power in the purest form. A labor movement builds solidarity along class lines, and the leverage it wields rests on the indispensable role of workers in capitalist production; the power basis for an environmental movement, conversely, rests on one's voluntary consent to certain green ideas. The extent to which environmental movements may exercise ideological power depends on their discursive and persuasive capacities. Successful movement making depends on certain combinations of structural and ideological powers that the movement may summon. Yet this point does not repudiate the fact that labor movements depend more on structural leverage, whereas ideological power is an environmental movement's forte. Over time, the issue becomes, once the existing power bases eroded, how to compensate the loss by acquiring new sources of power and consolidating the old ones.

Chapter 2 investigates disparate sets of existing works on the emergence of the four movements. Given that how to define "movement emergence" empirically is a contested issue in social movement literature, with most scholarly works on these four movements deploying different criteria to define movement emergence, I define the formation of social movements as a process of breaking out of existing institutional confines and then put forth a synthetic account in which "movement emergence" is conceptually and empirically understood as the synchronization of protest actions and oppositional consciousness. I present time series data to identify the periods of "protest escalation" and situate protest actions in the context of the rise of new public discourse and consciousness.

Chapter 3 tackles the discrepancy of movement emergence. If movement formation means breaking out of institutional confines, early-riser movements are those that state action and the pattern of industrialization were unable to prevent from consolidating their power base. Taiwan's incorporationist control scheme and decentralized industrialization "stunted" labor disputes to such an extent that the workers' chances of exercising leverage and extending solidarity were minimized. Workers at large corporations and strategic industries were closely monitored. Labor disputes breaking out at unorganized and geographically scattered small enterprises were so tiny that the system of compulsory arbitration easily hoovered them up. Yet at the same time, Taiwan's industrial structure entailed a spatial dimension rendering the same techniques of control much less effective at reducing the ideological power of an environmental movement. The fact that industrial establishments were geographically scattered led to numerous pollution disputes and shared pollution experiences by different sections of the population—a fertile ground on which to build ideological power.

The Korean case presents an opposite scenario. Korea's exclusionist approach and centralized industrialization undercut an environmental movement's ideological power for two reasons. First, pollution cases were geographically concentrated owing to uneven regional development, which also made pollution experiences less commonly shared. Second, the military junta resolved pollution disputes by relocating pollution victims elsewhere, a strategy that diminished the possibility of sustaining an urban–rural antipollution coalition. But ironically, the same control scheme placed workers in a better position to exercise leverage, given the size of industrial establishments and their geographical concentration. The government further thwarted the chances of class compromise by setting caps on wage increases, and repressive measures were resolutely out as laborers protested. This only led workers to build up leverage power so as to break out of the institutional deadlock. The more severely the government quelled workers by force, the more forcefully the next-round labor struggle bounced back.

Chapter 4 looks into the relationships between early-riser and latecomer movements. Early-riser movements would formulate a model of "how to do politics" that succeeding movements would imitate, and this very model would condition how succeeding movements situated themselves in relation to institutional arrangements and political authorities. In other words, the success of early-riser movements would induce latecomer movements to copy the formers' "home advantage." When Taiwan's environmental movement maneuvered its way by gaining limited concessions and building political allies through the electoral system, the labor movement immediately followed suit. As Korea's labor movement was historically excluded from the political arena and developed a strong ethos of self-organization and militancy, the environmental movement gained the propensity to organize aggressively. Conversely, the simple existence of early-riser movements may affect the state's treatment of successor movements. As those succeeding movements imitated the successful strategies of the early risers, governments reversed their policies to deal with latecomer movements, because the old strategy had clearly failed to extinguish the early risers. The Taiwanese government shifted

[handwritten margin note: labor is scarce to elites]

toward repression against labor from its previous position of noninterference in environmental matters, whereas the Korean government sought to incorporate the environmental agenda in contrast to its wholesale repression of organized labor early on. In response to such changes in state action, latecomer movements first engage in a new round of strategic adjustments to cope with new situations, only later seeking to strike a balance between applying the early-riser model and trying out other strategies that best serve to maximize their bargaining powers.

Chapter 5 compares the distinct trajectories of labor and environmental movements. Labor movements began by fighting for economic rights and then moved toward the realm of ideological struggles, whereas environmental movements started from ideological struggles and then shifted toward building leverage against economic–corporate power. The trajectories of labor and environmental movements are first steered toward maximizing leverage and ideological powers and subsequently toward transcending the limits that each of those powers has imposed. The maximization of movement power is most obviously seen in the shift of leadership. In the wake of movement expansion, labor unions in heavy or strategic industries—which were in the best position to exercise labor's leverage—became the dominant force inside both labor movements, replacing the leading role that workers in the labor-intensive sector had played early on. As for environmental movements, urban intellectuals and the "educated" class, who were best equipped to exercise discursive and ideological power, quickly replaced the central role of pollution victims and took the helm.

But maximizing one type of movement power comes with a price. The winning of wage negotiations through strikes was often construed as a self-interested action detached from general social interests. And as environmental discourses became so well accepted that even major developers began to appropriate environmental symbols, both environmental movements, ironically, faced the challenge of dealing with issues on which consensus was not easily reached, such as nuclear energy policies and distributive justice.

The paths that the labor and environmental movements have traveled in the past three decades in truth present a mirror image. The two labor movements strove to elevate themselves above economic–corporate struggles to winning ideological battles by presenting their interests as the interests of all under hostile, antilabor milieux; the two environmental movements, after successfully interweaving environment and nature into dominant ideologies, struggled to realize their ecological visions in concrete practices at the economic–corporate level, which revolved around troubling issues such as distributive justice.

The conclusion uses this strategic comparison to point out broader ramifications and reflect on the outlook of labor and environmental movements in the twenty-first century. This comparison, first, pushes us to think more systematically about the relationships between regime types and vanguard social movements and about whether political regimes have different Achilles' heels and come equipped with varied capacities to quell different insurgencies. Second, the fact that the contrast between leverage and ideological power is so far embedded in the context of late industrializers prompts us to ask if the pace, timing, and form of industrialization exert decisive impacts on how leverage and ideological powers are played out. The logical step is to look into the different historical experiences of early industrializers. Finally, it is still an open question whether we may apply the contrast between leverage and ideological power to other social movements. For future inquiry, one might analyze how each movement operates with a certain combination of leverage and ideology and take one step further and look for sources of movement power besides the two specified in this book.

In this "99 percent versus 1 percent" world of the twenty-first century, this study also points to the importance of cross-movement coalition, which many have discussed before (Evans 2005; Obach 2004; Rathzel and Uzzell 2011, 2012; Van Dyke and McCammon 2010). It certainly takes effort to recognize each movement's strength, weakness, and historical flaws to make genuine coalition building possible. For labor and environment, this book means to bridge the gulf.

1

The Power Bases of Labor and Environmental Movements

From the various historical accounts, labor and environmental movements appear quite different. If we make an ideal-typical distinction (see Figure 5), they have different constituencies, associational forms,[1] and targets of protection. In addition, they follow different organizing principles and seek to realize different types of solidarity to consolidate their power bases. They pose different degrees of threat to the authorities and are treated accordingly. They articulate different sets of social interests and construct distinct self-images, and as a result, the public perceives and receives them differently.

How are these differences connected to our reverse sequencing? In this chapter, I look for viable conceptual tools in the literature of social movements and sociology of development and engage in theoretical reconstruction. I suggest that we look for the specificities of labor and environmental movements, and by movement specificity, I refer to the essential characteristics that set labor movements apart from other social movements and separate environmental movements from the rest. I contend that each social movement has its unique power base and that the power bases of labor and environment vary in a patterned manner. By looking closely into the specific power bases of labor and environmental movements, we may begin to shed light on varying patterns of interaction between social movements and their institutional surroundings.

There are two sources for building a movement's collective power: one is structural positions, the other ideology. *Leverage* is the power derived from the indispensability of one's structural position, whereas ideological power derives from the persuasive works of ideologies. The way that labor movements

	Labor Movements	Environmental Movements
Power base	Leverage derived from structural positions	Ideology entailing universalistic ideas and broad persuasion
Constituencies	Wage laborers	Pollution victims and the educated class
Main associational forms	Labor unions	Voluntary civic associations
Target of protection	Labor power as private property embodied in individuals to be traded in the labor market	Environment/nature as collective good and communal properties, given its indivisible character
Organizing principles	Members' willingness to pay and to act (go on strike)	Swaying public opinion through the means of mass communication
Type of solidarity	Solidarity within the working class	Outreach and cross-sectional alliance

Figure 5. Differences between labor and environmental movements.

rely on the power of leverage is in direct parallel to the way that environmental movements rely on ideological power. Furthermore, the two types of movement power should be understood in the context of Gramsci's analysis of the formation of a collective actor—how it evolves from the economic–corporate to economic class and finally to the hegemonic (universal social interest) level (Gramsci 1971, 181–82). Leverage is rooted at the economic–corporate level, where the very location of a collective actor in an interdependent relationship with its opponents provides the foundation for its exercise of power. Ideological power, conversely, is situated at the hegemonic level, where transcendent and universalistic ideas elicit popular consent across different sections of the population by elaborating lived experiences and presenting a better working model in moving toward universal interests. Taking Gramsci's formulation as a point of departure, I maintain that labor and environmental movements begin their career of movement making at different entry points. Labor starts from the economic–corporate level and environmental movements from the hegemonic level. Furthermore, the progression between the economic–corporate and hegemonic moments is not a one-way street, as Gramsci originally prescribed. If labor movements have to transcend the limits of self-interested action to represent the interests of other subordinate groups, environmental movements face the challenge of moving from universal claim making to consolidating the basis of social support and dealing in concrete terms with the issue of redistributive justice.

Retrieving Movement Specificity

Working on two movements as different as labor and environment, one's first instinct is to look for any theorizing that captures the specificity of each movement and the differences between them. The next step is to explore whether their very specificities and differences play any role in the movement-making process. From the bulky corpus of social movement studies, we find two polarized approaches. Most empirical research is inattentive to the issues of movement specificity because research design and methodological choices prevent it from being so. Conversely, discussions of movement specificity are often featured in more theory-oriented works, but the criteria used to distinguish one type of movement from another oftentimes have trouble withstanding empirical scrutiny. In the following, I discuss in turn these two different approaches.

Empirical Works, Research Methods, Disappearance of Specificity

Social movement studies comprises four types of research designs, typologized by the number of movements and the number of locations under scrutiny (see Figure 6). Each is biased, in its own way, against the issue of movement specificity. The first type of research design documents the rise and development of one particular movement in one particular location.[2] This type of study may be historical in nature, but not always; this type may also study the internal variation within the movement in question, but again, not always. The most prominent examples include the civil rights movement (McAdam 1999b; Morris 1984; Payne 1995), environmental movements (Broadbent 1998; Jamison, Eyerman, and Cramer 1990; McKean 1981; Szasz 1994; Walsh 1981), labor movements (Chakrabarty 1988, 1989; Fantasia 1988; Voss 1993), women's movements (Freeman 1975; Staggenborg 1988; Taylor 1989), and student movements (Gitlin 1980; Zhao 2001). Single-movement studies as such are at a disadvantage when it comes to tackling movement specificity, owing to a lack of explicit, external comparison

		Number of locations covered	
		One	More than one
Number of movements studied	One	(I) Single-movement, single-location studies	(II) Single-movement, cross-location studies
	More than one	(III) Multiple-movement, single-location studies	(IV) Multiple-movement, cross-location studies

Figure 6. Four research designs of social movement research.

with other movements. McAdam's excellent work cannot illuminate the uniqueness of the civil rights movement and how it differs from women's, peace, and antiwar movements. Marc Bloch once said that we could never arrive at a complete understanding of "the English open field system, the German *Gewanndorf*, or the French *champs ouverts* by examining England, Germany or France *alone*" (Bloch 1969, 70). The same principle applies in that a complete understanding of any social movement cannot be achieved by studying the movement alone.

The second type of research design is the single-movement, cross-location study, and in my estimation, this is the most popular choice among students of social movements. Here I choose the word *location* on purpose, because the geographic units of analysis vary greatly, ranging from nation-states and subunits within a nation-state (counties, cities, regions, and provinces) through to continents. Prominent examples include labor movements in newly industrializing Asian countries (Deyo 1989, 2012; Y. Lee 2011), women's movements in the United States and Western Europe (Katzenstein 1987), the civil rights movement in various counties of Mississippi (Andrews 2004), women's movements in two Indian cities (Ray 1998), and antinuclear movements in four democracies (Kitschelt 1986).[3] The main line of inquiry centers on one question *only*: why does the same movement "perform" differently—in terms of levels of mobilization, issue selections, impacts on political structures, and relationships with established political players—in different locations? More often than not, single-movement, cross-location studies end up explaining movement variations in terms of the variation of external contexts. Characteristics of political opportunity structures (Kitschelt 1986), linkages with political parties and the role of labor within the state (Katzenstein 1987), characteristics of the field in which each movement is embedded (Ray 1999), repression and economic vulnerability of the black population (Andrews 2004), or the social organization of production and the types of state intervention (Deyo 1989) are all enlisted to explain the variation of movement performance in different locales.

This particular research design has two potential biases. First, because the movements compared are the same, explanations from "outside" are favored when accounting for different outcomes. By favoring external explanations, this research design tends to give a backseat to such internal explanations as leadership, political skills, membership compositions, factional struggles, and strategic capacities. Second, single-movement, different-location comparisons are biased toward explaining differences. The reason to be cautious of this bias is simple: apples and oranges are different, but both are fruit; cats and dogs are different, but they both belong to the order Carnivora. Beneath all kinds of differences, there are curious commonalities waiting to be explored, and vice versa. In a nutshell, the specificity of the movement remains obscure, owing to a lack of external comparison with other movements.

The third type of research design involves multiple movements at a single location and usually follows either of the two lines of inquiry. The first line brackets a group of movements emerging at different points in time into a particular protest cycle. This line of inquiry pushes for further understanding of mutual influences between early-riser and latecomer movements, the direction of such influences, and the mechanisms through which such influences are transmitted. The dominant formulae of the relationship between early-riser and latecomer movements are developed along the line of positive-sum relations, no matter whether from early risers to latecomers, or vice versa. According to Tarrow (1994, 155–56), early risers demonstrate the vulnerability of authorities and broaden the political space in which latecomers may maneuver. Early risers pretest a range of repertoires of collective action and explore possible allies that latecomers may selectively appropriate. The increase in collective action leads to the creation of new organizations and the radicalization of old ones. In a series of studies of the U.S. civil rights movement, McAdam (1988, 1995, 1999a) unequivocally takes the position that the civil rights movement was the root of later movements such as student, feminist, antiwar, and gay rights, forging a master frame on which latecomers depended. "Initiator movements encourage the rise of latecomers . . . by setting in motion complex diffusion processes by which the ideational, tactical, and organizational 'lessons' of the early risers are made available to subsequent challengers," whereas latecomers are "creative adapters and interpreters of the cultural 'lessons' of the early risers" (McAdam 1995, 226, 229). The theses on "social movement spillover" (Meyer and Whittier 1994) and "organizational density" (Minkoff 1997), furthermore, clarify the mechanism of transmission from early risers to latecomers: overlapped personnel, shared master frames, and so on. Another piece addresses the effect of latecomers on early risers (Isaac and Christiansen 2002), its authors maintaining that the newly ascendant civil rights movements revitalized the older, institutionalized labor movement, especially laborers in the public sector. The positive-sum findings, however, are far from conclusive, and deviant cases have been reported.[4] All in all, this approach has neither attended to the question of why certain movements arise early in the first place nor provided an explanation as to whether different early-riser movements impact succeeding movements differently.

In the second line, that of multiple-movement, single-location studies, multiple movements are purposely selected to illustrate a broader, common

theme. In other words, this approach means to get past the "illusory difference" to study "the underlying similarities between relatively dissimilar
objects" (Ragin 1987, 47). Thus two movements as different as Pentecostal-
ism and Black Power could still lead Gerlach and Hine (1970) to conclude
their similarity in organizational and ideological features. The juxtaposition
of civil rights, student, welfare rights, and women's liberation movements
can point to shared elements in movement formation (Freeman 1999). In
Poor People's Movements, the unemployed, industrial workers', civil rights, and
welfare rights movements were cited to prove the centrality of disruptive
powers in the struggles of the disadvantaged and the danger of substituting
direct action with formal organizations (Piven and Cloward 1979). In *The
Art of Moral Protest,* animal rights, ecological, and antinuclear movements
are used as examples of the "postcitizenship movement" to illustrate similar
cultural dynamics in the process of movement making (Jasper 1997). In the
first two cases (Gerlach and Hine 1970; Freeman 1999), multiple movements are used to construct general theses on movement dynamics. The
latter two cases (Piven and Cloward 1979; Jasper 1997) go one step further
to construct movement "subtypes." Even though multiple movements were
studied, the overall purpose was not to compare internally the selected movements but to highlight the distinctive features they shared. As a consequence,
among multiple-movement, single-location studies, the specificity of a single
movement remains a buried issue.

The fourth research design—multiple-movement, cross-location studies—still only rarely draws attention to the issue of movement specificity. In
the following, we examine in detail the works from Rucht (1996), della Porta
and Rucht (1995), and Kriesi et al. (1995), three separate studies on a variety
of "new social movements" in different countries. Rucht and della Porta
and Rucht place explanatory primacy exclusively on ultramovement, contextual factors, just as the single-movement, cross-location studies do. Kriesi
et al.'s study is so far the only exception, attending to both contextual explanations and movement specificity.

In his study of environmental and women's movements in France, Germany, and the United States, Rucht (1996) constructs three types of movement structure—grassroots, interest group, and party oriented—to capture
the cross-national variation of environmental and women's movements. Rucht
argues that, in each country, social movements' strategies and practices are
mediated through a unique movement structure inadvertently developed
in response to a peculiar yet relatively stable national context. Given the degree of permeability of political systems, state capacity in policy implemen-
tation, existence of movement alliance, and countermovement (190, 200),
"the French movement was strongest in the party-model, the United States

in the interest-group model, and the German movement a balance of all three" (202). Given the centrality of movement structures (as a mediating factor between micropractices of movements and broader contexts) and contextual structures, differences between women's and environmental movements are mentioned in passing yet carry no analytical or explanatory weight in the overall framework.

Della Porta and Rucht (1995) shift the focus of analysis from a single movement to a cluster of movements and examine a particular "social movement family"—left-libertarian students', women's, ecology, and peace movements—in Italy and Germany. Their main interest lies in explaining the parallel behavioral shift of left-libertarian movements in both countries according to the change of alliance systems (left-wing parties) and conflict systems (conservative parties and countermovement). They find that either a conservative party's move to the right or the presence of countermovement elicits radical responses from left-libertarian movements (261). If left-wing parties move to the center and leave left-libertarian movements with less access to political decision making, the movements tend to radicalize as well. Yet if the access to political power is granted and the left–right conflict is smoothed out, left-libertarian movements tend to deradicalize (269). Once again, differences between the four target movements—particularly the timing of movement emergence and the level of mobilization—receive no systematic treatment (256).

Kriesi et al. (1995), however, provide a welcome surprise. Though mainly aiming to explain the varying mobilization patterns of new social movements in France, Germany, the Netherlands, and Switzerland, they devote one whole chapter to discussing movement types (82–110). On the basis of the logic of action and general orientation of the movement, they use three movement types—instrumental, subcultural, and countercultural—to categorize the five movements studied. The most crucial point is that, within the same national context, movements of different types show varying levels of mobilization (87), develop different action repertoires (89), react to political authorities and the change of political opportunities in different manners, and receive varying degrees of support from political allies (91). Movement types matter, Kriesi et al. argue, because movements perceive and respond to their institutional surroundings in terms of their own logic of action and general orientation, and political authorities "have a specific reaction pattern to each movement type as well: authorities are well aware of the different degree to which the types of movements pose a direct challenge" (109). Besides movement types, they further differentiate the category of instrumental movements into "high-profile" and "low-profile" movements, based on the characteristics of policy agendas that different instrumental movements put forth, and they demonstrate the striking differences between the two types of instrumental movements (96–108).

Kriesi et al.'s work is the only empirical work to focus on broader political contexts without losing sight of individual movements' characteristics. They even enlist movement specificity as an independent variable to explain cross-movement variations. Several important lessons can be learned from their work. First, the reason that contextual factors are not movement-neutral is because of the mediating effect of individual movements' own characteristics and dispositions. Second, movement differences should not always assume the status of dependent variable; at times it can be an effective independent variable in explaining cross-movement variation. Despite my admiration for their work, problems arise if we squeeze labor movements into Kriesi et al.'s typology. Both labor and environmental movements will be classified as instrumental movements, with a mixture of high-profile and low-profile policy agendas. The extent to which Kriesi et al.'s typology, based on five new social movements, helps us differentiate labor and environmental movements is limited.

Theoretical Construction and Movement Typologies

When we turn to theory-oriented works for discussions of movement typologies that cover the specificities of individual movements and the differences between them,[5] the often encountered problem is that the criteria of distinction are empirically disputable. The most notorious case is probably the comparison between "old" and "new" social movements addressing different types of social contradictions in response to the transition from industrial to postindustrial societies (Cohen 1985; Melucci 1985; Offe 1985; Touraine 1981). Class-based and identity-based movements have distinct bases of social support and fight for different ends—economic distribution versus cultural transformation. Yet this distinction between old and new has been empirically challenged, if not discredited (Calhoun 1993; Pichardo 1997).

Later theoretical formulations of movement typologies are more modest compared to the sweeping new social movement approach. But the criteria used to differentiate social movements and to pinpoint movement specificity are very similar, including the social bases of movements (or social locations of movement participants) and movement goals.

Jasper proposes a distinction between citizenship and postcitizenship movements. The citizenship movements are organized by social groups excluded from full citizenship, including workers, women, and ethnic minorities. The ultimate goal of this type of movement is to achieve a state of full inclusion. The postcitizenship movements are composed of people who have already been fully integrated into the social system, and this type of movement pursues protections and benefits for others and includes movements around the environment, disarmament, and animal rights (Jasper 1997, 7).[6] According to another account, Morris and Braine (2001) maintain that the relationship between social movements and the system of domination are key to constructing movement typology. Those who are historically subjected to a subordinate position because of their social identifiers, such as race, class, gender, and ethnicity, are buttressed by a preexisting culture of opposition and strong group identification. Subsequently, they become the carriers of liberation movements aiming to overthrow a system of domination. Equality-based special issue movements are seen as a subset of the liberation movements, aiming at a limited battle, such as the pro-choice and the grassroots AIDS movements. Finally, the participants of social responsibility movements, such as antinuclear and peace, are not directly connected to any system of domination and voluntarily choose to assume the appropriate movement identity through self-education.

Yet in what ways these formulations help us understand the reverse sequencing of labor and environmental movements in Taiwan and Korea is not entirely clear. The new social movement theory subscribes to a linear understanding of societal evolution and in this unique context there is only *one* movement sequence: labor movements were by default the early riser movement, and this was only later challenged by identity-based movements such as environmental movements. This is exactly the type of argument that this book attempts to problematize. Though Jasper and Morris and Braine do not rest their movement typologies on the premise of grand social transformation, different bases of social support and movement objectives are not viable answers to either the discrepant timing of movement emergence in the same national context or a reverse sequencing across contexts. To argue that a movement arises early because its supporters belong to certain social groups or because it purports particular goals is not only logically unsound but also easily disproved by the empirical observation of the reverse sequencing of labor and environmental movements in Taiwan and Korea.

Grievances, Resources, and Institutions

After surveying different research designs and movement typologies, I now tackle the substantive explanations the literature puts forth to see how the reverse sequencing and movement specificity can be accommodated. I divide possible interpretations along three lines of explanatory primacy: grievances, resources, and institutions.

For a grievance-centered argument, movement sequences reflect the conditions, both objective and subjective, of labor exploitation and environmental degradation; the more severe grievance will arise earlier and the less severe later. As Polanyi argues that protectionist movements arose *in response to* the disruptive forces of market expansion, it is only logical that the greater the social disruptions affecting the labor market or the natural environment, the more likely the movement in question would arise earlier than its counterpart. One may thus argue that different movement sequences in two societies reflect varying degrees of urgency of labor and environmental problems. This version of Polanyi is akin to the Durkheim-inspired collective behavior and mass society theories, that is, that popular protests are a reflection of alienation, a lack of social attachment, and other structural strains induced by social transformations such as industrialization and urbanization (Kornhauser 1959; Le Bon 1982; Smelser 1963). What sets Polanyi apart from the early social movement scholars is that the latter tend to "pathologize" protest activities and protesters, a position that Polanyi does not endorse.

The grievance-centered explanations of popular protests are, curiously, based on assumed linkages between society types and movement types. In this regard, Kornhauser's statement is most illuminating: "mass society is characterized by an abundance of mass movements. Other types of society are characterized by different kinds of social movements" (Kornhauser 1959, 50). Interestingly, many (new social movement) theorists explicitly adopt this correspondence thesis—a correspondence between society and social movements—as well. In an industrial society, class-based movements dominate, whereas in a postindustrial society, new social movements—aka identity-based movements—prevail (Melucci 1985, 1996; Touraine 1981, 1985). These "new" movements "are not sparked by problems of distribution, but concern the grammar of forms of life" (Habermas 1981, 33). The way that societies and movements correspond with each other is as follows: (1) each type of society embodies its own social contradictions; (2) social contradictions govern the intensity and form of grievances; (3) different grievance structures lead to the predominance of certain movements in each type of society. Following this line of logic, the explanation for reverse sequencing rests on a macroanalysis of society as a whole. Society types shape grievance structures that in turn govern the order of emergence of different movements. We see two distinct movement sequences in Taiwan and Korea, given the grievance-centered approach, because they are fundamentally two different types of society; the answer for the reverse sequencing rests on identifying the very differences between Taiwan and Korea as two social systems and examining two separate grievance structures corresponding to each of the two societies.

The second explanation is about resource bases. There are two strands to this approach. The first strand—resource mobilization theory in the social

movement literature—maintains that movement emergence is not a function of the degree of grievance but is conditioned by the availability of
resources at one's disposal, be they cadres, leaders, organizational infrastructures, networks, allies, information, money, supplies, or office spaces (Cress
and Snow 1996). In contrast to Smelser, Gurr, and other grievance-centered
theorists, resource mobilization scholars argue that the level of grievance
and the capacity to act are not causally related (Oberschall 1973). In fact,
those who have the most grievances tend to be so powerless that they cannot
even act on their grievances.[7] Eventually, it is the availability of resources that
determines the rise of a movement. The overall volume of resources available
to be appropriated is conditioned by the increased size of the middle class,
who have spare money and discretionary time, or the rise of foundations
and the nonprofit sector (McCarthy and Zald 1987a, 1987b). Following this
reasoning, if there are significant differences in available resources for labor
and environmental movements both within and across national contexts, we
may expect different sequences of movement emergence.

The second strand of the resource-based argument is from the poststructuralist school in the literature of development (Agrawal 1996; Escobar
1995; Esteva 1992), whose focus is more on discursive struggles in the wake
of development. The appearance of local struggles against development projects imposed by national elites and foreign capital is conditioned by discursive resources at the command of the local. Traditions, conventions, and local
culture are possible, and potent, weapons to counter the dominant practices
and ideology of development (Baviskar 1995; Ferguson 1996; Keck 1995).
Besides local discourses, one can also argue that discursive resources are
poured in from the outside to legitimize local claims. International campaigns
on environmentalism, aboriginal rights, feminism, or human rights generally perform such functions. To apply the discursive resource argument to
our cases, it seems plausible that the sequencing of labor and environmental
movements might vary if they enjoy different degrees of discursive resources,
either domestically or internationally.

The third line of explanation rests on institutions, and this institutional-
ist approach also contains quite a few variations. From the perspective of
political opportunities—the dominant paradigm in social movement studies—
one might cite Tarrow: "collective actors' [movements'] political opportunities[8] vary between actors and change over time" (Tarrow 1988, 429) and
"national opportunity structures may be the basic grids within which movements operate, but the grid is seldom neutral between social actors" (Tarrow
1996, 51). By this logic, political opportunities are *not* movement-neutral.
Labor and environmental movements face different political opportunities;

interaction

the one offered more favorable opportunities would be likely to arise earlier than the one confronted with less favorable conditions. One type of political opportunity might favor a labor movement over an environmental movement, and another type of political opportunity would do the opposite. By comparing societies through their differing sets of political opportunities, we might be able to explain an observed reverse sequencing.

The second variation, moving away from political institutions, focuses on the institutional underpinnings of development and industrialization and their respective effects on labor and environmental movements. Simply put, the pattern of industrialization, facilitated by a series of development strate- *patterns or strategies* gies, changes domestic class dynamics, which in turn shape the terrain where social movements take off. A classic line of argument can be traced back to Marx as well as other works examining the relationship between economic structure, class dynamics, and popular protests (Brenner 1985; Hobsbawm 1967; Paige 1975). The most notable example might be Moore's (1966) monumental study of three routes from a preindustrial to a modern society. Scholars of new social movements (Kriesi 1989; Offe 1985) and development studies (Collier and Collier 1991; Deyo 1984, 1989; Koo 1990, 2001) continue this tradition. Here I provide two recent examples. On the labor movement side, Seidman argues that in two countries as different as Brazil and South Africa, the adoption of a set of similar development strategies led first to similar patterns of elite cleavage and labor–capital relations and then to the rise of social movement unionism (Seidman 1994). Evans's (2002) collected volume, addressing urban sustainability in late industrializers and postsocialist societies, also demonstrates the definitive impact of neoliberal, triumphalist development policies—be they attracting foreign capital in Vietnam (O'Rourke 2002), dumping chemical wastes in rural Hungary (Gille 2002), or managing water resources in São Paulo (Keck 2002)—on the alignment of opposition forces: the aggrieved communities, translocal nongovernmental organizations (NGOs), and opposition parties.

be aware of this

Following this line of argument, one may argue that the institutional underpinnings for development, just like political opportunities, are not movement-neutral either. The same set of development strategies and economic structures may exert uneven effects on the social bases of labor and environmental movements and facilitate or constrain the two movements differently. For example, centralized industrialization—where industrial facilities are concentrated in selected areas and the core of the economy consists of a few gigantic corporations—offers certain conditions conducive to the rise of labor movements, such as densely populated workers' neighborhoods favoring working-class solidarity. But at the same time, this type of industrialization

the right of neoliberalism AND the right of this

may hamper the chance of antipollution struggles customarily initiated by farmers and fishermen against modern industrial establishments, given the power differential between huge conglomerates and pollution victims. Thus the key to the reverse sequencing rests on identifying different sets of development strategies and institutional underpinnings that eventually lead to two different movement sequences. These three lines of interpretation, then, can be summarized as follows:

> *Grievance-centered explanations.* Two societies with different grievance structures result in different orderings of movement emergence.
>
> *Resource-based explanations.* The availability of resources at the societal level and the ability of the aggrieved to procure them condition the timing in which each movement arises; in two societies with different levels of resource availability and/or movements with varying capacities to procure resources, we observe variations over movement sequences.
>
> *Institution-centered explanations.* Institutions—political and economic—exert uneven impacts on different movements; two distinct sets of institutional grids are likely to produce different movement sequences.

All three lines of interpretation reveal partial truths. Given their different analytical foci and the baggage inherited from past debates, particularly between the grievance and resource approaches, it is not easy to reconcile them. I propose to look into the type of power each movement exercises to reorient the discussions of grievances, resources, and institutions. Instead of focusing on different grievance structures at the societal levels, labor and environmental movements elaborate different types of grievances that constitute their resource bases. Instead of focusing on the overall volume of available resources at the societal level and on individual movements' capacity to procure resources, labor and environmental movements simply need *different types of resources* to articulate their grievances and to advance their movement power under institutional constraints.[9] Finally, I fully recognize that one set of institutional arrangements may have differential effects on different social movements. And this observation can be taken further by allowing for interaction between movements and the political authorities. Labor and environment embody different types of movement power that pose different degrees of threat to political authorities, and as a result, the latter tend to treat them differently, as we have learned from Kriesi et al. (1995). Arguing that two institutional grids lead to two distinct movement sequences glosses over intranational variations. Instead, as I see it, each of the two movement sequences results from the interaction between one institutional grid and two types of movements rooted in varied grievances and resource bases. The benefit of adopting this angle is that both cross-national and intranational variations of movement performance are covered simultaneously. The explanatory power of each of the three lines of interpretation is in no way compromised. On the contrary, grievances, resources, and institutions stop being separate, competing lines of interpretation but rather become interactive components, properly rearranged from the perspective of movement power into an organic whole.

Leverage and Ideological Power

Comparing labor and environmental movements, I find that they draw their power from different sources. Labor builds leverage through structural positions, and environmental movements draw power via ideology. By exercising different types of power, labor and environmental movements articulate grievances and engage with rivals in distinct ways.

I highlight these different sources of movement power for two reasons. First, if we see the rise of social movements as the formation of collective actors who learn to command the powers they equip, it becomes clear that the exercise and actualization of each type of movement power require a specific set of structural conditions and that two movements relying on different types of power will perform quite differently under the same structural conditions. Second, we may also look into movement powers from an interactive perspective. If social movements pose varying degrees of threat in terms of the type of power they exercise, the differential treatment by political authorities of different movements, either before or after their rise, makes much more sense. Institutional measures and counteractions adopted to repress or coax different movements are not unilaterally decided by the logic of state apparatuses or corporate economies but are responses to different types of movement power challenging the Establishment in a variety of ways.

Movement power is anything but new. Many have discussed that the powerless often use protest—negative inducement (threat)—to pressure the authorities to engage in a bargaining process (Alinsky 1989a, 1989b; Lipsky 1968; Wilson 1961). Discussions of nonviolent action rest on the assumption that "the exercise of power depends on the consent of the ruled who, by withdrawing that consent, can control and even destroy the power of the opponent" (Sharp 1973, 4). Piven and Cloward (1992, 310) highlight the power of institutional disruption and make this point even more explicitly: "the lower-stratum protesters have some possibility of influence . . . if their actions violate rules and disrupt the workings of an institution on which important groups depend." Michael Schwartz (1976, 177) also maintains that those who are subjected to routinized power relations in fact "possess a latent power deriving from the possibility of refusing to abide by the power exercised over them." Flacks (2004, 114) says it even more explicitly: "the power of the powerless is rooted in their capacity to stop the smooth flow of social life" and "social movements . . . can be most fruitfully examined as social formations that seek, over time, to maximize the power available to their constituencies."

It is not just students of social movements who talk about movement power: scholars of social democracy and welfare states also have their eye on the power of organized labor that "provide[s] the ability to reward or punish another actor" (Korpi 1974, 1571). They also show obvious interest in the extent to which the shifting balance of power between labor and capital changes the strategies of class conflict (Korpi and Shalev 1979). Furthermore, they tackle the overarching theme of the relationship between working-class power and distributive, social-democratic projects (Esping-Andersen 1985).

But the preceding discussions imply that the "power of the weak" is monolithic; they do not really tell us how to distinguish the powers that labor and environmental movements wield, respectively. As a consequence, other sources must be supplemented. On the labor side, the entire literature of Marxism comes to our aid by specifying the leverage and structural power of the working class (Silver 2003; Wright 2000). On the environment side, it is most noticeable that, in fewer than thirty years, various discourses over "environment" and "nature" have been successfully instilled into the public psyche in most parts of the globe. Flipping through daily newspapers, we read about politicians pledging to clean up air, ecological disasters worldwide, and all sorts of debates over resource management, energy policies, or national parks, all with varying degrees of intellectual sophistication. There is a consensus on "saving the planet," and fighting for environmental causes is seen as politically respectable. As an ecological historian notes, "we all want to save the planet. That is, few, faced by an opinion poll, would declare themselves to be anti-planet, or pro-planetary destruction" (Bramwell 1994, 180). Environmental movements are one of the very few social movements that procure broad social support and successfully turn movement causes into dominant ideology. The ideological power that environmental movements wield is what I consider the most distinguishing feature of this movement. Melucci's (1996, 1) portrait of contemporary social movements also hints at this ideological power: "What they [social movements] possess is . . . the power of word. . . . They speak a language that seems to be entirely their own, but they say something that transcends their particularity and speaks to us all."

To elaborate the two types of movement power further, I maintain that leverage is positional power. When we say a group of people has leverage against its target, we first presume that these people are already positioned in an interdependent, if asymmetrical, relationship with their target. By withholding cooperation, they immediately obstruct what their target desires to achieve. The classic example is that workers halt their participation in the process of production, and capitalists are prevented from realizing profits. In other words, leverage can only be exercised by a group of people who are incorporated in a sustained social relation and whose role in the relation happens to be indispensable. When leverage is exercised, the party being protested against is pressured into making concessions or using force to elicit the crucial contribution these leverage holders used to perform.[10] Younis's (2001) study of two national liberation movements in South Africa and Palestine illustrates all these points. In the South African case, the black labor force was fully incorporated into the settlers' economy and thus enjoyed a certain degree of leverage against white colonizers; the Palestinian labor force was excluded from the settlers' economy and held no leverage against its oppressor.

Furthermore, corresponding to its positionality, leverage is target-specific and, as Lukes (2005, 75, 79) would term it, "context-bound." Industrial workers may launch strikes in the factories, college students may stage a building occupancy against university administrations (Heirich 1971), and low-ranking clerks may withhold information and sabotage the functioning of complex organizations (Mechanic 1962). Yet their positional powers do not automatically hold true if contexts and targets change. Student revolts do not directly hold leverage against capitalists, nor do industrial workers exert immediate influence on institutions of higher education. This is not to say that leverage is permanently delimited on its own turf. In some cases, leverage spills over. Students may not exercise leverage against capitalists directly, but they may do so indirectly by pressuring the universities to terminate agreements with any contractors who do not follow certain codes of conduct, or they may boycott sweatshop products directly as consumers (Bartley and Child 2011). Industrial workers may not have leverage against universities directly, but they may lobby against budget cuts in higher education, particularly in the area of labor research and outreach programs. Or they may engage in sympathy strikes in support of campus workers' demands for a living wage.

If leverage is about the power of positionality, ideological power is the power of ideas, or more precisely, the power of popular consent to "concrete phantasy which acts on a dispersed and shattered people to arouse and organize its collective will" (Gramsci 1971, 126). I am entering rough water by using the term *ideological power*, because ideology is chronically a term of abuse (Williams 1986, 157) and may have as many as sixteen different, mutually exclusive definitions in circulation (Eagleton 1991, 1–2). In this book, ideologies refers to "oppositional ideologies," specifically, that is, ideas and beliefs reflecting the interests and life experiences of subordinate social groups that stand in opposition to dominant ideologies reflecting opposing interests. Feminism and environmentalism are prime examples of such ideologies in contexts where patriarchy and developmentalism reign. These oppositional ideologies are situated in a field of ideological struggle "in which self-promoting social powers conflict and collide over questions central to the reproduction of social power as a whole" (Eagleton 1991, 29). In this vein, social movements produce and sustain oppositional ideologies that structure new meanings, ideas, beliefs, and practices.

The ideological power of a social movement first depends on the extent to which the movement converts a sizable population who formerly subscribed to dominant ideologies into taking on a new oppositional consciousness. It then depends on the extent to which that oppositional consciousness inspires converts into action to fight off possible attacks and to win more people over. As to why oppositional ideologies have the power to convert bystanders and organize collective will, Polanyi provides a succinct answer: when advocates of certain ideas stand for interests wider than their own (Polanyi 2001, 139, 159, 163), these ideas serve both as glue to bridge social differences and as magnets to win support from outside their natural constituencies. In other words, ideological power comes from the "universality" and "collective good" that these ideas articulate and claim to represent.[11] The working of ideological power from the oppositional camp essentially revolves around persuasive work right under the nose of dominant ideologies. The exercise of ideological power is contingent first on discursive capacities to forge an oppositional ideology and to initiate a cognitive revolution for a previously indifferent audience. The working of ideological power also depends on an effective appropriation of the means of communication to reach different sectors of the population. In most cases, the "means of communication" refers to radio, television, newspapers, and magazines with national circulation. As Therborn (1980, 80) has argued, "[ideologies] are always produced, conveyed, and received in particular, materially circumscribed social situations and through special means and practices of communication, the material specificity of which bears upon the efficacy of a given ideology."

The strengths and weaknesses of the two types of movement power are quite clear. Leverage affords one the ability to build solidarity and organization, but the power is not necessarily transferable across contexts and, worse, may be treated as a sectional interest. In contrast, ideological power may change the public psyche in profound ways, but it must deal with the sustainability of cross-sectional solidarity thinly based on ideas and discourses.

Movement Power on the Battlefield

Leverage and ideological power are not isolated concepts but need to be situated in the terrain of struggle. Here I am invoking Gramsci to deepen our understanding of the formation of collective actors (Gramsci 1971, 181–82). In his famous *Prison Notebooks,* Gramsci outlines the process in which, operating within the economic and military limits, a collective actor (in this case, the working class) reaches its maturity by moving from the economic–corporate to economic class and finally to a hegemonic level, corresponding to the elevation of political consciousness of the collective actor at each stage. Gramsci's formulation is clearly unidirectional and hierarchical. The elevation from the economic–corporate to the economic class level represents the broadened scope of solidarity among those who share similar economic interests. Yet the crucial moment comes at the transition from the economic class to the hegemonic level, through which the collective actor transcends "the corporate limits of the purely economic class, and can and must become the interests of other subordinate groups too" (181). It is also at this stage that the collective actor engages in decisive ideological struggles and exerts intellectual and moral leadership to subordinate groups as a whole. Gramsci's formulation also contains an interactive element between the collective actors and the external limits. The process of collective actors moving into different levels is accompanied by a different balance of forces within the terrain of struggle, as well as changed outer limits, both economic and military.

The progression from the economic–corporate to the hegemonic level contains a few important messages. First and foremost, it indicates the direction toward which working-class politics should head, which delivers an overall sense of the trajectory of labor movements. Second, each level features a new battle and a new battlefield, which requires the collective actor to arm itself with new maps to explore an uncharted territory. Besides political consciousness, the transition from economic–corporate to economic class demands a better organizational infrastructure, whereas the transition from economic class to the hegemonic level requires a high level of discursive and intellectual capacity so as to fight a cultural–political war across the terrain of ideology. Finally, the progression is evolutionary and cumulative. Gramsci certainly does not imagine a labor movement jumping around the three levels randomly but rather following a step-by-step process of maturation. But this is not to say a collective actor cannot retreat back to a lower level if its attempt to move up fails. All in all, what has been achieved at each level—skills, consciousness, and organizational bases—will serve as the groundwork for struggles at the next level. But it is equally clear that the dominant practice at each level (say, self-interested action at the economic–corporate level) also imposes difficulties on the transition to a higher level. Inertia and complacency are strong forces maintaining the status quo, even if the collective actor comes into being with the purpose of bringing change to the world. It takes serious self-transformation of the collective actor to break away from self-imposed confines.

Combining Gramsci's formulation with the two types of movement power discussed here, I reformulate a bidirectional and nonhierarchical model of the formation of collective actors and their movements in the terrain of struggle (see Figure 7). I collapse the levels of economic–corporate and economic class into one, because both revolve around the issue of economic interest, the only difference being the scope of social organization. The contrast between economic–corporate and hegemonic levels is maintained, and they represent two types of battle—economic and ideological—that collective actors must confront. This model accommodates different types of collective actors: one is leverage based, the other ideology based. The leverage-based movements enter the terrain of struggle at the economic–corporate level and strive to develop ideological power in the process of moving in the direction of the hegemonic level. The ideology-based movements begin a cultural, ideological struggle at the hegemonic level and, over time, head toward the economic–corporate level and pursue leverage power.

This reformulation immediately poses questions. If in Gramsci's formulation a labor movement's ideological struggle at the hegemonic level is buttressed by the skills, knowledge, and organizational bases developed through

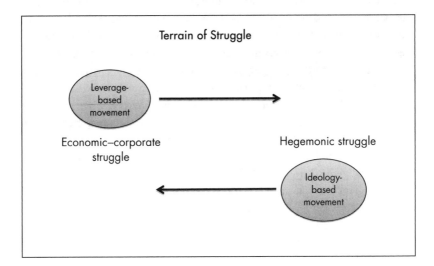

Figure 7. Movement trajectories in the terrain of struggle.

struggles at the economic–corporate and economic class levels, what would an ideological struggle without such groundwork be like? Furthermore, if an ideology-based movement does gradually engage in struggles at the economic–corporate level, as we speculate, what exactly is its leverage? For the first question—the nature of ideology-based movements' struggles at the hegemonic level—my current diagnosis is that such movements need to appropriate organizational resources elsewhere to take off. But in the long run, ideology-based movements are prone to be organizationally unstable and to suffer from a fluctuation in grassroots support. This type of movement may maintain an integrity when the universalistic ideas promoted can still stimulate enough public passion; but if the tide of popular consent recedes or universalistic ideas become so well accepted that even opponents begin to appropriate them, the movement might stagnate.

The second question—that of the leverage that ideology-based movements may develop—is a difficult one. The long-term goal of an ideology-based movement is somehow less defined than that of a leverage-based movement, and it becomes difficult to picture the kind of leverage required to achieve the goal. For example, if a labor movement aims to achieve a socialist revolution via force or a social democracy via electoral victory, there exist concrete historical cases from which we may examine different combinations of the leverage and ideological power deployed to accomplish either goal. But in the case of environmental movements, the prototype of ideology-based movements, the precedent of a planned "green society" is lacking. The movement's overall vision of an economic order and social institutions is less elaborated, and there are multiple and competing paradigms inside the green movements. At this point I am inclined to suggest that the leverage of ideology-based movements is not a question one can answer a priori. Instead, one must look into the concrete cases at hand for possible answers.

Leverage and ideological power, and their opposite paths within the terrain of struggle, are ideal constructions. The purpose is neither to squeeze social reality into a small, analytical black box nor to subject historical knowledge to the status of "a servant of theory" (Weber 1949, 102). The crucial task is to evaluate how our analytical tools in each empirical case "approximate to or diverge from reality" (Weber 1949, 90). Before embarking on the journey of empirical inquiry, I want to clear up possible confusion as to the distinction between leverage and ideology and to elaborate on the contrasting trajectories that labor and environmental movements undergo.

The dichotomy of leverage and ideological power might provoke some suspicion. Both labor and environmental movements, some may argue, simultaneously possess and deploy both types of power. Hobsbawm (1967, 13,

16–17) states plainly that machine breakers in the eighteenth and nineteenth centuries received overwhelming sympathy from all parts of the British population, including many manufacturers. Others also talk about how early craft radicalism was tied to broader communal life (Haydu 1988; Thompson 1966; Voss 1993). Though whether cross-sectional social support is garnered in the process is not clearly stated, it nevertheless signifies certain "ideological moments" of this leverage-based movement.

Environmental movements, conversely, adopt militant tactics such as site occupancy and boycotts against commercial products, and this can also be read as the exercise of leverage. Going one step further, it can also be argued that there are no pure economic or ideological struggles, a rephrasing of E. P. Thompson's (1995, 231) famous line that "every contradiction is a conflict of value as well as a conflict of interest." All struggles contain both economic and cultural components. To successfully carry out a strike requires ideological work to persuade members both within and without the working class. Environmental protests also pose a threat in disrupting the normal function of social institutions. In this vein, one can even contend that leverage and ideological power are in fact mutually constituted. Ideological power is the precondition of the exercise of leverage, and vice versa. It is, in this line of reasoning, artificial to make a clear-cut distinction between leverage and ideological power. By doing so, one runs the risk of losing sight of the complexity of reality and the interplay between economy and culture–ideology.

I am in full agreement with the statement that all material struggles are ideological struggles, and vice versa. It is not my intention to suggest that labor movements do not exercise ideological power at all or that environmental movements have no leverage. The question is in what proportion each of the two movements exercises leverage and ideological power. That a movement mainly relies on one type of power but summons another type of power at times as an auxiliary tool is a more informative expression than that the movement in question exercises both types of power. Second, if the exercise of leverage and ideological power should be understood in terms of proportion, the distinct trajectory that either labor or environmental movements undergo in the terrain of struggle may also be regarded as a series of changing configurations of the two types of power. This implies a growing importance of ideological power in labor movements and that of leverage in environmental movements over time.

Further elaborations are also needed as to whether labor and environmental movements move between the economic–corporate and hegemonic levels according to the directions I have indicated in Figure 7 and, if they do, what motivates them to progress as such. In many case studies of labor movements, their portrait of, or plea for, the transition from business unions to social movement unionism is a nice parallel to the transition from the economic–corporate to the hegemonic level. As for what prompts labor movements to transform as such, this varies historically. In some cases, labor movements and socialist parties have grown strong enough to seize the office of the state, and thus they "sought support beyond the working class as soon as the prospect of electoral victory became real" (Przeworski 1985, 25). In other cases, the combined assault of business offense and regressive labor laws under neoliberal globalization eroded the institutional security that the working class had once enjoyed. Labor unions were pressured into looking for broader social support to secure workers' economic well-being (Clawson 2003; Fantasia and Voss 2004; Lopez 2004). In the industrializing context, a specific set of development strategies laid out the foundation for the rise of social movement unions, characterized by sudden waves of strike activities, rapid escalation of demands from work-related issues to broad political goals, and an alliance between labor movements and urban communities (Seidman 1994).

Though empirical works on environmental movements are less systematic than those of labor movements, we can still extract a few general points. Let us use the unfolding of environmental movements in the United States as an example. As far as mainstream environmental movements are concerned, they reveal a process of "universalizing" environmental issues to make a clear break from "sectional interests" where environmental protests originated. Later on, the concerns over resource distribution and social equality were gradually brought back through struggles against toxic waste and environmental racism (Bullard 1990, 1993; Szasz 1994). The issue of unequal distribution of the "environmental bad" was brought to light much later than general concerns over the integrity of the ecosystem and conservationism. The term *environmental justice* appeared in the United States in the mid-1980s (DiChiro 1998, 122), decades after the rise of ecological movements in the late 1960s. In many industrializing countries, environmental activism started from antipollution activities and communal rights toward natural resources. Ecological issues, conservationism, and green consumerism surfaced quickly and became the main themes of the movements. As the movements evolved, economic issues gradually reentered the realm of public debate. If it is indeed the general pattern of movement trajectory, the maturation of environmental movements seems to involve concrete coordination of diverse economic interests surrounding environmental issues, and the direction of progression seems to fit our projection.

As to why environmental movements unfold as such, again, this is a question that can be answered only by analyzing concrete historical situations.

Nevertheless, a normative, universalistic vision of nature eventually has to confront acute questions such as "whose nature" and "whose vision," which are directly tied to the economic interests of different social groups. I suspect that under certain circumstances, the tension between "nature for nature's sake" and caring for the economic well-being of different collectivities would be most severe within environmental movements, and the progression toward the economic–corporate level might be accelerated. One possible situation is that, when the urgent need for developmental projects to solve the problem of scarcity is coupled with a distributive scheme reproducing a huge gulf between the haves and the have-nots, environmental movements will be more likely to directly entangle themselves in economic conflicts. Such scenarios are most likely to take place in developing countries plagued with persistent inequality, as illustrated through case studies like the rubber tappers' fight in Brazil (Keck 1995), indigenous groups' struggles against dam construction in India (Baviskar 1995), and other marginalized groups' fight for their livelihoods (Friedmann and Rangan 1993; Guha 2000; Martinez-Alier 2002; Rangan 2004).

There must be other critical issues within the ideal construct of movement power and trajectories that I fail to tackle. But this is already too long an exposition of theory. It is time to let history have its say.

2

The Tangles of Movement Histories

As outlined in the Introduction, this book divides the reverse sequencing into three areas of empirical inquiry: who it is that becomes an (early riser) what the impact of the early risers is on the latecomers; and which trajectory labor and environmental movements undertake. Before tackling them with full force, I want first to make empirically my case that the timings of emergence of the four movements are indeed in reverse order. This will require some preliminary explanations of movement histories and the social surroundings from which the movements arose. I first survey the existing literature on the contested issue of movement emergence, then move on to examine different criteria used to identify the timings of emergence of the four movements. Given the need to evaluate the four movements in terms of a consistent criterion, I suggest that we see movement emergence as a process of synchronization between protest actions and collective consciousness. I will present numeric data on protest activities over time and further situate them in the respective contexts of consciousness raising and discourse production.

Movement Emergence in the Literature

To determine at what point in time a movement has emerged is one of the most difficult questions. On one hand, this difficulty has a definitional aspect. Social movements have been and are still defined in various ways. The timing of movement emergence may vary depending on which definition one uses. On the other hand is the typical difficulty of any historical inquiry. Given the indivisible nature of historical time and the interrelatedness of social events, to declare that a movement emerges in a particular period of time or right after certain major events is often a contested business. Many monographs in social movement studies hesitate to make clear declarations as such. Rather, they present many "turning points" of a movement. If one focuses only on a single social movement, the genesis issue can be compensated for by presenting "historical fullness," that is, tracing the root causes of the movement way back, over several decades or even a century. This book, however, compares four movements all at once, and "historical fullness" is not a realistic option. I thus opt for formulating a set of indicators of movement emergence and apply them consistently to the four movements.

Explaining why a movement emerges is quite different from empirically confirming the existence of the movement and declaring the timing of emergence. If one can explain movement emergence through protesters' grievances, grievances in turn can hardly be an empirical indicator of movement emergence, because on too many occasions, grievances prevail without the presence of social movements. The same logic equally applies to resource mobilization and political process or opportunities: the availability of resources and the opening of political opportunities do not necessarily indicate the existence of social movements. On occasions, movements emerge while resources are scarce or political conditions objectively remain the same (Kurzman 1996).

Nevertheless, the social movement literature tackles the empirical indicator issue in the following way. Social movement scholars first spell out the constituting elements of social movements and then trace a series of historical events to see when these elements surfaced. Here are a few items from a very long list:

sustained collective action (Tarrow 1994, 5)

large-scale, widespread, and continuing elementary collective action (Lang and Lang 1961, 490)

collective defiance (Piven and Cloward 1979, 5)

uninstitutionalized collective action and general beliefs (Smelser 1963, 73, chapter 5)

organized action in pursuit of cultural innovation or "historicity" (Touraine 1981, 31)

organizations capable of taking action (Gamson 1975, 14)

a collectivity with indefinite and shifting membership (Turner and Killian 1957, 308)

a set of opinions and beliefs (McCarthy and Zald 1987a, 20)

activities creating new social identities and ideas (Eyerman and Jamison 1991, 2–3)

public efforts of claim-making employing a specific repertoire of action
and displaying participants' WUNC (worthiness, unity, numbers,
and commitment) (Tilly 2004, 3–4)

the mobilization of a collective actor who is sustained by solidarity and
engages in a conflict with an adversary for the control of resources
and whose action entails a breach of the limits of compatibility of the
system (Melucci 1996, 29–30)

Once these elements are located in real time, students of social movements try
to reconcile inconsistencies—different elements might not come into being
simultaneously—and decide which elements are the primary indicator in
proclaiming the birth of a movement. Tilly (1978, 10) pertinently describes
the difficulty of indicator selection:

> The fact that population, belief, and action do not always change together
> causes serious problems for students of social movements. When they
> diverge, should we follow the belief, whatever populations and actions they
> become associated with? Should we follow the population, whatever beliefs
> and action it adopts? Should we follow the action, regardless of who does
> it and with what ideas?

Nevertheless, judging from existing empirical works, the indicators most
often used to confirm movement existence and the timing of emergence are
protest activities, organizations in the loosest sense, and collective consciousness or beliefs—or any combination of the three. Protest activities, with
no doubt, have been given more analytical weight than the other two. One
only needs to recall the centrality of the event-centered approach in the
social movement literature. This approach is basically built on analyzing protest events collected from newspapers or other sources, and most "classics" in
social movement literature (Eisinger 1973; Kriesi et al. 1995; Lieberson and
Silverman 1965; McAdam 1999b; Olzak 1989b; Paige 1975; Tarrow 1989;
Tilly 1995; Tilly, Tilly, and Tilly 1975) rely heavily on this approach. The
number of classics focusing on protest groups and organizations seems fewer,
the most famous example probably being *The Strategy of Social Protest* (Gamson 1975).

With this piece of knowledge in mind, we may begin to examine the
empirical works on labor and environmental movements in Taiwan and Korea.
Studies of the four movements are predominantly situated in the context of
democratic transitions in the late 1980s. These movements are seen as part
of "the democratic project" in their own spheres, and the rise of social movements in general is treated as a sign of a slowly resuscitated civil society that

has long been subjected to an overdeveloped, repressive state apparatus. In this vein, the foremost concern of scholarly inquiry rests on understanding the changing dynamics between civil society and the state. Scholars proceed by examining how labor and environmental movements have contributed to the transition from authoritarian regimes to democracies (Buchanan and Nicholls 2003; Ho 2000; S. Kim 2000; Tang and Tang 1997), their relationships with political authorities—both the ruling and opposition parties (Fan 2000; Lee 2009; Weller and Hsiao 1998; Wu 1990)—and finally how the posttransition "new politics" facilitates or constrains the course of action of organized labor and environmentalists (Ho 2003; Huang 2002, 2003; Kim 1994; Kuo 2003; Y. Lee 2011; Shin 2010; Song 1994; Terao 2002; Wu 2002). Democratic transition and consolidation have remained the theoretical backdrop of most discussions of labor and environmental movements for nearly two decades, yet there exist quite a few disagreements, the timing of movement emergence being one of them.

Regarding Taiwan's environmental movement, the main disagreement is over which types of protest activity should be used to mark the birth of the movement. The dominant interpretation is that this movement—consisting of local antipollution action and conservationist campaigns initiated by urban intellectuals—took shape in the early 1980s in response to the state's mismanagement of various public health issues. Later, local actions grew in both intensity and scope, and the battle against DuPont's transnational investment in 1986 signaled the maturation of a national environmental movement (Chang 1989; Hsiao 1988, 1999; Hsiao, Milbrath, and Weller 1995; Tseng 2008; Wei 1987). Other works view the genesis question differently. Some argue that the movement arose in the mid-1980s as different environmental actions converged and "went national" (Fan 2000; Ho 2001), and in this case protest activities at the national level are the marker of movement emergence. Others maintain that the cultural root of the movement can be traced back to the 1970s and that the lived experiences of, and sense of indignation over, being subjected to environmental hazards constituted the foundation of sustained environmental activism (Lii and Lin 2000).

In the case of Taiwan's labor movement, the debate is over whether protest activities or movement organizations should be used as the primary indicator of movement emergence. The majority opinion would say protest activities. The first wave of labor protests in the postwar period broke out between 1987 and 1988, and the 1970s and the first half of the 1980s were considered an era devoid of genuine labor activism (Chang 1989; Chao 1995; Chu 1996, 1998; Dzeng 1994; Hsiao 1992; Huang 1999; Shieh 1997; Tung 1996; Wang and Fang 1992; Wu and Liao 1991). The minority opinion is that the founding of the first independent labor organization in 1984, consisting of concerned intellectuals, marks the birth of the labor movement (Kuo 2003; Lee 1991). Some even proclaim that the labor movement began in 1977 when the first independent labor union was formed (Minns and Tierney 2003), but Chao (1991, 15–16) argues that this union neither shrugged off management control nor engaged in confrontational actions until 1986. Among monographs documenting the history of a particular trade union, we occasionally see slowdowns or walkouts in the 1970s (Chao 1991, 47–58; Lin 2000). So far, the documentation on labor activism in the 1970s is, overall, extremely thin (Liu 2010): wildcat strikes and random protests did exist, but there is no compelling evidence attesting to organized efforts of movement building and networking among these protests.

As for Korea's labor movement, the genesis debate centers on two issues: (1) whether the left tradition continued despite the interruptions of World War II and the Korean War and (2) the nature of labor activism in the 1970s. On the first issue, many activists in the student and labor movements and scholars following a social history tradition advocate the continuity of the left tradition and argue that the root of the Korean labor movement was in the colonial period. Others, however, point out that the left tradition was severely interrupted in the late 1940s with the prosecution of the "reds" and the mass exodus of leftists to North Korea (Cho and Kim 1998; Lee 2005). From this perspective, postwar labor activism should not be conflated with activism prior to the founding of the First Republic of Korea in 1948.

On the second issue, some dismiss the 1970s labor protests as spontaneous, inconsequential actions that did not build class solidarity or elevate political consciousness. On the basis of this position, Korea's labor movement was revived by the Kwangju massacre in 1980 and the following politicization of students (Sonn 1997). Or, from the vantage point of how labor struggles contributed to democratization, this movement simply tagged along with the democratic project in the late 1980s (Jung 2000). Yet the dominant interpretation contends that Korea's labor movement began to take shape in the early 1970s, triggered by the self-immolation of Chun Tae-Il in 1970 and the subsequent democratic union struggles led by female workers (Chun 2003; Koo 2001; Y. Lee 2011; Song 2000). The documents of the Korean Confederation of Trade Unions (KCTU)—the leading organization of democratic unions—are also in line with this position (Korean Confederation of Trade Unions 2001).

Concerning the rise of Korea's environmental movement, interpretations diverge, again, over the issue of placing explanatory primacy on environmental discourses, protest activities, or movement organizations. Some argue that it began in the early 1970s "when a handful of university professors and conservationists began to worry openly about the declining quality of the natural environment" (Eder 1996, 99). A different opinion is that this movement started in the 1970s as an antipollution campaign demanding material compensation for farmers who lived near industrial complexes (Lee 2000). Others define the rise of the movement, consisting of both antipollution and ecological streams, by the appearance of the first professional environmental organization in 1982—the Korean Pollution Research Institute (PRI)—and the antipollution campaigns it initiated in the mid-1980s (Ku 1996a, 2011; Lee 1999; Lee and Smith 1999). But some also argue that this movement took shape in the late 1980s, because the proliferation of green ideas and organizations did not take place until the era of democratic transition. The rise of the movement was impacted by the opening of political opportunities, and it became one of the major players in the so-called *simin* (citizen) movements, in contrast to traditional *minjung* movements consisting of laborers, farmers, and urban poor (S. Kim 2000; Ku 1996b).

As I noted earlier, the empirical criteria of movement emergence generally fall into three categories: protest activities, movement organizations, and collective consciousness. The discussions of the four movements are no exception. Some use protest activities to mark movement birth; others see the rise of major movement organizations as the launching of a movement. Even among those who define movement emergence in terms of protest activities, disagreements persist. Some maintain that only national campaigns count. Others say that local protests can be a fine indicator in claiming the existence of a movement as long as they are widespread and publicly visible. Some say that the birth of a movement is associated with the realization of material interests at the economic arena; others contend that only elevated political consciousness may mark movement emergence. Amid a variety of interpretations, what I want to do is synthesize the four sets of scholarly works to find a coherent definition of movement emergence and weigh the four movements against it to see if the reverse sequencing thesis can be confirmed.

Movement Emergence as the Synchronization of Action and Consciousness

A movement emerges when we simultaneously witness two things. The first is that, outside institutionalized procedures, protest activities escalate conspicuously. Which forms protest actions and campaigns may take vary widely. They may be spontaneously formed or carefully organized. They may be situated at either the local or national level, depending on different national conditions.

The second thing observed during movement emergence is the formation of some sort of "new consciousness," which may also take different forms. In the case of environmental movements, new consciousness was the result of discursive efforts by scientists and environmentalists to organize social understanding and consensus on natural or man-made disasters—say, Three Mile Island, Hurricane Katrina, mudslides, factory explosions, or other environmental incidents—that were both unfamiliar to the public and triggered public worries. Mainly mediated by media, journalists, and experts, such public worries were later channeled into a new consciousness critical of the state's development project and corporations' profit-driven practices. In the case of labor, new consciousness took the form of revealing hidden injustice resonating with the lived experiences of a group of workers. Working-class consciousness was mainly organized by labor activists and ideologically advanced workers through workplace interactions, small-group meetings, night schools, and other educational campaigns. No matter whether it was mediated by media or activists, and no matter whether the target was the general public or a specific group of workers, the shift of consciousness indicates a movement-building project in its embryonic form.

To put the two things together, the criteria I use to define movement emergence are the synchronization of protest action and new consciousness, similar to the assertion that "the emergence of a protest movement entails a transformation both of consciousness and of behavior" (Piven and Cloward 1979, 3).[1] The reason I emphasize the "synchronization" process is that consciousness and action do not always go hand in hand, and it takes years of effort to bring them together. To bridge the gap between action and consciousness can be anything but a smooth and linear process. Sometimes action lags forever behind radical consciousness—Malaysian peasants' clearsighted understanding of their threatened well-being in the process of agricultural mechanization was decoupled from "onstage," open confrontation (Scott 1985). At other times, radical action is not backed by mature visions of alternatives—the shenanigan-like revolts initiated by the British working-class "lads" led them nowhere (Willis 1977). In these two scenarios, we simply do not see the rise of conventionally defined social movements.

By placing emphasis on action and consciousness, I remove the founding of major organizations from the equation of movement emergence. This is not to say that organizations do not play an important role in coordinating consciousness and action. Yet action and consciousness remain the defining elements of a social movement, and we simply should not "confuse a movement's collective action with the organizations and networks that support the action, or even consider the organizations and networks to constitute the movement" (Tilly 2004, 6).

To study the synchronization between action and consciousness, we need to track the parallel development of (1) how scattered protests escalated in both frequency and intensity and (2) how intellectuals and activists conjured up discursive resources to reach the target audience by fighting off dominant ideology and so result in a shift of consciousness. Using escalated protest activities to indicate movement emergence is fairly common among social movement scholars. For example, McAdam uses the first peak of protest actions in 1955 to mark the birth of the civil rights movement (McAdam 1999b, 121, Figure 6.1). Yet numbers of protest events should be situated in the context of discourse, meaning, and consciousness, with social protests eventually becoming part of the process of consciousness raising and discourse production. It is at the point of convergence of escalated protest activities and the shift of consciousness that we declare the emergence of a movement.

I use two empirical indicators to identify the dual development of action and consciousness. On the part of action, I trace newspapers, government statistics, and other secondary sources to locate protest activities on record to identify the period in which the number of protest activities suddenly increases for the first time. I also use self-accounts from movement activists as points of cross-reference. On the consciousness front, I first identify when discourses on labor rights and environmentalism began to surface through academic or underground publications. Then I check national newspapers to see when environmental discourses began to be widely appropriated and track movement publications for labor activists' educational campaigns. The sources I use are a mixture of primary and secondary data, including (1) time series data on labor and environmental protests between 1961 and 1990 collected through trawling two national newspapers, the *China Times* and the *Korea Times*; (2) reports of protest events and movement organizations in other scholarly works that used systematic trawls of national newspapers (Chang et al. 1992; Hsiao 1988, 1997; Ku 1996a); (3) more than four thousand news reports collected through keyword searches of the full texts of major national newspapers between 1950 and 2000 on labor and environmental controversies; (4) government statistics on labor and environmental disputes; (5) movement publications and historical documents, such as campaign flyers and eighteen documentary films; (6) sixty-eight interviews with activists and academics, totaling roughly 140 hours of audio-taped discussions; and (7) personal notes on multiple sessions of informal conversations, small-group meetings, and public events, taken during my two years of fieldwork in Taiwan and Korea.

I begin with the numeric data on each movement's protest activities over time to identify the first peak of protest escalation. Figure 3, in the Introduction, is a comparison of the distribution of Taiwan's environmental and labor protests. Taiwan's environmental protests first experienced a small peak around 1970, and then two more obvious peaks in 1977 and 1984, in contrast to labor's first wave of protests taking place between 1984 and 1985. This has Taiwan's labor movement lagging behind its environmental counterpart by more than a decade. Figure 4 contains information on Korea's labor and environmental protests. Looking at the frequency data of Korea's labor protest in the twenty-two-year period, we identify three waves of protest; the first peak appeared around 1970–71. It is also obvious that the subsequent waves of labor protest—the second peak in 1981 and the third around 1987 and 1988—were more forceful and sweeping than the previous ones.

For Korea's environmental protests, the trend is flat, and we simply cannot find an obvious peak of protest action. Only sixty environmental protests were reported by the *Korea Times* and the *Korea Herald* between 1969 and 1990, with the number of protests each year remaining in single digits. Consulting other secondary sources, I would mark the late 1980s as constituting the birth of Korea's environmental movement. All the historical narratives on record confirm that the first major antipollution campaign was initially publicized around the mid-1980s. They also confirm that antipollution protests reached their height in 1990: "there were 73 anti-pollution protests in the first seven months of 1990 . . . more than 24,000 people took part in environmental demonstrations which were concentrated in the heavily industrial southeast part of this country" (Clifford 1990a, 72). It is probably more precise to argue that the first peak of Korea's environmental protests emerged between the mid- and the late 1980s. This shows Korea's environmental protests lagging considerably behind their labor counterparts. Using the synchronization of protest action and oppositional consciousness as the marker of movement emergence, the respective timing of the four movements' rise is presented in Figure 8.

In the following, I situate the protest activities within a context in which protest action and oppositional consciousness were mutually reinforcing: counterhegemonic discourses fueled protest activities and ideologically justified the legitimacy of noninstitutional action; in turn, labor and environmental protests solidified the challenge these nonofficially certified discourses posed to the dominant ideology. Here I particularly want to emphasize the contextual difficulty of articulating action and consciousness, because, in Taiwan and Korea at this time, any oppositional discourse was censored and so-called antigovernment action was severely punished.

Given what we have learned from the four movements, the articulation of protest action and oppositional consciousness shows the following pattern. In the "premovement" stage, protest activities and systematic reflections on the plight of labor and environmental degradation remained separate. Early labor and environmental protests started exclusively from immediate,

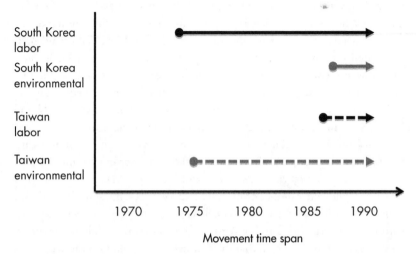

Figure 8. The rise of four movements.

everyday lived experiences and were not inspired by grand discourses or counterideologies. In these early protests, officially certified ideologies were con-
veniently appropriated to justify the extrainstitutional actions. When we
examine Taiwan's antipollution protests prior to the late 1970s and Korea's
environmental protests prior to the mid-1980s, few of the early protests in
either country proudly waved the banner of environmentalism. Protesting
farmers and fishermen cried out to defend threatened livelihoods: dying crops,
dying fish, damaged property, contaminated soil, and poisoned human bodies. One's right to private property and concerns over public health were the
cornerstones that ideologically sustained early antipollution struggles. By
the same token, Korea's labor struggles prior to the mid-1970s and Taiwan's
labor disputes prior to 1984 emphasized illegal activities on the part of employers and invoked "legality" under the capitalist system (labor protection
offered in the *existing* legal framework)—instead of Marxism, socialism,
communism, or social democracy of any sort.

Ironically, protest activities permeated by conventional thoughts and
vocabularies created a new, oppositional consciousness challenging dominant ideologies. The Korean worker Chun Tae-Il's self-immolation in 1970
provides the best example attesting to how protest activities became the decisive fuel for the rise of radical thoughts. This twenty-three-year-old textile
worker, having only an elementary school education, burned himself to death
while holding a copy of Korea's Labor Standards Law and shouting,

Follow the Labor Standards Law.
We are not machines.
Let us have Sundays off.
Don't exploit the workers.
They are not machines. (Cho 2003, 315)

Chun's final words "don't let my death be in vain" heralded a decade of independent union movements (Cho 2003; Chun 2003), and his longing for college friends who would have helped him understand the Chinese characters in the labor laws[2] radicalized a whole generation of youth, workers, and nonworkers alike. Shocked and shamed by Chun's death, college students launched hunger strikes, organized joint rallies, and adopted various resolutions in demanding the improvement of working conditions. Some of them began to work in factories or teach workers at night schools. Christian communities also broadened the involvement in labor organizing and education that they had started in the mid-1960s. It was through night schools, church activities, small-group discussions in the dorms, and educational campaigns with workers as the target audience that radical consciousness began to burgeon among Korean workers.

Taiwan's labor movement, though suffering from a more difficult birth, demonstrated the same point from the flip side. Even though the number of labor protests increased slowly in the late 1970s and the beginning of the 1980s, they were resolved mainly through the official system of conflict resolution. What prompted the first escalation of Taiwan's labor protests in 1984 was a string of workplace tragedies.[3] When the two worst coal-mining accidents in Taiwan's history happened one after another in 1984, one leading to 74 deaths and the other to 102 deaths (*The United Daily* 1984a, 1984b), charity donations for the families of the deceased hit a record high; government officials stepped down, taking responsibility; and news pages were full of long harangues against coal mine owners. Lawyers and left intellectuals began to congregate to fight for workers' rights. Yet in the mid-1980s, labor action remained moderate, taking the form of petitions and lawsuits. No strikes, demonstrations, or other forms of open defiance were observed. Horrifying stories emanating from workplaces did not change the fundamental framework through which the public understood industrial relations.

That the convergence of action and consciousness did not take place until 1987–88 partly resulted from a lack of significant protest activity that radicalized existing labor discourses or created counterideologies, whether symbolic action like Chun Tae-Il's death or substantive action like noticeable slowdowns, walkouts, or strikes. It is around 1987–88 that we witness the first wave of public demonstration of labor power. Workers from Far Eastern Chemical Fiber and a Japanese-owned electronic engineering company engaged in slowdowns and disrupted the production line (*The United Daily* 1988g). Another four-day strike of transportation workers—demanding wage increases, time off, and arrears of wages stipulated by law—not only paralyzed a county of more than one million people (*Economic Daily* 1988) but also inspired workers elsewhere to follow suit. In just twelve months, sixteen more strikes broke out, all initiated by transportation workers and all illegal (Council of Labor Affairs 1996). Besides strikes, textile workers protested against plant closures, various campaigns to reorganize yellow unions—pro-company unions—emerged inside workplaces, and local unions began to build regional networks and form interunion solidarity. This outbreak of labor protests called on workers elsewhere to fight for their basic rights. More importantly, their protest activities prompted a handful of intellectuals to defend the workers' position, inspired college students to become labor organizers, and stimulated more extensive educational and organizing campaigns targeting Taiwan's working class. All of these attest that both labor movements relied on different forms of protest action to change workers' consciousness and recruit potential allies.

This is not to say that radical thoughts can be introduced only after protest activities have emerged. In other cases, counterhegemonic discourses have been in circulation for some time but have not made direct connection with early protests. In both countries, extensive reports on water and air pollution began to appear in major newspapers in the mid-1960s (*Central Daily News* 1965; *China Times* 1965; *United Daily* 1967), and green thinking was introduced by natural scientists in the early 1970s. Experts on industrial relations, starting from the 1960s, also frequently pointed out the possibility of labor–capital conflicts and the functioning problems of existing unions, and Taiwan's first leftist magazine, *Xiachao*, was published in 1976, years ahead of the outbreak of the first-wave labor struggle.

A more accurate characterization of this scenario is that early protest activities, though developing within the confines of existing labor laws at the time, opened a small window for counterhegemonic discourses to be rediscovered by the workers and put into wider circulation. In other words, protest activities not only created new radical thoughts but also gave the preexisting underground oppositional discourses a chance to gain strength against the dominant ideology and to capture the target audience.

Besides protest activities, unexpected disasters affecting a sizable population can also help formulate radical thoughts and contending discourses. This point can be best illustrated through the two environmental movements.

When it first appeared in the early 1970s, green thinking was popularized in Taiwan through a series of natural and man-made disasters: ship wreckage and a serious oil spill in 1976; multiple casualties caused by a hydride gas escape in 1978;[4] and, in 1979, a case of cooking oils being contaminated with harmful chemicals, affecting thousands of consumers and, worse, pregnant women and infants (*United Daily* 1979). These disasters occupied news pages for weeks or months at a time. Experts were interviewed and invited to deliver op-ed pieces from a variety of perspectives. Two things clearly shine through from the early coverage of pollution news: heartfelt sympathy toward pollution victims and unrestrained harangues against the government's mismanagement. It was by interpreting the causes of such disasters that environmental consciousness began to prevail in the public mind. In Korea, even though discussions of environmental protection also began in the early 1970s, the convergence of action and consciousness did not occur until a public hazard case involving hundreds of victims of "Onsan illness" in 1985. Onsan illness was a bone and joint disease caused by cadmium poisoning (Moon and Lim 2003, 55), identified as "a Korean version of Japan's well-known '*Itai-itai* illness'" (Lee 1999, 94). Carefully planned public campaigns were conducted by environmental NGOs, and the Onsan case for the first time brought environmental degradation and public health issues extensive media coverage and public attention. Later, immense public pressure forced the government to relocate thousands of Onsan residents and provide financial compensation. Another disaster that further incorporated environmental ideas into public discourse was a phenol emission case in 1991. A chemical company spilled phenol into a major river, subsequently affecting the water supply in the third largest city in Korea, Taegu, and its surrounding areas. This pollution case led to an unprecedented boycott event for environmental causes and the nationalization of environmental protests (Eder 1996, 108–9; Moon and Lim 2003).

With protest activities or disasters as a catalyst, contending discourses on labor and environmental problems with wider circulation served to legitimize and stimulate future protest activities. On one hand, more protest activities were "instigated," because these nonofficially certified discourses tackled the failures of the existing institutional arrangements and helped explain how injustice worked. On the other hand, protesters began to appropriate these counterhegemonic discourses. New demands, more in line with the counterhegemonic discourses, were adopted and advanced through protest activities. Stricter environmental regulations and the closing down of polluting facilities replaced financial compensation; workplace democracy and revisions of unreasonable labor laws replaced demands for arrears of wages stipulated in labor laws.

In addition, protesters not only memorized the lines of counterideologies but also actively rewrote the scripts. The portion of counterhegemonic discourses that proved to be effective in legitimizing protest activities was repeatedly appropriated, including the slogan of "down with the collusion of government and corporations" and the concepts of eco-tourism and sustainable development. Other portions that did not fit the needs of action, or that threatened to bring bad results, were dropped like a hot potato. Under the anticommunist atmosphere at that time, early labor struggles in both countries never employed explicit socialist language but invented their own substitutes. The famous Korean term *minjung*—"common people as opposed to elites and leaders or even the educated or cultured" (N. Lee 2011, 42)—in the 1970s and 1980s was sometimes used as a code word for socialism; the Chinese *caogen* (the grassroots) and *minjian* (the civil sphere), connotating bottom-up social forces, might or might not have an implication of socialism, depending on the context.

The impact of a contending ideology on subsequent protest activities can be best illustrated by both Taiwan's and Korea's environmental movements. In the case of Taiwan, after environmental discourses had been disseminated in the early 1970s and popularized in the second half of the decade, both the frequency and intensity of protest activities grew, and pollution victims were provided with new discursive weapons—the number of environmental protests quadrupled in 1977 and tripled in 1984 compared to the previous year, respectively. More and more reports appeared in the early 1980s documenting how angry residents had rushed into polluting facilities and smashed up the offices. By that time, the right to live pollution-free was firmly incorporated into the repertoire of protest action. We also observe more organized efforts to advocate environmental causes. Lawyers managed to get involved in the cooking oil case and brought lawsuits against the wrongdoers (Hsiao, Cheng, and Lei 1982); 116 farmers initiated the first antipollution lawsuit, seeking financial compensation for crop damage, and won their case in 1981 (*China Times* 1982e); and natural scientists and writers successfully collaborated with major media outlets to launch a yearlong conservationist campaign to save an ecologically sensitive area (Chou and Yao 1980; Ma 1980).

Korea's environmental movement followed a similar path. More and more open confrontations were observed after the Onsan case in 1985. Antipollution lawsuits were pursued and won in the late 1980s. A variety of campaigns—against golf courses, airport development, and nuclear waste dumping facilities—were waged with varying degrees of success. The movement's overall capacity to shape public opinion grew exponentially throughout the 1990s.

To sum up, the synchronization of action and consciousness is a dual battle. On one hand, scattered protest activities must escalate to break away from existing institutional arrangements and open the floor for counterhegemonic discourses to reach the target audience. On the other hand, isolated discourses on labor rights and environmentalism must be ready to take on dominant ideologies that had been finely honed and widely practiced for years and, more importantly, either to win over a portion of targeted workers or, in the case of environmental protest, to be translated into public consciousness.

Two themes emerge from the preceding crude sketch of the relationship between action and consciousness: structural constraints placed on labor and environmental movements and the unique paths that the four movements chart. On the first theme, it is most obvious that, in the case of early-riser movements (Taiwan's environmental and Korea's labor movements), the synchronization of consciousness and action went more smoothly than for the latecomer movements (Taiwan's labor and Korea's environmental movements). We are immediately prompted to ask what stood in the way of the convergence. The key to understanding particular constraints placed on movement emergence is to analyze the pattern of government intervention in settling labor and environmental conflicts, either through co-optation and compromise or by engaging in ideological warfare to absorb or discredit oppositional agendas. We deal with this issue most closely in the following chapter.

The second theme is that labor and environmental movements underwent the synchronization process somewhat differently. On the part of labor movements, it was protest activities that inspired further elaborations of oppositional consciousness and counterhegemonic discourses. Be they self-sacrificing gestures (self-immolation) or the display of collective power (strikes, slowdowns, walkouts), the gravity of both labor movements revolved around the capacity to *act* (Offe and Wiesenthal 1980). The way that new consciousness and counterideology came into the picture of both labor movements was through resonance with lived experiences and associative activities among workers. Efforts to shift working-class consciousness specifically targeted two subsets of workers: those who were most likely to act and those who posed most threats to the powers-that-be if they did act. If we observe the early organizing efforts of both labor movements, the formation of working-class consciousness and the adoption of counterideology among workers were mediated through workplace interactions, small-group meetings, night schools, and semisecretive cadre training programs. Consciousness-raising efforts in these settings were meant to sustain future mobilization and strengthen workers' will—and willingness—to act on their interests and beliefs, even under precarious conditions.

In contrast to the centrality of protest activities to labor movements, the dissemination of a new ideology called environmentalism was of greater importance to the development of the two environmental movements. It was through highly publicized public hazard cases that environmentalists finally got their message out, and protest activities began to be understood in a brand-new light. The formation of both environmental movements revolved around—paraphrasing Offe and Wiesenthal—the capacity to *persuade*. The work of persuasion targeted everyone, not just potential pollution victims, and, as a consequence, was heavily mediated through media outlets. Local means of communication—neighborhood networks or village meetings— were of importance only when mobilization for specific protest events at particular locales was concerned. As environmental activism moved into the arena of national politics, it depended on mass media to reach a broader audience. Protest activities at the formative stage of environmental movements functioned as testimonials to a national audience of the authenticity of the new ideology, in both the scientific and philosophical senses, to convert previously indifferent bystanders into believers.

The contrast here is that the counterhegemonic ideology sustained a specific segment of workers to act collectively and to strengthen the labor movements that advanced their class interest, whereas environmental protests persuaded an amorphous, general public to entrust to environmental movements the duty to realize universal interests and the collective good.

3

The Emergence of Early-Riser Movements

You won't be arrested for pursuing environmental issues. You won't and you can't.

 —Korean labor activist, personal interview

Taiwan's and Korea's movement emergence stories began in the early 1970s, twenty-some years after anticolonial struggles were won and a system of divided nationhood was firmly established in the Cold War era.[1] Unlike European workers and other protesters whose experience of industrialization preceded the struggle for citizenship, the political rights of Asian workers and other aggrieved populations predated "the development of a stable economy" (Lipset 1959, 101). Macro socioeconomic conditions—a universal suffrage that did not, however, guarantee genuine power sharing, and young, capitalistic economies aspiring to rid themselves of poverty and stride toward great wealth—set the stage for labor and environmental movements to make their entry.

Against this backdrop, this chapter begins with two long quotations from movement activists regarding the discrepant timing of movement emergence. One Taiwanese activist involved in both labor and environmental movements remarked,

> To organize pollution victims was much easier than organizing workers. . . .
> If this place had pollution problems, we just went there and investigated a
> little, checked the statutes and ordinances, called a village-wide meeting.

Everybody came, discussed a little and decided to protest, then we went on protesting. . . . The ideological basis of an environmental movement was solid, well accepted like the idea of democracy, human rights or the love for one's hometown, and these could easily be used in environmental mobilization. The ideological struggle in the factory was very difficult. "What's wrong if bosses want to make more money?" "When times are bad, factory owners have no choice but to sack people and cut wages." In labor movements you constantly had to battle such ways of thinking. But in environmental protests, none of the local residents would say it was OK for factories to pollute. (interview with Taiwanese labor scholar, January 9, 2003)

In contrast, a seasoned Korean labor activist commented,

Talking about environmental issues wouldn't harm you, it's like talking about democracy. . . . Labor movements are about conditions inside the factory. . . . Environmental groups protested about toxins getting out of factories and damaging the environment. I wanted to ask: what about those working *inside* the factory? Workers were dying from the toxins! I think environmental groups decided to deal with pollution issues from outside and didn't talk much about pollution inside the factory. . . . Environmental groups only care about water, waste, that sort of thing. . . . The labor movement is only for workers. The environmental movement is for everybody, and it involves no danger. But for workers, we have to expect penalties and prison terms if we really get involved. (interview with Korean labor union leader, April 17, 2003)

These two quotations are a prelude to a discussion of the unveiling of early-riser movements. In the first, the contrast was between the varying degrees of difficulty in combating dominant ideologies and securing certain successes at pollution sites and workplaces. Taiwan's environmental movement was in an advantaged position because its ideological basis was solid, in the sense that environmentalism had a certain affinity with existing beliefs, which people embraced without question. Labor, in contrast, lacked such an ideological buttress. The second quotation highlights the different levels of repression that labor and environmental movements confronted in Korea. It is asserted that the Korean environmental movement was leniently treated, in contrast to constant witch-hunts against labor. If the first quotation indicates the significance of ideological breakthroughs in the development of Taiwan's environmental movement, it does not tell us the process and mechanisms through which environmentalism as a new ideology was propagated and accepted.

The second quotation points to the ambiguous effect of repression on im-
peding movement emergence. It was the heavily repressed labor movement
in Korea that first broke free from institutional confines. It seemed to be an
ironic twist that repression turned out to legitimize rebellion. If repression
alone cannot dictate the timing of movement emergence, we need to explore
further what enabled Korean labor to evolve into a collective actor and, at
the same time, what prevented the environmental movement from achieving
a similar level of success.

In the following sections, these two quotations will be placed in their
historical contexts. This chapter argues that Taiwan and Korea showed two
distinct "structures of grievance," conditioned by how the project of industrialization had been geographically organized, and two different schemes of
"conflict management" through which the authorities intended to prevent
labor and environmental conflicts from escalating. Taiwan's incorporationist scheme and decentralized industrialization weakened the consolidation of
labor power yet were incapable of resolving environmental grievances and of
preventing them from engendering a rural–urban alliance. Korea's exclusionist approach and centralized industrialization, by contrast, resolved early environmental conflicts by relocating pollution victims and so undermining their
chances of forming a wider coalition, but they failed to quell intense labor
conflicts aided by students and churches. Through exploring the two sets of
infranational variations of labor and environmental movement, this chapter
demonstrates the interactive effects between government interventions and
movement powers and the resulting movement sequences.

The Patterns of Industrialization and the Structure of Grievances

Petitions, lawsuits, demonstrations, and other forms of collective action are
barometers of social grievance. Government documents on disputes and newspaper coverage of protest activities provide a starting point for readers to
get a glimpse of how grievances are structured. In a nutshell, Taiwan's labor
and environmental disputes were geographically scattered in rural and urban
areas. The size of each dispute, measured by the number of participants,
tended to be small and the overall number of yearly disputes numerous. In
Korea, labor and environmental disputes were geographically concentrated.
The size of each dispute was larger and the number of yearly disputes fewer.

On the labor front, early labor disputes in Taiwan and Korea all started
from nonstrategic, labor-intensive export sectors. If we take a look at the
distribution of labor disputes recorded by both countries' labor administrations between 1966 and 2001 (see Figure 9), Taiwan had 67,720 occurrences, whereas Korea had 12,152.[2] Taiwan's total number of labor disputes

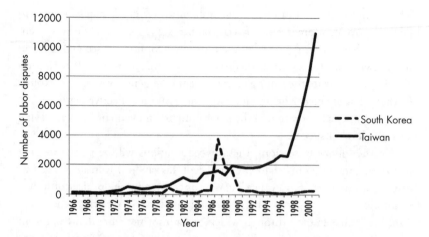

Figure 9. Distribution of labor disputes, 1966–2001. Data for Taiwan: 1966–70 from Djang (1977, 287) and for 1971–2001 from Yearbook of Labor Statistics *(Directorate-General of Budget Accounting and Statistics). Data for Korea: 1966–80 from Deyo (1989, 60–61), Huang (1999, 115), and Koo (2001, 159); 1981–2001 from the International Labour Organization's labor statistics (http://laborsta.ilo.org/).*

was five times its Korean counterpart; yet these figures are misleading in the sense that they indicate neither the strength of nor the solidarity among the Taiwanese workers. The size of the average Taiwanese labor dispute was incredibly small, at 12 workers per dispute, in contrast to Korea's 392 workers per dispute (see Figure 10).

On the environmental front, environmental protest data are used as an imperfect proxy because of a lack of comprehensive early statistics (see Figure 11). Taiwan had 1,957 occurrences of environmental protest between 1961 and 1987, with an average of 72 incidents per year. These environmental protests took place in five out of twenty-two counties and cities on the Taiwanese mainland in 1961, the number increased to fifteen out of twenty-two by 1971, and finally, in 1980, environmental protests broke out in every county and city (Liu 2011, 9–10). In Korea, 60 environmental protests were recorded between 1969 and 1990, with an average of 2.7 per year. Concerning the geographical expansion of Korea's environmental protests, Ku's comprehensive study of the history of Korea's environmental movement provides some clues. Throughout the 1970s, there were eleven major pollution events (Ku 1996a, 146, Table 5-1), and the majority of these were located in industrial

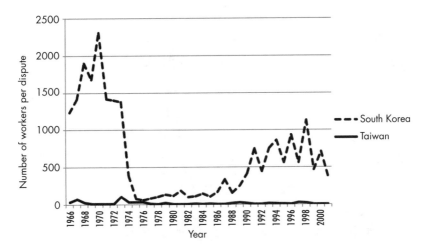

Figure 10. Size of labor disputes, 1966–2001. Data for Taiwan: 1966–70 from Djang (1977, 287); 1971–2001 from Yearbook of Labor Statistics *(Directorate-General of Budget Accounting and Statistics). Data for Korea: 1966–80 from Deyo (1989, 60–61), Huang (1999, 115), and Koo (2001, 159); 1981–2001 from ILO's labor statistics (http://laborsta.ilo.org/).*

centers (Seoul, Incheon, Pusan, and Ulsan). Only two cases out of the eleven were in rural areas, and these concerned pesticide-related pollution.

These contrasting structures of grievance resulted from the different patterns of industrialization that the two countries had undertaken. Taiwan's development strategy was to achieve international competitiveness through flexible subcontracting systems. This led to a decentralized industrial structure. In contrast, Korea's development relied on an economy of scale, which led to a spatially concentrated, *chaebol*[3]-dominated industrialization and the aggregation of workers in a handful of urban areas. By examining income and occupation data on farming households in rural areas, Ho contends that "in Korea industries are concentrated in or near the principal cities of Seoul and Pusan, whereas Taiwan's industrialization has followed a more decentralized pattern" (Ho 1979, 77). Between 1956 and 1966, rural Taiwan absorbed a very large share of the increase in employment in labor-intensive industries, such as textiles, apparel, food, wood products, and nonmetallic mineral products (Ho 1982, 984). By 1971, manufacturing establishments located outside sixteen urban centers "accounted for 50 percent of the manufacturing employment and produced 48 percent of the manufacturing value-added" (Ho 1979, 83).

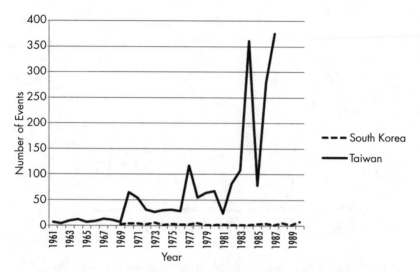

Figure 11. Distribution of environmental protests, 1961–90. Data for both countries compiled by the author. Data for Taiwan from the China Times Fifty-Year Images Databank *(http://140.112.152.45/ttsweb/); data for Korea from the* Korea Times *and the* Korea Herald *microfilms archived in Harvard-Yenching Library, National Assembly Library of Korea, and National Taiwan University Library.*

By contrast, in 1974, 44 percent of Korea's labor force outside of agriculture and mining worked in Seoul and Pusan, and the figure jumps to 62 percent if we count the adjacent provinces of the two cities (Ho 1979, 77n3). In 1984, "approximately one-half of all manufacturing workers were found in the Seoul-Kyungin area . . . and another 40 percent were in the Yongnam region, which includes two major cities, Pusan and Taegu" (Koo 2001, 42–44). The patterns of industrialization, first, conditioned the process of proletarianization—part-time proletariat in rural Taiwan versus rural labor force flocking into urban areas for employment in Korea (Gates 1979; Koo 2001)—and, second, affected the spatial patterns of industrial pollution: geographical dispersion in Taiwan but concentration in Korea.

The patterns of industrialization entail both spatial and organizational dimensions. For the spatial dimension, this distinction of centralization and decentralization refers to the physical locations of industrial establishments and the geographical dispersion within a specific territory. Taiwan's industrial establishments spread rather evenly along the west coast, in urban and rural areas alike (see Map 1). In the 1960s and 1970s, two-thirds of thirty-eight newly established industrial estates were located away from Taiwan's

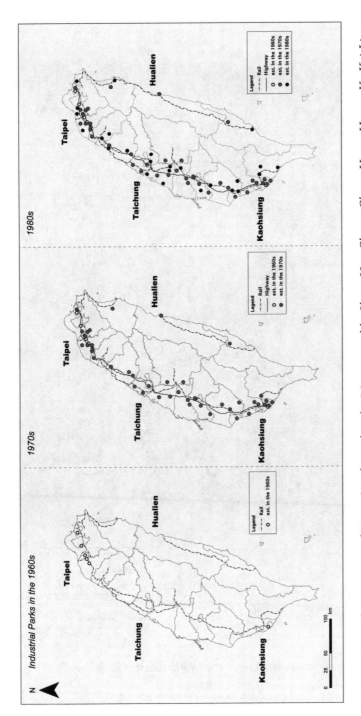

Map 1. *Geographic expansion of Taiwan's industrial parks. Maps created by Sheng-Han Chang, Chung-Hsuan Huang, Yu-Kai Liao, Chieh-Ting Tsai, and the author. Data from the Industrial Development Bureau MEA (1997), Lin (2007), and the web page of the Industrial Development Bureau (http://www.moeaidb.gov.tw/), which included information on each industrial park.*

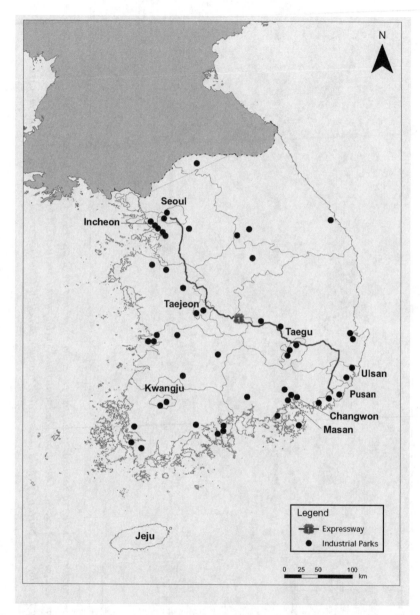

Map 2. Korea's industrial complexes in the 1980s. Adapted from Koo (2001, Map 1).

major cities and their suburbs (Ho 1982, 984). As a consequence, "Taiwan's countryside is studded with small factories in industries which . . . pollute badly, such as leather tanning, wire stripping, and electroplating. The number of factories increased 10-fold, from 5,623 to 62,474 between 1950 and 1980" (J. Moore 1988, 45).

Korea's industries were mostly concentrated in the metropolitan areas—Seoul-Incheon, Pusan, and other cities (Taegu and Ulsan) along the expressway connecting Seoul and Pusan (see Map 2). The spatial distribution of industrial establishments had profound impacts on the disparities in rural–urban income (Ho 1979), domestic migration patterns, and the process of proletarianization (M. Kim 2003, 83; Koo 2001, 41–43). When industrial employment was concentrated in urban areas, it involved a rural-to-urban migration of agricultural surplus labor. The result was the spatial concentration of industrial workers at particular locales and the gradual rise of densely populated working-class communities, as indicated in Table 2.

The following lines from Kim Ji-ha's poem poignantly capture the domestic migratory pattern:

> . . . don't cry, I must go
> on the painful road to Seoul,
> climbing the many hills which make even the sky weary,
> to sell my labour (cf. Chun 2003, 73)

By contrast, Taiwan's decentralized industrialization and industrial employment in the rural areas "made it possible to transfer labor services from agricultural to non-agricultural activity without at the same time moving laborers

Table 2. Geographical concentration of Korea's industrial workers

Region	Number of workers (thousands)		
	1970	1980	1989
Seoul	291 (33.9%)	445 (22.1%)	526 (17.0%)
Incheon/Kyunggi	104 (12.1%)	478 (23.8%)	982 (31.8%)
Pusan	137 (15.9%)	319 (15.8%)	383 (12.4%)
Kyungnam	60 (7.0%)	231 (11.5%)	407 (13.2%)
Taegu/Kyungbuk	99 (11.5%)	263 (13.1%)	382 (12.3%)
Total for Seoul, Incheon/Kyunggi, and Pusan	532 (62.0%)	1242 (61.8%)	1891 (61.2%)

Source: Hong (1997, 151, Table 5-1).

from rural to urban areas" (Ho 1982, 984). This produced what Gates called Taiwan's "part-time proletariat":

> When factories shut down, lay off, automate, or for some other reason need fewer workers, these young people can be sent back to farms and shops where large, frugal households will absorb them. . . . Industry has the use of them when they are young and cheap, and is not obliged to contend with an angry out-of-work proletariat massed *near* the factories when its own interests dictate layoffs and firings. (Gates 1979, 401–2, emphasis mine)

Beside the spatial dimension, there is also an organizational dimension to the distinction between centralized and decentralized industrialization, indicating how economic power was distributed among enterprises of different sizes in different sectors and how capital and human resources were organized to push forward developmental projects. It is widely acknowledged that the vitality of Taiwan's economy has rested on the manufacturing exports of numerous small- and medium-sized enterprises (SMEs). It was an economy sustained by SMEs in the private sector, while large-scale public enterprises[4] at upstream sectors functioned as policy instruments to influence downstream private firms. Korea, by contrast, "has acquired one of the world's most concentrated economies" (Amsden 1989, 122), in which large, private business groups, benefiting from public subsidies, became the driving force of the economy.[5] In 1984, Korea's top three *chaebol* alone accounted for 35.8 percent of GNP, and the combined sales of the top five and top ten *chaebol* accounted for 52.4 percent and 67.4 percent of GNP, respectively (Amsden 1989, 116, Table 5.1). Amsden further shows that, in 1982, 82 percent of 2,260 commodities were produced under monopolies (more than 80 percent of market share held by one company), duopolies (more than 80 percent of market share held by two companies), or oligopolies (more than 60 percent of market share held by three companies) (120–21). Table 3 summarizes the contrast between the top business groups and SMEs in both countries. Even though the data are from the 1980s and 1990s, the infrastructures for Taiwan's SME-centered industrialization and Korea's *chaebol*-dominated economy were already well laid out by the late 1960s and 1970s.

One may reasonably surmise that occurrences of labor and environmental conflict were conditioned by patterns of industrialization. Spatially, labor exploitation and "negative externalities" like pollution took place where industrial establishments resided. When sources of pollution and exploitation were geographically spread out, labor and environmental conflicts tended to be found across the map. If industrial establishments were geographically

Table 3. Shares of economic contributions of top business groups and SMEs

| | Sales of top business groups in 1994 (% of GDP) | | | SME share of total exports (%) | |
	Taiwan	Korea	Year	Taiwan	Korea
Top 5 groups	12.3	49.0	1982	69.7	22.1
Top 10 groups	19.7	60.4	1986	66.4	35.3
Top 30 groups	31.3	73.7	1991	56.9	39.3

Source: Abe and Kawakami (1997, 395, 397, Tables V and VII).

concentrated in major metropolitan areas, labor and environmental protests tended to be confined to these areas as well. In a nutshell, the spatial distribution of industrial establishments roughly corresponded to the spatial distribution of labor and environmental conflicts.

Concerning the organizational aspect of industrialization, the scale of labor disputes was conditioned by the size of industrial establishments, whereas the effect of the size of production units on the scale of environmental protests was rather unclear. In the case of labor disputes, it was unlikely for a labor dispute to be filed by one hundred workers when only thirty workers were employed at the workplace. In an SME-dominated economy like Taiwan, one was likely to observe numerous labor disputes at any given time, but their size was rather small. The relatively large size of industrial establishments in Korea provided a setting in which labor disputes had the potential to involve more workers. As for environmental protests, the polluting capacity of an industrial establishment was not solely determined by its scale of production but was also affected by its physical location (e.g., being sited on a river upstream of a densely populated city) and its financial capacity to invest in pollution control.[6] The total volume of toxic waste produced by a small factory may be less than for a large-scale production unit; yet the small factory may be less likely to invest in pollution control and more likely to externalize production costs such as waste management, not to mention the effect of the factory happening to shed waste into a river serving as a water supply for densely populated areas. It is safe to suggest that levels of air and water pollution produced by either SMEs in Taiwan or large corporations in Korea have been quite high since the 1970s, given the available statistics.

The crucial point is that the pattern of industrialization, whether centralized or decentralized, set the parameters within which labor and environmental conflicts took shape and were structured. Labor and environmental conflicts mattered because, on one hand, they signified firsthand experiences of labor exploitation and environmental degradation on the ground and, on the other, they were caught between governmental efforts to quiet disobedience and movement organizers' efforts to magnify their impact. If such conflicts could be easily resolved through existing institutional procedures, the effectiveness of government intervention was reaffirmed and labor and environmental activists lost a chance to advance their causes. If such conflicts remained "unresolvable," they became a showcase for pinpointing institutional failures and reframing public discussions. Broadly put, movement powers retreated as government intervention worked out fine and advanced when institutional processes failed to settle conflicts. There was a clear zero-sum relation between government intervention and movement powers as far as labor and environmental conflicts were concerned. How the delicate tango of two opposing forces—government intervention and movement powers—was played out in Taiwan and Korea becomes our immediate concern.

Two Opposing Forces: When Regime Control Met Movement Powers

From the patterns of government intervention in labor and environmental conflicts, a *second* difference between the ways in which Taiwan and Korea controlled dissent now needs to be noted. Taiwan deployed an "incorporationist" scheme, whereas Korea used exclusion and repression to contain social protests. Taiwan's Kuomintang (KMT) was a very stable, quasi-Leninist party-state (Amsden 1985; Cheng 1989). Backed up by superior organizational capacities, it extended its party branches into rural and urban sectors and occupied most of the public space available for dissent. KMT rule was based on one principle: it claimed to represent the interests of all groups and all strata and laid out the organizational infrastructure to achieve this. By contrast, Korea's military regimes between 1961 and 1987 were highly unstable, marked by coups, loose-then-tight control schemes (Deyo 1989, 72–82), underground antigovernment resistance (Lim 2000), and fitful outbursts of popular discontent (Choi 2000). The general logic of the military junta was not about strengthening party machinery and other organizational infrastructures that could endure the rise and fall of any particular general-turned-president[7] but rather about consolidating power in the strongman's hands and prolonging his political career indefinitely by any means—quite drastic means, in fact, such as revising the constitution, declaring a state of emergency, suspending national elections, or kidnapping opposition leaders whenever the incumbent felt threatened. When openly challenged, the regime generally restored order by force, and the intensity of repression grew with time. Incorporation and repression as two contrasting principles of authoritarian rule yielded, as we will see later, quite different results, while meeting labor and environmental challenges.

Taiwan's Incorporationist Control

As an increasing number of geographically dispersed labor and environmental conflicts began to surface in the early 1970s, Taiwan's ruling KMT deployed its "incorporationist" approach to settle local conflicts. This incorporationist scheme was part and parcel of the KMT's attempt to solve a crisis of legitimacy triggered by a series of international and domestic events. In October 1971, the political claim that the KMT put forth to justify its authoritarian rule in Taiwan—"we are the only legitimate representative of China"—was decisively undermined by United Nations Resolution 2758, in which the governmental seat of China was transferred from the Republic of China (Taiwan) to the People's Republic of China (PRC). The following year, Nixon visited China and the Joint U.S.–China Communiqué was issued. International setbacks reached a peak in 1979 when formal diplomatic relations between the United States and Taiwan ended. Domestically, Generalissimo Chiang Kai-shek died in 1975, and his Soviet-trained, one-time-Communist son took over power. With an overall sense of national crisis, student activism broke out in the early 1970s but was subsequently rechanneled and taken over by the KMT's Youth Corps. Both oil crises of the 1970s led to serious economic recessions. Problems such as the pricing of agricultural products, plant closures, inflation, and unemployment developed (Li 1992, 95).

In response to this national crisis, the KMT reconsolidated its support base on two fronts. Economically, it launched new national development projects for industrial restructuring—a shift from a labor-intensive to a capital-intensive mode of development (Gold 1986, chapter 7; Haggard 1990). Government officials stated quite bluntly that Taiwan was losing ground diplomatically. It must succeed in international markets. Less than two weeks after being kicked out of the United Nations, the vice minister of economic affairs proposed that "maintaining economic growth and further exploring international markets are the only ways to protect us given the current international situation." He further gave detailed suggestions for providing investment incentives and fixing the inflation problem (*United Daily* 1971b). Top party and government officials convened and reached a similar conclusion that "the most urgent task now is to win the economic war over the Communist PRC" (*United Daily* 1971a).

Politically, the KMT strengthened existing systems of interest representation. The most pronounced actions were this émigré regime's project of

"Taiwanization" (Gold 1986, 114)—opening up a channel for indigenous politicians to move up the power hierarchy (J.-H. Wang 1989)—and an all-out effort, beginning in 1973, to organize labor unions (Dzeng 1994, 72–82; Li 1992, 95–101). This was not the first time that the KMT had tried to tame organized labor. As early as 1951, the KMT began its first wave of drives toward unionization, promulgating the Labor Movements Directive, in which it was stipulated that "labor sentiment should be reflected back to the party at all times, so that the decision-making of the party can accurately represent workers' interests and also receive support from workers" (Fan 2004, 257). Twenty years later, the aims of a second union drive in the 1970s were to (1) direct the founding of new unions, (2) recruit non-KMT union activists into the party, (3) reserve leadership positions for party members, and (4) plant party cells inside workplaces to monitor labor activities (Huang 1999). Between 1973 and 1983, the average annual increase in the number of newly founded unions was ninety-three, almost fivefold the figure between 1960 and 1972, which was only twenty (Li 1992, 97). A KMT cadre testified as to how the KMT managed the labor sector at that time:

> I started working on union organizing in 1970. I was responsible for visiting factories to organize unions and to protect those who were interested in forming a union. Whenever there was a slight sign of labor disturbance, I would be the first one to be there. . . . As a KMT labor movement organizer, you had to go out and organize unions. Each of us was assigned to and responsible for organizing certain industries. We even had a yearly union organizing competition, those who organized the most unions each year won. And you got a sales commission for organizing each union. (interview with a former KMT labor movement organizer, February 20, 2003)

The KMT organizers handled both public and private enterprises and simultaneously planted party cells in factories along with the founding of labor unions. The KMT organizers were given an official title in the Taiwanese provincial government and acted in an official capacity to inform factory owners about the governmental policy on promoting union organizing. In cases where factory owners were cooperative, the owners often ordered plant managers to give the KMT organizers a list of workers' names as the founding members of unions. In cases where owners resisted, the KMT organizers would get workers involved through educational campaigns. A 1971 KMT document titled "Suggestions on Guiding Union-Organizing at Private Mining and Manufacturing Industries" stipulated that, if workers who joined the union drive were threatened by employers with job transfers, layoffs, or other disciplinary action, all relevant agencies should step in to protect the workers and help them regain their posts and back salary (Fan 2004, 322). As for how the party cadres dealt with wildcat strikes and slowdowns:

> There were no strikes in the 1970s, maybe slowdowns, but no strikes, no demonstrations. At that time, in big factories, we had party-organized cells. Any sign of labor disturbance would be reported to the upper branch and we would intervene immediately and solve problems quickly. *We would not let things deteriorate into workers taking to the streets.* (interview with a former KMT labor movement organizer, February 20, 2003)

The KMT's second union drive was sensitive to enterprise size. The same KMT organizer noted, "We were handed a list of companies with basic information such as factory locations, numbers of workers, etc. Then we chose from this list. First we organized factories employing more than five hundred workers. Once these were unionized, we moved down the list to organize factories employing fewer than five hundred but more than three hundred. *Always starting from the big ones*" (interview with a former KMT labor movement organizer, February 20, 2003). It is also worth noting that the Labor Union Law of the time "prohibit[ed] unions in workplaces with fewer than 30 employees, even though these enterprises account[ed] for 95 percent of the total and employ[ed] 70 percent of Taiwan's workforce" (Cohen 1988, 128). If the "organized" workers at large corporations were under the KMT's patronage, the labor problem at the "unorganized" SMEs was handed to a system of mediation and compulsory arbitration:

> The city or county government may set up the Labor Dispute Arbitration Board "to expedite the settlement of labor disputes so that production may be kept in good order." . . . No lockout, strike, or work slowdown are [*sic*] allowed before or during the period of arbitration. When the case becomes serious, the competent authorities may resort to compulsory arbitration. The decision of the Arbitration Board is final, and any one or party which infringes upon the contents of the decision will be punished under the Provisional Regulations for the Punishment of Persons Obstructing National Mobilization. (Djang 1977, 286–87)

Besides organizing labor unions, the KMT had, since the 1950s, organized farmers' and fishermen's associations and set up hundreds of "service stations" *(fuwuzhan)* in almost every township in the countryside and every district in the cities throughout Taiwan. By 1969, there existed 401 such service stations hiring 28,731 full-time party cadres to "service the needs of the masses." The ratio of full-time party workers to the overall population was 0.24 percent, that is to say, there were just over two full-time party cadres for every one thousand people (Wu 1987, 54–55, 58). Their service activities ranged from "scholarship, emergency aids, medical care, legal assistance, [and] employment, to various kinds of leisure activities" (76). Party branches disguised as "service centers" actively participated in all types of conflict resolution at the local level, including environmental disputes. In many antipollution cases, party cadres, along with local politicians, sat on mediation committees to help settle the amount of compensation for damage caused by pollution. Mediation activities also took place in the offices of service stations.

The KMT adopted an "incorporationist" approach to handle both labor and environmental conflicts, but the same approach yielded divergent results. Labor conflicts were settled through institutional means and labor's power was contained, whereas government intervention provided no long-term solutions to environmental conflicts, which led to the rapid expansion of environmental protests. Recurring pollution protests in the same old locations, and spreading to other areas, constantly questioned the legitimacy of a developmental state.

Labor Discontent Smothered

The KMT's labor control was multilayered. Workers at large-scale corporations and strategic industries were under the KMT's patronage. "The presence of security agents and ruling party activists in many workplaces has an incalculable restraining effect on collective action by the workplace" (Cohen 1988, 130). On the rare occasions that signs of labor grievance were detected in those big corporations, "we would not let things deteriorate into workers taking to the street," as the interviewed party cadre said. Party cells inside the workplace and labor unions worked with the goal of quieting discontent and speeding up conflict resolution. Anecdotes like the following were often heard:

> In 1975, 7,000 female workers intended to launch a strike at General Instruments, a US-invested company. One week later, the vice-president revealed the secret of how to have workers concede. He just told the KMT intelligence agents in the company that, if the thing was not settled quickly, they were going to divest. The KMT agent promptly pressured the union, and a 7,000-worker strike was immediately dissolved. (cf. Cheng 1988, 53)

The strike began with the American management's failure to pay a promised bonus, which "led to a one-shift strike, but government officials and the pro-KMT union forced a return to work, and even singled out strike leaders, who were prosecuted. The bonus was not paid" (Cohen 1988, 130). Because labor discontent at big corporations was closely monitored and promptly intervened in by party cadres and unionists, labor conflicts and open defiance in big corporations were extremely rare before the mid-1980s.

The numerous labor disputes mainly took place at un-unionized SMEs in labor-intensive, nonstrategic industries. Thus the average size of each dispute was extremely small. In Shieh's study on 215 labor disputes, 70 percent were one-person disputes, 92 percent had fewer than ten workers involved, and in only one case out of 215 were there more than thirty workers involved (Shieh 1997, 208). Furthermore, both labor statistics and empirical studies repeatedly confirmed that the major causes of labor disputes were termination of contract and arrears of wages (Hsiao 1992, 159, Table 7.2). Labor disputes often took place at a time when employment relations had been terminated or bordered on being terminated. When Shieh reinterviewed the petitioners, he found that in 93 percent of cases (200 out of 215), employment relations had been terminated (Shieh 1997, 174). Considering the number of workers involved and the timing of labor disputes, Taiwanese workers were granted little leverage against employers and may have only grudgingly relied on the system of mediation and compulsory arbitration to seek minimal justice.

The effectiveness of the mediation system can be verified by a closer reading of Taiwan's yearbooks of labor statistics. Among piles of figures and tables, the numbers of unsettled disputes are displayed side by side with the total number of labor disputes each year. The sheer presence of such items speaks volumes. This is evidence not only that a mediation system was at work but also that this system was so well documented that the outcome of each case could be crisply presented in statistical terms. Taiwan and Korea both adopted the system of mediation and compulsory arbitration in labor disputes, but one simply does not see such figures in Korea's labor statistics. Looking into the figures more closely, it is astonishing how successfully the mediation system resolved Taiwan's labor disputes. In bad years—also bear in mind that any dispute dragging on longer than a month would be counted as unsettled—the percentage of unsettled cases was between 3 and 7 percent. In good years, there were no unsettled cases. Even in 2001, as the number of labor disputes hit a record high (more than ten thousand), the percentage of unsettled cases was 0.9 percent.

Furthermore, the mediation system was only a small part of the KMT's effort to tame the working class. Under *no pressure from organized labor*, in 1950, the KMT enacted labor insurance—health care for the employed—to cover public enterprise workers and transportation industries. One year later, the coverage of labor insurance was extended to all enterprises hiring more than ten workers (Huang 1999, 63), covering roughly 70 to 75 percent of the labor force. Under *no* pressure from organized labor, but with some protest from capitalists, the KMT enacted the Labor Standards Law in 1984 to provide guarantees "concerning maximum hours, vacation time, pensions, severance pay, minimum wages, pay equity, maternity leave, bankruptcy protections, and occupational safety and health" (Cohen 1988, 131).[8] This is in stark contrast to the experience in Western Europe, where pro-labor measures resulted from the long-standing struggles of organized labor. Legal protection and health coverage came as a free gift for Taiwan's workers. Though never thoroughly implementing the pro-labor measures to protect workers' interests, the KMT carefully positioned itself between labor and capital to create the facade that workers could look up to this party-state for help. Some also argue that Taiwan's labor laws were just "a stand-by mechanism" (Shieh 1997, 189). On paper, all the basic rights were guaranteed and legally protected. In practice, workers' collective organizations were manipulated and controlled by the party-state. The KMT intervened in labor disputes not to redress unequal power relations between capital and labor but to let the logic of the labor market reign. If a worker was treated badly, the KMT helped her get payments in arrears or injury compensation and then sent the worker back on the labor market to find another job.

Workers in large corporations and strategic industries were preemptively organized by the KMT, meaning that workers in the most advantaged positions were prevented from exercising their bargaining power in the 1970s and the first half of the 1980s. At the same time, workers who were not under constant state surveillance did voice their discontent in the form of petitions and direct action. The structural location of these workers—labor-intensive SMEs in nonstrategic industries—granted them less leverage vis-à-vis the state and capitalists given the abundance of the labor supply. The small size of labor disputes further diminished these workers' bargaining power, which enabled the existing mediation system to reach a quick resolution. As Moore (1978, 97) clearly points out, social support received sustains one's defiance toward the authorities. The size of labor disputes directly affected, on one hand, the breadth of workers' solidarity and, on the other, the extent to which workers were able to exercise leverage vis-à-vis the opponents in each microconfrontation. The smaller the size of a dispute, the less support workers received from their peers, the less leverage they had, the more likely they would be to opt for a way out of the dispute on an individual basis, and the easier the system of mediation could smother potential rebellion. The more workers let the KMT mediate individual labor disputes, the less likely the workers were to challenge yellow unions in the workplace or build genuine labor power of their own. The choice offered to Taiwan's workers in the early days was between "play by the book and get something back, no matter how unsatisfactory" and "play with fire and risk getting fried." Judging from history, Taiwan's workers chose the former.

Environmentalism Unleashed

Overwhelming concerns over the environment in the 1970s originated from two sources. On one hand, it was from direct, simple perceptions that one's little world was being threatened by unknown forces. Crops withered and fish died in ponds overnight; clothes hung outside became stained with suspicious dust, noises from nearby factories were so loud that the windows rattled; air smelled bad, water tasted awful, and bodies fell ill. On the other hand, environmental concerns came from imported thoughts, mediated by foreign PhD holders. The first generation of foreign-trained natural scientists returned to Taiwan in the early 1970s. Shocked by the state of environmental degradation, they began to voice their concerns over industrial pollution and the lack of conservationism and later on supplied their expertise to justify the cause of environmental activism.

But the success of the incorporationist scheme in settling labor disputes did not transfer over to environmental conflicts. Among 1,957 environmental protest events that erupted between 1961 and 1987, 35 percent were initiated by farmers and fishermen whose livelihoods were threatened by the operations of nearby industrial establishments. Omitting those cases in which protesters' occupations were unreported, farmers and fishery workers initiated almost 90 percent of environmental protests (see Table 4). Roughly 20 percent became serious pollution disputes involving recurring, multiple protests.

In the 1970s, it was rather common for factories to "[take] advantage of irrigation and drainage canals in the rural areas to discharge the industrial waste water without treatment. In a few cases, industrial waste has resulted in soil contamination so bad that surrounding farmland had to be abandoned" (Sun, Knutson, and Lee 1998). Such practices infuriated the highly advanced and commercialized agricultural sector. After the postwar land reforms, the KMT "followed the traditional sequence of first developing its agriculture and rural infrastructure and then rapidly expanding its industrial sector with the help of resources . . . diverted from agriculture" (Ho 1982, 983). The agricultural sector, as Hobsbawm has argued, performed three fundamental functions in the process of industrialization: it fed an increasingly nonagricultural population by raising its productivity; it supplied surplus

Table 4. Occupational distribution of Taiwan's environmental protesters

Occupation of environmental protesters	Occurrences	Percentage
Professionals	27	3
Legislators, senior officials, and managers	54	7
Clerks, technicians, and associate professionals	5	1
Service and sales workers	2	0
Agricultural and fishery workers	688	88
Craft workers, plant and machine operators	7	1
Unreported (missing)	1,174	–
Total	1,957	100

Source: *China Times* Fifty-Year Images Databank.

laborers for industries; and it provided "a mechanism for the accumulation of capital to be used in the more modern sectors of the economy" (Hobsbawm 1962, 31). Thanks to this agriculture-then-industry policy, a diversified agro-industry was developed, which had benefited from improvements in rural infrastructure (transportation systems and rural electrification) and extensive government programs supplying technical assistance to the small and intensively worked farms (Ho 1982, 982–83). Farmers and fishermen engaging in antipollution protests were, in truth, a petite bourgeoisie well connected with a commercial world from which they drew their not-so-meager incomes. Thus they did have a stake in defending their livelihoods. News reports in the 1970s often documented the amount of agricultural loss due to industrial pollution. It was also not uncommon in environmental struggles for farmers and fishermen to distribute flyers documenting the net profits from agricultural product exports in their region and denouncing the damage that industrial pollution had done to local agricultural interests.

As to the process of conflict mediation, before the public nuisance arbitration committees *(gonghaijioufen tiaojie weiyuanhuei)* were set up in each municipality and county in 1993, the regular township mediation committees *(tiaojie weiyuanhuei)* handled local pollution disputes. These mediation sessions in pollution disputes were similar to those used for labor disputes. Politicians, KMT party cadres, and local notables stood between pollution victims and polluting factories in negotiating for damage compensations. They further used their formal and informal influence to pressure both parties into abiding by the terms of the agreement. This method of mediation succeeded in ending labor disputes by helping workers get some compensation and move on to other jobs. But it could never fully resolve environmental disputes if the source of pollution remained, so long as pollution abatement equipment was not installed and pollution victims did not move elsewhere. The crucial difference was that, whereas the mediation system channeled workers to take the option of an individual "exit" and thereby close a case for good, it only afforded short-term solutions for ongoing environmental disputes, which in the long run merely achieved "forced coexistence" between polluters and victims.

The following case exemplifies the ineffectiveness of official mediation in settling pollution disputes. An industrial district with seven chemical factories in Miao-li County had a thirty-year-long environmental dispute with about one hundred farming households nearby. As early as 1973, the county government and township administrations settled a compensation agreement in which the seven factories agreed to jointly pay for crop damage twice a year (*United Daily* 2000). But instead of this settling the pollution dispute permanently, antipollution protests became endemic. Newspaper archives show that protest activities related to this case recurred in eight separate years between 1974 and 2000, sometimes with multiple protests in any one year.

Not all environmental disputes centered on material compensation. Quite a few focused on removing the source of pollution, and in such cases official mediation was even less effective. Without stringent environmental regulations in place, local governments could only enforce minimal pollution standards, and the penalties for air and water pollution were so low that it was much cheaper to pay fines than to invest in pollution abatement equipment. Local governments' inability to alleviate pollution problems only led to heightened clashes between conflicting parties and a more acute sense of indignation among victims. Most pollution cases, in fact, began with complainants seeking institutional solutions. In one particular case, victims petitioned 269 times within four years (an average of 1.3 petitions per week) with no effect. It was only after exhausting all available means that they took matters into their own hands and adopted extreme measures, such as blocking the entrances to polluting facilities or rushing in to destroy the production units (Hsiao 1988, 131).

The geographic dispersion of SMEs led to equally dispersed environmental disputes, which translated into firsthand pollution experiences among a sizable population. It also meant that relocating victims to unpolluted areas was not an option. As existing institutional means could only impose "forced coexistence," over time, victims began to demand the closure or relocation of polluting facilities. Sometimes people even acted preventively by opposing development projects in the pipeline or by refusing to accept suspicious facilities in their communities.

In a context of frequent, repeated, and widespread occurrences of manmade environmental hazards where institutional procedures failed to produce long-term solutions, pro-environment discourses provided by urban intellectuals were circulated by print media and found wide resonance. Starting from the mid-1960s, the media reported not only antipollution protests but also air and water pollution problems in Taipei (*United Daily* 1964, 1965): the intense debate between the Department of Health and the Ministry of Economic Affairs over water pollution,[9] warnings from World Health Organization experts of Taiwan's pollution problem, detailed reports on the government's effort to curb water and air pollution, and the progress of proposed environmental regulations in congress could all be followed in the press. Mediated by national newspapers, lived experiences and pollution-related information became the building blocks of a popular consensus for environmentalism. Press coverage gave victims a new language and discourse to name the source of their everyday problems. It also revealed the severity of pollution around the country. In the face of ineffective mediation systems and intensified conflicts over pollution, the KMT's vow to safeguard public health and get rid of industrial pollution was challenged and doubted again and again. Environmentalism provided a new framework that put things in perspective, and this media-facilitated discursive intervention gradually gained ground in public opinion. By the early 1980s, the demand to live pollution-free was so widespread that even KMT-affiliated politicians jumped on the bandwagon to support the antipollution cause.[10]

Korea's Exclusive Repression

In contrast to Taiwan's incorporationist approach, the Park Chung Hee regime in Korea shifted away from its early soft version of social control and adopted an exclusionist scheme to deal with social turmoil in the late 1960s and early 1970s. In the first period of the Park regime (1963–71), civil liberties were not entirely stifled, and so a facade of electoral competition was maintained. This system remained in place until the late 1960s and early 1970s, as a series of crises hit. Economically, export growth slowed throughout the 1960s owing to U.S. protectionism, the GNP growth rate dropped dramatically in 1970, inflation was up, and real wage increases were down (Haggard and Moon 1993, 73–74). "The first crisis of export-oriented industrialization . . . [was] caused by serious balance of payments problems and widespread business failures in foreign-invested firms. Massive layoffs, a wage freeze, and delayed payments caused many labor protests in the export sector" (Koo 1993,

138). Politically, Park Chung Hee amended the constitution in 1969, allowing him to seek a third presidential term, which stimulated a sizable political opposition. Two years later, Park defeated the opposition candidate Kim Dae Jung by only a narrow margin, indicating a growing political opposition. The changed geopolitical climate also alarmed Park. Nixon's "rapprochement with China and détente with the Soviet Union . . . seemed to portend the beginning of the end of the global system of American economic and military hegemony on which the ROK [Republic of Korea] had been founded and continued to depend" (Eckert et al. 1990, 364). Also, in response to North Korea's frequent espionage and small military actions at that time, the United States proceeded to withdraw about twenty thousand troops from South Korea.

Confronted with regime crisis, the military junta reconsolidated its power through the following measures. Economically, Park announced the Heavy and Chemical Industry Plan in 1973, targeting shipbuilding, automobiles, the petrochemical industry, and steel as strategic industries of national development, to boost the national economy. Politically, in the name of national security and to establish a more efficient "Korean-style democracy" (Im 2011, 233), Park declared a state of emergency in 1971, set up the Yushin regime in 1972, and issued a total of nine emergency measures[11] in the following three years. This marked the end of a "more confined structure of democratic party politics" between 1963 and 1972 (Eckert et al. 1990, 361). Under the Yushin regime, Park relied heavily on intelligence agencies and other repressive state apparatuses to rule, and his executive power expanded exponentially at the expense of the legislative and judiciary branches. He had the authority to ban public demonstrations; to control wages, rents, and prices; and to mobilize any material or human resources for national purposes. He was also given the right to "appoint one-third of the National Assembly, to dissolve the National Assembly at will, to appoint all judges, and to appoint all members of the constitutional committee" (Lee 2001, 73). The post-1972 Park regime quelled social unrest by force, punished dissidents with arbitrary arrests and physical torture, and intensified the politics of exclusion. Quite simply, post-1972 Korea was in a state of "wholesale repression" (Song 2000), and the Yushin regime imposed an unvarnished dictatorship and turned Korea into "a garrison state" (Im 2011).

This "wholesale repression" yielded contrasting results on labor and environmental conflicts. The most repressed—labor—bounced back more fiercely, and its open confrontation with the regime increased with intensity and militancy every time it resurfaced from the underground. Korea's compulsory arbitration was unable to resolve labor disputes and smother workers' discontent, nor did repressive measures destroy the organizational infrastructure of opposition and solidary networks built through past struggles. In contrast, the less repressed antipollution protests were settled through relocation subsidies. The government negotiated with polluting facilities to pay such subsidies, and victims took the money and moved elsewhere. The dissemination of pro-environment discourses was undercut by victims' taking this "exit" option, and the formation of a rural–urban alliance on environmental causes was delayed.

What Does Not Kill You Makes You Stronger

Under the Yushin regime, the official policy was to suppress the expansion of trade unions (Cho and Kim 1998, 142). Korea's workers confronted a situation in which official wage guidelines undermined their economic struggles, previously exercised rights were taken away, and official channels to articulate grievances were shut down one by one. The Park regime assumed that a wage increase would have impeded domestic savings and export growths, and "the primary goal of state labor policy was to tie export production closely to a low level wage" (Choi 1987, 269). The regime thus adopted a "wage restraint" policy to control inflation and external equilibrium (Song 1996), and wage guidelines were set up to dictate the upper limit of yearly wage increases. Firms whose wage increases exceeded the guideline risked losing government subsidies (Cho 1987, 46). As far as industrial wages were concerned, the Korean state did not facilitate but instead obstructed the attainment of a class compromise—in the form of wage increases—between capital and labor.

So far as lost rights were concerned, a special law was promulgated in 1969 to ban labor disputes in foreign-invested firms. Two years later, the newly enacted Special Measures Pertaining to National Security restricted workers' rights to collective bargaining and action (Choi 1987, 88). "In practice, this has taken the right to strike away from workers, and those who involve themselves in labor disputes take considerable risks, such as multi-year prison terms" (Cho 1987, 45). In 1973 and 1974, labor laws were revised substantially so as to be in line with the Special Measures. All collective bargaining and labor disputes were subject to compulsory arbitration managed by the labor administration. As to those channels for addressing labor discontent that had been closed off, the only umbrella organization, the Federation of Korean Trade Unions (FKTU), was stripped of its mediating role in collective bargaining. The progressive portion of the FKTU leadership was purged and replaced by Park Chung Hee's supporters. The Korean Central Intelligence Agency (KCIA) began to intervene heavy-handedly in bargaining and union organizing.[12] With the aid of the state's repressive industrial policies, employers grew more resistant to unionization and openly engaged in antiunion actions and unfair labor practices (Choi 1987, 91).

Simply put, Korean workers were cornered, disarmed, and repressed on all fronts. Hard-pressed by a harsh economic reality and frustrated by the ineffectiveness of existing unions, a portion of Korean workers moved toward organizing autonomous unions at the grassroots level in the 1970s. In a clandestine manner, workers established liaisons with church-based groups—Urban Industrial Mission (UIM) and Jeunesse Ouvrière Chrétienne (JOC)—students, and outside political opposition and engaged in establishing new unions and taking over company-controlled unions while escaping the attention of employers and the state intelligence agencies. Choi also argues that, in the mid-1970s, labor unions at the grassroots level were split into the pro-FKTU and pro-UIM/JOC camps and that the gravity of the labor movement was shifting toward the latter (Choi 1987, 315).

As the Park regime regressively revised labor laws and deployed repressive measures to control labor unrest, workers responded by going underground and preparing to strike back. Toward the end of the 1970s, big labor disputes such as Dongil Textile and Y. H. Trading exploded one after another, a sign that the mediation system had failed and that repressive measures were unable to contain labor discontent. The Y. H. Trading case in 1979 triggered a series of chain events resulting in Park's downfall. It began with female workers protesting inside the building of the opposition party, leading to a police crackdown. One opposition leader, Kim Young Sam, was expelled from congress, and sixty-nine opposition congressmen resigned in protest, followed by huge riots in Pusan and Masan, martial law, and Park's assassination. During the so-called Spring of Seoul in 1980, labor disputes quadrupled in one year according to official figures. Unofficially,

> at that time [of the assassination of Park], the majority of workers were already involved in some form of . . . strikes all over the country. According to one former Blue House [Presidential Palace] official, when the Pusan-Masan rallies of workers and students occurred in 1979, more than 70 percent of the factories in the Kyongin [Seoul-Incheon] province alone were facing strikes. (Song 2000, 15)

The preceding events provide a sketch of the distinguishing characteristic of Korea's labor struggle under the dictatorship: a long period of quietude followed by an intense wave of strikes and collective action. Labor struggles in the 1970s were led by female workers in the labor-intensive, export-manufacturing sector and took place in a handful of metropolitan areas with a considerable working-class population. The size of industrial establishments breeding labor disputes tended to be large, and so did the size of labor disputes. The Peace Market where Chun Tae-Il worked held several hundred small workshops and twenty thousand workers in close proximity. Pangrim Textiles was one of the largest firms, employing about six thousand workers; Dongil Textiles employed thirteen hundred in 1972 (Ogle 1990, 82, 84); Y. H. Trading employed roughly four thousand in 1970 (M. Kim 2003, 89). Many labor disputes also took place at a time when jobs were threatened because of plant closures. Strictly speaking, the structural position and the timing of disputes did not grant Korea's female workers much leverage. Korean workers thus attempted high-risk, disruptive actions to compensate for their lesser leverage. Chun Tae-Il's self-immolation is one example, Dongil Textiles female workers' spontaneously protesting in the nude another, along with twenty-one textile workers' seizure of the office of the Asian-American Free Labor Institute and detention of its American director (*Korea Times* 1981b).

What sustained such feisty struggles for an independent union movement? Faced with state-sanctioned wage guidelines, with a mediation system with little credibility, with a political regime with no intention of absorbing workers' interests but instead doing its best to exclude the working class politically and repress them by force, and with a capitalist class safely upheld by the state and unwilling to make compromises, Korean workers had no way out. With no way out, some surrendered, others fought—and fought as fiercely and as collectively as the situation allowed. It was this kind of desperate, fighting spirit that laid the foundation for Korea's labor movement.

What happened between 1981 and 1987 repeated the same pattern as between the early 1970s and 1979: repressive measures led to underground labor organizing, and suddenly all hell broke loose. Chun Doo Hwan staged a coup in 1980, and his coming to power caused considerable bloodshed in Kwangju. To secure a contested legitimacy, Chun Doo Hwan declared martial law and adopted ultrarepressive measures, and Korea entered its most repressive period ever. The National Assembly was dissolved and political parties were banned (Croissant 2002, 236). The state attempted to seize control of public life:

> A total of 67,000 people were arrested between August 1980 and January 1981 and, among them, 39,786 were sent to concentration labor camps. More than 500 former politicians were banned from political activities by a "Special Law for Political Purification." . . . Around 200 Periodicals and newspapers were banned, more than 800 journalists fired. . . . Furthermore, radical university professors were dismissed and as many as 600 student

leaders in Seoul and 2,000 nationwide were estimated to be arrested. (Chu 1995, 353)

And the regime cracked down particularly hard on labor. Under the sweeping purification campaign to "'purge impure elements,' 'rectify amoral business activities,' and 'purify the nation by rooting out various social vices'" (Clifford 1998, 164), the Chun regime demanded that companies establish "purification committees" that would root out "troublemakers" among the workers (Ogle 1990, 104). Labor laws were revised so as to outlaw regional and district unions in an attempt to prevent cross-workplace networking among unions. The new labor laws also stipulated that bargaining would be carried out at the enterprise level, literally forbidding any bargaining at the industrial level. "Third-party intervention" was prohibited. Neither UIM/JOC nor FKTU/industrial federations were allowed to partake in local union actions. Furthermore, based on the Guidelines for Purification of Labor Unions promulgated one week after Chun was designated president, "eleven of the seventeen national industrial union presidents were forced to resign. One hundred and six regional leaders and almost two hundred local officers were forcefully evicted from their unions" (Ogle 1990, 102). "Agitators"—workers or activists—were blacklisted and cut off from employment opportunities across industries.

Chun Doo Hwan's "reforms" resulted in the sudden death of more than half of all labor unions. The number of registered unions dropped from 4,947 in 1979 to 2,618 in 1980, then to 2,141 in 1981. Almost 60 percent of existing labor unions lost their legal titles overnight, including progressive unions active in the 1970s, such as the Cheonggye Garment Workers Union, founded where Chun Tae-Il used to work. Furthermore, "employers took advantage of this anti-labor atmosphere and fired thousands of workers who had actively participated in the democratic union movement. The fired workers were then blacklisted by the security agency and barred from gainful employment" (Koo 2001, 102). Hundreds of regional union leaders and officers were either forced to resign or expelled from their unions. Between 1980 and 1985, nearly twenty-seven hundred workers were sacked from their jobs under this antilabor repression (Korean Confederation of Trade Unions 2001).

The labor movement again went underground and was aided by students radicalized by the Kwangju massacre of 1980. Interested in overthrowing the Chun regime, different factions of student activists identified labor as their strategic partner. Students either fled to factories en masse to organize the shop floor at both strategic and labor-intensive industries (the "shop floor" faction) or stayed outside to form broader alliances as labor struggles broke out (the "political struggle" faction) (interview with former student movement leader, May 12, 2003). Furthermore, "the periodic purges of labor union leadership . . . had created a substantial number of men and women dedicated to the improvement of the labor movement" (Ogle 1990, 108).

The working of repressive measures in Korea took an ironic turn. Forged IDs were widely used by students-turned-workers to sneak into factories, physical torture created more martyrs to be admired, prisons provided a space for networking among different opposition groups, and serious confrontations between riot police and hard-pressed workers turned indifferent spectators into sympathizers with those who suffered. Between 1985 and 1986, major labor disputes broke out again, including the 1985 Daewoo Motor strike that resulted in favorable wage increases and the 1986 Kuro strike that involved sympathy strikes and broad social support from students and community groups. "The country witnessed a rash of unprecedented student suicide protests, and massive, violent confrontations broke out between the police and demonstrating students and workers" (Eckert et al. 1990, 380). In the crucial year of 1987, a sophomore Seoul National University linguistics major, Park Chong-chol, was tortured to death during police interrogation, and the whole country was outraged (*Korea Times* 1987). That President Chun decided to handpick his right-hand man, Roh Tae-woo, as the next president added insult to injury and finally pushed matters to the boiling point. After two weeks of nationwide street fighting filled with tear gas and Molotov cocktails, Chun and Roh relented. During and immediately after the regime crisis, more than three thousand strikes broke out, and big corporations were hit particularly hard:

> Some 69 percent of firms that hired a thousand or more workers were confronted with work stoppages. 38.5 percent of those hiring less than a thousand had the same experience. This wave began in the south in the big industrial concentrations of Ulsan (dominated by Hyundai), Kojedo (dominated by Daewoo and Samsung) and Changwon (dominated by Goldstar and Hyundai) and spread north. (Ogle 1990, 116)

The workers' status as a major political force was confirmed. The year 1987 heralded an era in which unions in strategic industries, consisting of semi-skilled male workers, took the helm of the labor movement, while the female vanguard from the labor-intensive sector was marginalized.

Stifled Environmental Discourses

From the outset, Korea's environmental issues were manipulated by the military junta as a deliberate distraction from political issues. In general, environmental issues were conceived of as politically safe and less dangerous than labor and oppositional movements. For this very reason, they were marginalized and looked down on by labor and student movement activists. University professors and conservationists began to voice their concerns in the early 1970s about the declining quality of the natural environment in Korea, though restricting "their activities to the publication of research, professional conferences, and small-scale publicity campaigns aimed at cleaning up trash in national parks" (Eder 1996, 99). Furthermore, environmental issues were not short of media coverage in the 1970s. Major media outlets began to comment on pollution cases in 1973 and advocated for public health (Ku 1996a, 375–76, appendix 4). Park Chung Hee himself promoted the "environmental protection movement" and led government officials and millions of Koreans to clean up trash and fertilize trees (*Korea Times* 1974, 1977, 1978). The constitution was amended in 1980, adding Article 35 to protect environmental rights.

One anecdote illustrates this point nicely. Yul Choi, the leading figure in Korea's environmental movement, was imprisoned in the 1970s over his involvement in antidictatorship protests. While serving the term, he read more than 250 books on global environmental issues, sent by Amnesty International simply because such texts were not considered "political" and so were not banned by the prison authorities. After being released from prison, he founded the first environmental NGO and became an environmental activist (Anbarasan 2001, 48). Another activist's personal experience also confirmed this point:

> Most Korean parents worried about their children joining student movements. When I got involved in the environmental movement, my parents thought that was a bad thing. Student movements, environmental movements, they were all the same. My parents expected me to quit after graduation. But I didn't. They were so disappointed, and they burned my books. But a relative who went to a prestigious university with a very good job approached my father, saying "Hey, this [environmental movement] is not the same as labor or student movements, this is very important and necessary, so don't worry. Of course it's not easy to make good money, but it's very good. Don't be angry at your son." Two or three years later my father even joined an [environmental] demonstration. (interview with an environmental activist, April 18, 2003)

Another Korean activist reported the following:

> A: When people asked me what I did for a living, I said I worked for the environmental movement, and they would say something like, "Oh, you're doing a very nice job!"

Q: Do you think labor activists would get the same praise?

A: I don't think so. We have had the legacy of militant trade unions for a long time. People still think those who participate in labor movements are dangerous, a very risky job.

Q: Would people think that labor activists work for good things?

A: It depends. If they have a pro-democratic orientation, that might be the case. But it's not like what they would say to an environmental activist. Although labor unions are much bigger than environmental organizations, people's support for [the environmental movement], not material but emotional support, is much stronger than their support for labor movements. (interview with an environmental activist, March 26, 2003)

Ironically, from the perspective of the "serious" activist, the reputation of environmental issues was tainted. The environmental cause's "political neutrality" affected the standing of this movement in the wider social movement circle. For activists, "political liberty, labor rights, and social and economic equity were far more important than smoke in the atmosphere and brown streams of water in Korean rivers" (Eder 1996, 100). Up to the mid-1980s, environmental campaigns revolved around either consciousness raising or "soft" programs like trash picking. Mainstream activists resisting the military regime looked down on this kind of environmentalism because it "looked too much like the government's own citizen participation programs that sponsored and funded many 'safe' NGOs" (Eder 1996, 101). Several interviewees working for the Korean environmental movement hinted at their sense of marginalization in the early days. A former student movement leader remarked,

A: Like those who worked for environmental movements in the 1980s, we were rather suspicious of their motive. They were serious antidictatorship activists at the beginning, but why did they suddenly rush to work on environmental issues . . . ?

Q: Why were you suspicious?

A: Because they *betrayed* the need of that time, they escaped to a safer place to do their activities. When I met [the environmental] people like them in the mid-1980s, I'd berate them! (interview with a former student movement leader, May 12, 2003)

Such reactions by mainstream activists toward the environmental movement, particularly by those from labor and student movements, had historical precedents:

> It is unfortunately true that Marxists and others on the "traditional" Left have often given the impression that they viewed the strivings and struggles of these [new] movements as of no great consequence, or as an unwelcome "diversion," at best, from the "real" struggle. Sometimes the grievances and demands expressed by new social movements have been dismissed as mere bourgeois and petty-bourgeois preoccupations. (Miliband 1989, 95)

Although environmentalists fought to distinguish themselves from government-sponsored campaigns and prove their good standing to other movements, a handful of pollution disputes broke out, concentrated in Seoul and in the vicinity of the industrial cities of the southeast (Ulsan, Onsan, Pusan, and Yeocheon), where big corporations and strategic industries were stationed. Industrial cities like Ulsan and Onsan were originally agricultural areas that "had good harbors and fisheries until industrialization began in 1962" (Jeong and Cho 2002, 60). Ulsan became the fastest-growing industrial city in Korea during the postwar period only after the Park administration designated it a special industrial development district and built two gigantic industrial complexes for the heavy chemical industry, an oil refinery, fertilizer plants, automobile production facilities, and shipbuilding wharfs. The rise of Korea's pollution disputes was embedded in the process of imposing large-scale industrial production on top of agricultural areas. Intersectoral tension over the use of natural resources was inevitable.

Pollution cases in the 1970s usually started from crop damage and public health issues (Ku 2011, 208), and the conflicts between farmers and pollution facilities intensified later—a similar dynamic to the pollution cases in Taiwan. Yet behind these pollution disputes, the socioeconomic reality was quite different. Korea's agricultural sector had been in decline ever since the drive for industrialization began in the 1960s. In contrast to Taiwan's extracting surplus from a well-developed agricultural sector to subsidize industry, "Korea . . . is an example of an economy where rapid industrialization, supported by foreign saving (import surplus), preceded rural development and where industry was used to support agricultural development" (Ho 1982, 983).[13] After land reform, Korea's farm units did not develop commercial farming or agricultural modernization, and many farmers lived at the subsistence level (Whang 2001, 23). In this sense, Korea's early pollution disputes were a fight between a less well-off agricultural population and a much bigger industrial giant backed by capital and the state. With such background information in mind, the resolution of early pollution disputes begins to make more sense.

In the sixty environmental protests collected from the *Korea Times,* victims repeatedly appealed to the authorities for intervention, initiated lawsuits, or organized direct action in the 1970s and 1980s. Victims often received compensation through court rulings or government orders, or the polluting facilities paid voluntarily. Figure 12 lists major compensation cases in the 1970s. Yet one thing stands out in Korea's early environmental disputes: the final solution was the out-migration of pollution victims, not the relocation of polluting facilities. The government handed out the cash collected from polluting factories, and victims moved elsewhere. In dramatic fashion, in 1981, the Ulsan City administration announced a massive evacuation plan to relocate as many as ninety thousand residents (*Korea Times* 1981a). In a 1982 dispute, Onsan residents complained that polluting factories from the Onsan Industrial Complex had not paid them the relocation subsidy as promised back in 1976 (*Korea Times* 1982).

An interviewee explained the whole situation like this: "Compensation was the number one issue of the local pollution cases. The local leaders didn't have the power to kick the factory out. They had to negotiate for compensation. Local governments were involved, and they devised a plan for moving them [pollution victims] out and gave them money" (interview with an environmental researcher, March 9, 2004). This kind of resolution was highly unacceptable to many environmental activists, and it was not uncommon to hear complaints that "in the 1970s the main agent of anti-pollution was [rural] residents . . . they wanted compensation, they demonstrated only for more money" (interview with an environmental activist, March 26, 2003). Being asked why pollution victims did not stay on and fight, an interviewee responded,

> In Korea farmers were very poor, social mobility was rare, and . . . *most of them wanted to move to the city.* In one particular development case, local residents even supported the construction project, as they could then receive the relocation subsidy and move. (interview with an environmental researcher, March 9, 2004)

In Korea's early antipollution struggles, demands for relocating pollution facilities were rarely heard. This seems to indicate that the power differential between Korea's pollution victims and the large corporations producing the pollution was quite insurmountable. It was in stark contrast to Taiwan's antipollution action: in only 28 out of 3,457 (0.8 percent) antipollution events in Taiwan between 1980 and 2000 did a demand to relocate pollution victims arise. In at least 10 percent of the 3,457 events, there were demands to close down or move polluting facilities elsewhere, and in quite a few cases, local communities did successfully achieve this goal (Hsiao 2002, 43). This indicates that the power differential between Taiwan's farmers and small- and

Year	Victims and polluting facilities	Polution type	Amount of compensation (in Korean won)	Agent of arbitration
1969	700 residents against Honam Oil Refinery Corp (Yosu)	water	150 million	provincial government
1971	150 laver farm owners and 640 workers against the Chinhae Chemical Co	water	300 million	unreported
1971	An orchard owner against the Korea Electric Co. and the Korea Oil Industry Corp. (Ulsan)	air	9 million	court ruling
1973	20,000 members of fishing co-ops against the Taehan Oil-Tanker Co. (Cholla-namdo)	oil leakage	66 million	ongoing lawsuit
1975	10 clam cultivators against the Honam Oil Refinery Corp. (Yosu)	water	380 million	court ruling
1975	890 fishermen against Hyundai Shipbuilding (Ulsan)	water	530 million	ongoing lawsuit
1975	70 fishermen against ten textile companies (Pusan)	water	211 million	ongoing lawsuit
1976	5 marine farmers against the Kyung In Energy Co.	water	48 million	court ruling
1979	500 farmers against Ulsan Industrial Complex (Ulsan)	air	300 million	provincial government

Figure 12. *Major Korean pollution compensation in the 1970s. Data from Korea Times and Korea Herald microfilms. The nominal exchange rate between 1975 and 1979 was 484 Korean won per U.S. dollar (Nam and Kim 1999, 238).*

medium-sized enterprises was not as insurmountable as that between the Korean farmers and giant conglomerates.

It is worth noting that, in both Taiwan and Korea, workers' potential to extend solidarity and to increase leverage power grew positively with the size of the workplace, whereas the power of pollution victims to bargain with polluters diminished with increasing size of the polluting facilities. Furthermore, pollution victims' out-migration meant that the Korean government and *chaebol* bought their way out of the nuisance of antipollution protests. The exit option for pollution victims posed an acute problem to building a broader urban–rural antipollution alliance. Victims wanted to find the quickest way out of the trouble, yet environmentalists aimed to get rid of the sources of pollution entirely. As an observer commented on the situation, "victims and environmentalists helped each other but *they had different interests.* The authorities also tried to divide them, compensating the victims and moving them to other places" (interview with an environmental researcher, March 9, 2004).

Relocation subsidies and out-migration of victims became viable solutions for Korea's early pollution disputes only because pollution-affected areas were geographically concentrated. The fact that these early antipollution protests neither inspired people elsewhere to engage in similar struggles nor quickly drew a sizable group of sympathizers prior to the mid-1980s did not result from the fact that environmental discourses were in short supply. Nor could the lack of popular support be attributed to underreporting of pollution events by media outlets. The issue was that environmental discourses and media coverage did not resonate with people's daily experiences derived from rampant pollution problems, as was the case in Taiwan. The crucial nexus translating abstract discourses into everyday beliefs was missing. In addition, even if major environmental disasters might effectively organize collective fear without the buttress of firsthand pollution experience, such cases did not appear until much later. Prior to their occurrence, the Korean government was successful in arranging individual solutions for pollution victims and so quieting things down. As victims moved away and antipollution alliances drifted apart, the Korean government's "pro-environment" facade remained unchallenged and unquestioned, leaving Park Chung Hee peacefully picking up trash at national parks, as the head of government.

Lessons from the Early-Riser Movements

We are in a position to revisit the two quotations appearing at the beginning of this chapter. Both activists deftly identified the different conditions of labor and environmental movements in their national contexts. That Taiwan's environmental movement had a solid ideological basis enabling it to break out of institutional confines was not simply the result of the power of universal ideas. The ideological power of environmentalism had the chance to unfold because pollution experiences were widely shared owing to a decentralized industrialization and to a KMT incorporationist scheme that failed to curb the recurrence of pollution problems. In the case of Korea, repression failed to contain labor because workers were caught in an institutional deadlock where compromises on wages and working conditions rarely occurred through negotiation. Densely populated industrial facilities further granted a social space to build strong solidarity to engage in high-risk, disruptive actions. Taiwan's environmental and Korea's labor movements arose early because the subjects of both movements confronted a no-way-out situation and their interests could not be properly accounted for through compromises and negotiations within existing institutional settings.

As for the two latecomer movements, their late arrivals did not result from a lack of structurally induced discontent. Nor is it because those who suffered did not act on their grievances, considering the frequency of Taiwan's labor disputes and antipollution actions initiated by Korea's farmers and fishermen. The two movements came late because the struggles in the early days were institutionally contained by a mediation system that, to some degree, answered to the interests and demands of protesters. Taiwan's workers had been placed in a position where it was difficult to exercise leverage, while the ideological power of pro-environment discourses in Korea was compromised by the government's window-dressing work and a lack of resonance with the general public. In addition, both Taiwan's workers and Korea's farmers were customarily granted an exit option, and the majority of them accepted the offer—the former took compensation through the mediation system; the latter took the relocation subsidies from the government and capitalists—which further impeded the formation of a potential coalition either with fellow workers or other social groups. As a result, we see the two contrasting pictures of movement emergence in Taiwan and Korea.

This should not simply be read as a story in which unaddressed grievances led to early movement emergence. Korea's labor and Taiwan's environmental movements perhaps trod more difficult waters, their pleas were unanswered, and both rose earlier than their counterpart movements. The key question becomes one of what Korea's workers and Taiwan's pollution victims did after learning that their grievances would not be addressed within the given institutional framework. Lying down to play dead was one option, and fatalism often had its charms. But they somehow managed not to do so. When Korea's labor was heavily repressed and its grievances ignored in every single campaign, unionists were "forced" to strengthen organizational infrastructures and build more ties of solidarity among workers; that is to say, they were forced to pursue leverage power. When Taiwan's rampant environmental pollution could not be solved by the KMT, pollution victims and environmental advocates were "forced" to work more closely to petition at higher administrative levels, to take up confrontational action, and to expound their causes to whomever was willing to listen, including media outlets. The result was the dissemination of environmental ideas and, for the movement as a whole, the gradual building of ideological power. The causal link between grievances and early emergence is not a direct one but is mediated through the unfolding of different movement powers (see Figure 13). This also points to the irony of the story: more constrained institutional settings might not deliver favorable results to either a single pollution case or to a single wage struggle, but it might inadvertently lead to the consolidation of distinct power bases favorable for the early emergence of a movement.

If workers and pollution victims acted as the protagonists in early-riser movements in both the 1970s and the first half of the 1980s, they did not nurture movement power on their own but received much help from allies. The coalition of workers, student activists, and churches in Korea was crucial in terms of raising workers' class consciousness and uplifting their fighting spirit. The alliance between pollution victims and urban intellectuals in Taiwan greatly facilitated the dissemination of environmental discourses by fusing everyday experiences with scientific language. It is not unfair to say that succeeding in coalition building separates both early-riser movements from their counterpart movements.

Yet coalition building is greatly impacted by the pattern of industrialization. To use labor organizing as an example, external supports from students and churches, which energized Korea's labor movement in the context of a *chaebol*-dominant economy and geographically concentrated industrial areas,

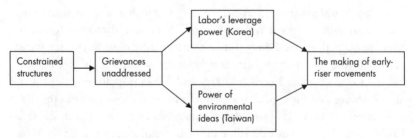

Figure 13. The unfolding of different movement power.

may not activate the Taiwanese workers so effectively in an industrial structure consisting of large enterprises closely monitored by the KMT and small capital scattered all over urban and rural areas. If there were thousands of students-turned-workers migrating into Taiwan's factories to organize workers, they would have confronted a completely different reality. To access and organize workers in state enterprises and big private firms on the shop floor, one had to first pass an entrance examination and background checks, and then elude the constant surveillance of the KMT party cell implanted in each large industrial establishment. To access and organize workers in the "unorganized" sector would be much easier, but even these helping hands from outside may not structurally increase the limited leverage of workers at geographically scattered factories that employ fewer than ten workers.

The story of early-riser movements further shows the limit of political control. Incorporation or repression does not always work, nor is either one effective in soothing all types of grievance. The true irony is that the state's intervention in directing the path of industrialization at an earlier time created problems that the same state apparatus could not solve later. If the KMT, guided by state ideology, historical experience, and political necessity, intentionally adopted an industrial policy of restricting the scale, concentration, and influence of private capital in the 1960s (Fields 1995, 27), it probably could not envisage that, years later, these geographically scattered SMEs would inadvertently call on an army of antipollution guerrillas determined to defend their lived environment. If Korea's military junta believed in "economy of scale" and offered massive subsidies and other incentives to encourage corporate growth (Kim and Park 2011), this tightly organized, like-minded group of military leaders and technocrats did not consider the possibility that the bigger the *chaebol,* the more workers would be employed, and the more likely it would be that the size of workers' organizations and their solidarity could withstand assaults from capitalists and the state. Maybe this is just a less dramatic way of saying that one creates one's own gravediggers, but the lesson nevertheless remains that no matter how carefully thought out and planned, any political design has its Achilles' heel. There are no invincible political–economic arrangements capable of simultaneously containing myriad social protests, each pursuing different types of movement power and each based on a different logic of action.

4

Movement Legacy and Latecomer Movements

Bounded by the spatial and organizational patterns of industrialization, Taiwan's environmental and Korea's labor activism slowly emerged as early-riser movements out of difficult battles against the state's incorporationist or repressive measures in the mid- to late 1970s. The previous chapter analyzed solely the interaction between early-riser movements and state actions. As the focus shifts to latecomer movements, a few things change.

First and foremost, the contexts change. Early-riser movements fought for restricted survival space in a relatively stable system in which the ruler was yet to show its vulnerability, whereas the rise of latecomer movements was situated in a context where early-riser movements expanded quickly and political elites scrambled to deploy more effective strategies to regain the status quo. The very expansion of early-riser movements indicates the weakened capacity of the state to "contain" civil initiatives and to direct action via old strategies (Tarrow 1994, 155–56). In response to the early-riser challenges, both authoritarian states launched a series of political projects to prevent things from getting worse. Through the readjustment and transformation of institutional orders, new strategies of restraining civil unrest were formulated and tried out. In this sense, both early-riser movements prompted certain regime responses that shaped the subsequent conditions from which latecomer movements arose.

The sheer existence of early-riser movements and the legacies they bequeathed must be incorporated into an understanding of latecomer movements. Early-riser movements left distinct cultural and organizational legacies to succeeding movements. The former set the tone for an emerging

oppositional culture, formulated a working model for grassroots organizing, and explored possible allies and the most viable strategies to success.
This oppositional culture and those organizing models were not invented
out of thin air. Different historical experiences and interaction with political
authorities channeled early-riser movements to develop varying oppositional
cultures and organizing models, which in turn shaped the range of options
from which latecomer movements could choose. Early-riser movements further gave the state-capital bloc the first taste of "what social movements were
like," and such exposure shaped how the state-capital bloc would respond to
latecomer movements. The rise of latecomer movements is embedded in the
process of mutual penetration between early-riser movements and political
regimes: their "political opportunity structure" is the regime's response to the
early risers' challenge, while the pool of movement resources—"the ideational,
tactical, and organizational 'lessons' of the early-risers" (McAdam 1995,
226)—is equally shaped by the early risers' encounters with political regimes.

The experiences of Taiwan and Korea show two contrasting patterns
of interaction between early-riser movements and political regimes. Under
the incorporationist KMT, Taiwan's environmental movement was deeply
entrenched in local electoral politics and actively sought political allies at
the national level to advance environmental causes. In contrast, Korea's labor
movement, conditioned by the military junta's repression and political exclusion, was from the outset deprived of any chance of political representation
and forced to strengthen workers' self-organization to gain concessions. Growing out of such interactive patterns, each early-riser movement settled into its
own organizing model. Taiwan's early riser, benefiting from limited concessions gained through existing institutional channels, familiarized itself with
the arts of negotiation, political exchange, and public relations campaigns
that would pressure political elites to incline toward its side. All of these were
contingent on the movement's ability to summon enough public support via
the existing networks of kinship and neighborhood, voluntary associations,
and the media. Korea's early riser lived a culture of militancy and self-reliance.
Its pronounced distrust of political elites and private capital was based on repeated past experience of repression and betrayal, and hence this movement
deployed a model of fighting tooth and nail in any economic struggle and
did everything it could to consolidate its only backup: a solidly organized
laboring population.

Once realizing that the old strategies had failed to extinguish the early-
riser movements, the KMT began to use repressive measures against the burgeoning labor movement while the Korean government sought to co-opt and
incorporate the agenda of the environmental movement. Both dramatically

reversed the policies they had adopted when dealing with the early-riser movements. Both latecomer movements imitated the early risers' strategies in the hope of success: Taiwan's labor movement zealously pursued an electoral route to consolidate its base of support, whereas Korea's environmental movement took on militant action to advance its cause. What worked for the early-riser movements, however, did not necessarily work well for the latecomer movements because of the change of state action and the latecomers' need to develop their own movement power distinct from the early risers' power. The Taiwanese labor movement's pursuit of political power via the electoral route was first undercut by state repression and later faltered between building leverage power through labor organizing and looking for political allies to present working-class interests. In contrast, Korea's environmental movement gave up militant action to reach a truce with the state and capital. It collaborated extensively with media outlets to sway public opinion and exercise its ideological power. At the same time, it engaged in serious membership drives to consolidate its grassroots base, a strategy very much under the influence of its labor predecessor.

In the following, I present two sets of narrative on Taiwan and Korea. In each, I start with the early-riser legacy, then analyze the change in state strategy, and finally look at how each latecomer movement balanced contradicting demands and aspirations.

Taiwan: Incorporation through Electoral Avenues and Voting Games

Taiwan's environmental movement emerged out of the failure of the institutional order to settle pollution disputes permanently. Given its propensity to exercise its power through discursive production to build public support and broad alliance, this movement, working within Taiwan's electoral politics, fashioned a movement model of solving problems through elite intervention.

The Early Riser's Legacy

The most important development in the Taiwanese environmental movement in the 1980s was the systematic involvement of the middle class and the changed class composition inside the movement. From 1971 to 1986, the number of farmer-initiated protests as a proportion of all protests dropped continuously (see Figure 14)—from 53 percent in the period 1971–77 to 35 percent in 1978–84, and then to 26 percent in 1985–87. If farmers and fishermen were the main actors in the antipollution protests of the 1970s, by the mid-1980s, we could even observe Lions Clubs, on many occasions, launching independent campaigns against water and air pollution (*China Times* 1984, 1985).

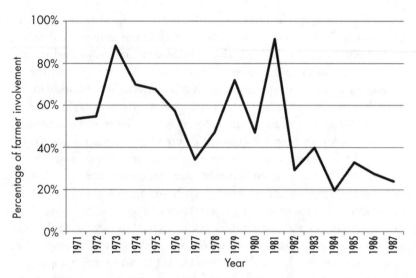

Figure 14. Proportion of farmer-initiated environmental protests. From China Times *Fifty-Year Images Databank.*

The making of Taiwan's environmental movement rested on a coalition between urban intellectuals and protesting farmers over lawsuits and cases relating to public health between 1979 and 1981, whereas the expansion of the movement in the mid-1980s relied on a solidified connection between the middle classes and the farming population. Journalists, ecologists, medical doctors, chemists, and lawyers in urban areas lent their expertise in discursive production to provide ideological-scientific backing for antipollution, conservationist, and antinuclear campaigns. Lions Clubs, shop owners, and schoolteachers residing in the pollution-plagued areas simultaneously translated environmental discourses into local settings and actively joined direct action. Through this process, voluntary associations on environmental issues at all levels began to emerge in the mid-1980s. The metropolitan-area Consumers' Foundation, founded in 1981, became involved more intensively in environmental issues in 1984. *New Environment Monthly* was first published in 1985 and, in 1987, transformed into the New Environment Foundation. Hundreds of college professors founded the Taiwanese Environmental Protection Union (TEPU) in 1988, and middle-class housewives formed the Homemakers' Union and Foundation in 1989. Civil associations on pollution prevention, spearheaded by the middle class, were also formed at the local level, particularly in areas near major pollution disputes. Local antipollution associations were organized around existing kin networks, neighborhoods, and temple affiliations (Weller and Hsiao 1998).

This cross-class connection—both the urban–rural nexus and the cross-class alliance in the polluted areas—was crucial. The public sympathized with farmers' threatened livelihoods, yet their antipollution action had to combat a powerful developmental ideology that linked industrial production and the accumulation of national wealth to collective betterment. The farming population, on one hand, lacked the discursive capacities necessary to counter that dominant ideology. On the other hand, the agricultural sector's political and economic influence was declining in proportion to its waning contributions to net domestic product and total exports. Given all these factors, the antipollution struggle was likely to be a losing battle if new alliances were not formed.

The involvement of urban intellectuals and the middle class provided the much-needed resources that farmers and fishermen lacked. With the input of "cultured" and "resourceful" social forces, early claims over crop damage and compensation were substituted with more universal messages, including those of public health, the integrity of the island's ecosystem, community preservation, sustainable development, the green economy, and intergenerational justice. These constituted a politically charged frontal assault on state developmentalism. In short, Taiwan's environmental movement rested on an organic connection between small-scale protests from a "dying" class whose political-economic significance was falling and the ascending "new class" whose discursive capacities were the best weapon to advance their interests. As Gouldner has written, environmentalism is one of the ideologies often manifested by new classes (Gouldner 1979, 42–43). Neither the "educated" class nor the farming population alone had sufficient leverage against the state and capital. Alliance, public support, discursive innovations, and news making became key words of the movement. The greater the degree to which the movement could make environmentalism a part of public discourse, and the more social support it could command in terms of public opinion, sympathetic action, and elite intervention, the more likely their opponents would be to back off or relent. We thus observe a *bifurcated* structure in Taiwan's environmental movement: urban intellectuals dominated discursive production, whereas farmers, fishermen, and the pollution-plagued middle class, backed by these discursive weapons, engaged in direct action, bargaining, and political dealings deeply entrenched in local electoral politics.

From here we begin to see the cultural and organizational legacy that Taiwan's environmental movement left. This movement grew out of local antipollution struggles and consisted of a loosely coordinated, geographically decentralized network of environmental activism that did not have its own grassroots base but was tacked onto preexisting networks. The support bases for the environmental movement coincided with important voting blocs that structured Taiwan's local elections: kinship networks, neighborhood organizations, and local voluntary associations within specific geographic territories. Its discursive capacity to frame environmental issues in universal terms so as to affect public opinion via mass media also put direct pressure on the KMT and incumbents at the national level. This movement thus pressured political elites on both fronts: by mobilizing these "voting blocs" and by galvanizing public support through mass media. By virtue of these organizational structures, Taiwan's environmental movement created a model of solving problems via political routes, mostly by the intervention of political elites seeking electoral success.

From these discursive campaigns and consolidated social networks at both local and national levels, the immediate impact of the environmental movement was the swift incorporation of environmental platforms into electoral politics. Since the early 1950s, open elections for executive and representative organs at the local level had been regularly held at nearly eight thousand villages, more than three hundred townships, and twenty-some counties and cities. Elections for seats at the Provincial Assembly were added in 1954. Even though it placed strict restrictions on national legislative elections, the KMT gradually allowed competition for a limited number of seats at the Legislative Yuan and National Assembly, starting in 1969 (Cohen 1988, 22; Lay 1992, 228–29). The number of legislators elected through this semi-competitive "supplementary election" process increased gradually, from 11 in 1969, to 51 in 1971, and to 130 in 1989. Simply put, elections had from early on been a part of Taiwan's social life, and the process of democratic transition in the 1980s only supplied more electoral opportunities and made the game more competitive.

Local politicians and national elites responded to antipollution issues through action and rhetoric. Election races at the lower levels of the administrative districts (village and township) often coincided with areas already suffering from pollution or under the threat of possible pollution. Goaded by voter pressure, local politicians rushed to defend the right to live "pollution free." For example, on March 28, 1982, Chungmen villagers from Kaohsiung County in southern Taiwan rushed into the Taiwan Amino Acid Co. They smashed windows and office equipment with clubs and rocks and poured liquid waste discharge all over the office to protest Amino Acid's long-delayed promise to relocate its factory. This protest action was led by the village head, Lin Ben-yuan, and authorized by a resolution passed by the general village assembly two days previously (*China Times* 1982b). Two months later, Chungmen villagers chartered buses to the Legislative Yuan in Taipei to settle the pollution problem. Three township council representatives fought fiercely to pay for the cost of the transport, because it was "right before the election of township representatives and village head" (*China Times* 1982a). Not surprisingly, Lin Ben-yuan was reelected village head in the June election (*China Times* 1982c).

Another similar case from 1982 concerned garbage disposal in Taoyuan County, northern Taiwan. Li Wen-ji, chief of the township designated to receive thousands of tons of garbage, solemnly swore,

> Our town has already suffered from water pollution, noise, and waste water and exhaust fumes from nearby industrial parks. With garbage added to it, this town is becoming unlivable. As the township chief, I absolutely oppose the "garbage invasion." I and the chairman of the township council will sit in the lifting crane [a piece of equipment that villagers had used to block the road that garbage trucks would have to pass], *we will fight against this with our lives.* (*China Times* 1982d, emphasis added)

This township chief certainly did not die fighting the "garbage invasion," but his bombastic language reflected the pressure he was receiving from townspeople.

One final example is from the landmark protest against DuPont's investment in a titanium dioxide plant at Lukang, an ancient port famous for aquaculture and as a religious center. Li Dong-liang, the leading figure of the anti-DuPont struggle, was first elected as a county council member and later as Lukang township chief during and after the antipollution campaign (Reardon-Anderson 1992, 27).

For representatives at the national level, such as the Provincial Assembly or Legislative Yuan, pollution-plagued voters constituted only a portion of their electoral base, and their demands had to be balanced against pressure from industries and other demands for development and employment. High-level politicians usually played the go-between in pollution disputes, mediating between polluters and protesters. Both incumbents and electoral candidates engaged in such political brokerage. Especially in tight races, incumbents and candidates would pressure polluters to strike a better deal that they could bring back to pollution victims in exchange for their political support.

Environmental activism was clearly entrenched in national politics. Middle-class, national organizations collaborated with media outlets on environmental campaigns to organize public opinion. Backed by growing public support, this movement further pursued political alliances in representative organs to stop development projects, revise existing legal codes, or enact new environmental laws. Less controversial issues such as pollution prevention and procedures for environmental impact assessment (EIA) became part of electoral platforms, regardless of party affiliation, as early as 1983 (*United Daily* 1983).

For controversial issues such as national energy policies, the environmental movement found a political ally in electoral candidates running against the KMT, especially the *dangwai* (literally "outside the [KMT] party") movement and its offspring—the opposition Democratic Progressive Party (DPP) founded in 1986. *Dangwai* legislators began to interrogate the executive branch on nuclear power plant safety as early as 1980 (*United Daily* 1980a). *Dangwai* candidates competing for seats at the National Assembly also advocated nuclear safety as one of their policy platforms (*United Daily* 1980b). Between 1982 and 1985, a series of accidents at nuclear power plants added fuel to the fire. In 1985, antinuclear sentiments were articulated by "leading academic experts, the Presbyterian Church . . . and the private Consumer Foundation" (Cohen 1988, 100). As the environmental movement gained momentum and public opinion tipped toward the antinuclear side, KMT legislators also chimed in. A KMT legislator threatened to sabotage the budget for energy research funds if the state-owned power company could not provide a satisfactory account of nuclear safety measures (*United Daily* 1982a). In 1985, fifty-five KMT and six *dangwai* legislators, practically all of them supplementary-election legislators, joined forces to demand the executive branch stop the construction on a fourth nuclear power plant (*United Daily* 1985). One year later, the election platform of the opposition party "included a plank calling for an eventual phase out of nuclear plants" (Cohen 1988, 100).

Besides traditional lobbying, environmental activists actively joined in the game of electoral politics. According to an empirical study (Ho 2000, 110, 167), in 1989 alone, fourteen environmental activists stood for the legislature, county magistrates/city mayorships, or provincial assembly, three of whom were elected. The majority ran on the DPP ticket, with only two running as independent candidates. Furthermore, when the opposition party became mayors or county magistrates, an environmental activist was commonly recruited to head the Environmental Protection Agency (EPA). Such political appointments started taking place at the county and city level in the late 1980s and early 1990s, and not long after at the national level as well. Movement leaders were geared toward electoral competition and accepted political appointments from their allies.

These examples illustrate that, from the outset, Taiwan's environmental movement was deeply entangled in electoral politics. Pollution problems at the local level forced local politicians to respond to direct voter pressure; environmental policies at the national level were swayed by the direction of public opinion and mediated by the movement's political allies in representative organs. This movement's success in garnering public support via traditional kinship and neighborhood networks, voluntary associations, and mass media gave it a certain bargaining power via electoral competition at various levels.

The legacy that the environmental movement bequeathed was a culture of pragmatism, accepting the necessity of political exchange and compromise while simultaneously working within and around the system. Owing to its reliance on electoral politics and political alliances, this movement pursued a peculiar organizing model of building horizontal linkages between preexisting solidarity networks and staging public campaigns via the media. With preexisting solidarity networks available to be "borrowed" and tapped into, Taiwan's environmental movement never pursued any serious organizing work on its own at the grassroots level, and organizing was a rather alien issue that received no systematic discussion inside the movement.

The KMT's Responses

In the face of the new challenges from environmental activism, the KMT's responses changed over time. In the late 1970s and early 1980s, the attitude of the KMT toward environmental protests was one of nonintervention, letting the conflicting parties fight it out in the realm of local politics. As the frequency and intensity of environmental conflicts increased and pollution disputes began to encroach on national politics, the KMT responded with an ensemble of strategies aimed at reincorporating the dissidents into the political system, three of which were of particular importance.

First, as Wu and Cheng (2011, 257) accurately put it, the KMT reconstituted its legitimacy basis through democratization in the 1980s. Good economic performance, governing experience, and strong electoral machines gave the KMT the confidence that it would not be replaced in free and open elections. The KMT "normalized" the political system by lifting martial law in 1987 and abolishing restrictions on participation in national politics:

> The KMT regime in Taiwan entered the 1970s with a proven formula for maintaining the entrenched political dominance of the mainlander elite at the national level and for controlling a limited popular electoral process at the local level. Formally the KMT state maintained a complicated five-branched national government, with a functioning legislature claiming to represent all the provinces of China with its life-term members elected in

1948 on the mainland. It also intentionally retained a cumbersome four-tier administrative system designed for all of China, from the national down to provincial, county/city, and town/borough levels. Native Taiwanese were allowed to elect their own representatives up to the provincial levels, and executive officials up to the county/city level. (Chu 1994, 101)

By rescinding the restrictions, lifetime members of the national representative organs retired and a new round of political competition began. Local political elites with national aspirations, the leaders of the opposition, and movement leaders with national reputations were lured into the electoral game. The old, truncated "career ladder" for local elites was rebuilt by opening up national representative organs to electoral competition. The KMT's move earned it a good name for democratization and, in the long run, narrowed elite dissidents' challenges to the electoral arena. The opening of electoral opportunities was part of the KMT's political strategy of incorporating local grievances and absorbing elite dissenters, as Wu's (1987) study has shown. The KMT's response in broadening the channel of political participation further encouraged existing practices of incorporating an environmental agenda into electoral platforms, of looking for political allies in representative organs, or even of pulling movement activists into the game of electoral politics.

Second, the KMT consolidated all environment-related affairs. Previously they had been assigned to different bureaucratic agencies, but now the EPA, a special agency with elevated status in the administrative hierarchy, was created as antipollution protests became a prominent problem.[1] The KMT overhauled a series of legal codes to handle grassroots grievances and imposed new procedural rules on demonstrations, public assemblies, and other protest activities. The decadelong discussion between government agencies over how to handle environmental grievances was only resolved with the promulgation of the Environmental Impact Assessment Act and the Public Nuisance Dispute Mediation Act (*United Daily* 1982b).[2] For regulating extrainstitutional civil disobedience generally, martial law restrictions on speech, assembly, and association were gradually replaced with civil codes stipulating when, how, and where protest activities could take place and the penalties for violations. These legal and administrative measures aimed to rechannel mass action back into acceptable institutional confines.

The first and second strategies aimed to rechannel dissident elites and to discipline mass action through new institutional measures. When all else failed, of course, the state could always fall back on force. By observing the interaction between the KMT and the social movement sector, another key strategy at the KMT's disposal was its selective use of repressive measures against the most threatening contenders, to warn others not to step out of line. Activists, cadres, and leaders from the targeted movements were singled out, isolated from their support bases, and prosecuted. This "selective repression" strategy had a profound impact on Taiwan's labor movement, as discussed in the following section.

The Succeeding Labor Movement

Taiwan's labor disputes, limited by enterprise size and by the KMT's preemptive mobilization, mainly came from "unorganized" SMEs. The scattered, small-scale conflicts throughout the 1970s and the first half of the 1980s were well absorbed by the compulsory arbitration system and resolved on an individual basis. But then, against the backdrop of an expanding environmental movement and the regime's new political openness in the late 1980s, we began to observe subtle changes on the labor front. The first sign of labor's "collective power" was shown not through work stoppages or slowdowns but through electoral success. In 1986, two DPP-endorsed candidates were elected as labor representatives at the Legislative Yuan and National Assembly, defeating two KMT candidates for the first time in Taiwan's electoral history. The KMT's candidates were high-ranking officials from the government-certified umbrella organization the Chinese Federation of Labor. Both were also high-profile labor leaders who, for twenty years, had coordinated labor education, monitored the progress of labor legislation, and performed diplomatic functions with international labor organizations. In contrast, the DPP candidates had no national reputation, ran no campaigns, and lacked any organizational backing, and yet were miraculously elected (Chang 1987). The result of the 1986 election could be read as the anonymous venting of labor grievances through electoral means and served as a prelude to subsequent protest actions. Following the electoral victory, a wave of escalated labor protests broke out around 1987–88, right after the lifting of martial law.

Furthermore, precisely because small-scale labor disputes and conflicts were unable to break out of the tight web of institutional containment, labor activism in the late 1980s was spearheaded by workers at a handful of large corporations and workers occupying strategic positions in transportation and public utilities. Some of the largest private firms were affected by open labor unrest at this time, including Yue Loong Motors, Li Ho-Ford, Funai Electronics, Formosa Plastics, Tatung, Taiwan Cement, Far Eastern Textiles, the local Philips affiliate, and Hwa Tong Synthetic Fibers (Cohen 1988, 134). Aided by the Labor Standards Law of 1984, workers at large corporations began to demand overtime payments and increased Chinese New Year bonuses.[3]

Workers from the "organized" large corporations engaged both in union reform, actively fighting for leadership positions to "purge" the KMT's influence, and in strike action. In 1988, workers at the state-owned China Petroleum elected a president who was "the first non-KMT member to head a major labor organization" (Cohen 1988, 135). Union reform, democracy, and leadership accountability became major platforms at individual unions' elections. In the same year, the first railroad strike broke out since the KMT took over Taiwan in 1949 (Japan Economic Newswire 1988). One thousand four hundred workers joined strike action that caused an estimated loss of around one million U.S. dollars per day (*Min sheng bao* 1988).

Within one or two years of its inception, the labor movement quickly jumped onto the arena of electoral politics. The first political organization for labor, the Workers' Party, was founded in November 1987, scarcely three months after martial law was lifted. It was the first labor party in Taiwan's history and staked the labor movement's claim to political participation and power sharing (Chen and Wong 2002, 37). Labor candidates actively joined the race to become legislators, National Assembly members, city councilpersons, and other elected officials.

The most dramatic aspect of Taiwan's labor movement between 1987 and 1989 is that the escalation of labor protests and the growth of labor organizations were immediately followed by retreats and defeats. Two events were of profound significance to the subsequent development of the movement. The first was the split of the Workers' Party. Scarcely one year from its founding, a group of activists left the Workers' Party to form a new political party, the Labor Party. A labor movement veteran remarked on this split,

> Before it [the Workers' Party] matured, internal strife just destroyed it. This is truly regrettable. . . . When the Workers' Party was first founded, many workers just showed up on their own and gave us a stack of applications [to become party members]. After the split, even those who were party members became much less enthusiastic [toward the party]. There was a sharp change in workers' attitudes toward the party. . . . The split was really a watershed event. The Workers' Party had originally had the chance to build up and strengthen class consciousness and to make advances politically, but after the split Taiwan's labor lost their own political representation and workers' political power was greatly diminished. (interview with labor activist, January 29, 2003)

Both Workers' and Labor party candidates participated in elections for various posts on multiple occasions. None of them was ever elected in the next twenty years, and the votes any candidate received were, with one or two exceptions, embarrassingly few. Continuous electoral defeats provided a negative exemplar for building labor's own political organizations. Such experiences also cautioned workers and activists to think twice before trying to build their own political power, channeling them instead toward the pragmatic route of allying with existing political parties.

The second major event was the defeat of the FECF strikers in 1989, the largest strike action in postwar Taiwan's history. Despite two thousand workers being on strike, with organizational and personnel backing from all of the independent unions and labor activists in Taiwan, this strike was crushed by the joint action of the KMT and the textile industry, who rallied around the country's largest textile firm. While the FECF strike showcased the most significant solidary action by Taiwan's independent unions, the KMT repressed it by force:

> The order to put down the [FECF] strike came directly from the National Security Council. . . . The KMT mobilized all the police forces in this region, dispatching riot police and law enforcement from three of the neighboring counties. The number of police was several times that of workers. This meant that the KMT was determined to put down the labor movement, starting with the FECF strike. Why this particular strike? Because the FECF union took the lead in this movement. *Putting down this union would greatly dampen workers' faith in this movement.* (interview with an FECF strike activist, January 27, 2003)

Furthermore, this strike also made capitalists at the textile and synthetic fibers industries engage in their own solidary action. It was reported that the Association of Synthetic Fibers decided to hold down the price of production materials to help the FECF plants get through the strike (*United Daily* 1989). As the confrontation came to an end, union leaders were fired, labor activists helping the strike were prosecuted, and the most organized and strongest union in the private sector collapsed. The defeat of the FECF strike is considered a watershed, in the sense that it discouraged workers from exercising the most powerful weapon at their disposal. Strike, as a means to engage in economic struggles, became highly unpopular in the following decade. From the sixteen strikes that broke out in 1988 alone, *after* the FECF, defeat strikes declined to only thirteen between 1989 and 2002, with zero workdays lost in seven of those years (1991, 1993–94, and 1999–2002) (Council of Labor Affairs 1996, 2003).

The defeat of Taiwan's labor movement on both electoral and protest fronts was closely related to a change of strategy within the KMT, which shifted away from what had been its standard treatment of the environmental movement. Realizing that its noninterference in minor environmental disputes had led to the rise of a national environmental movement, the KMT became more decisive and efficient in undercutting the growth of the labor movement from the outset. Though the KMT broadened electoral space so as to absorb dissenting elites, and renovated labor-related administrative organs and legal codes, it played the "selective repression" strategy against the labor movement. Labor and farmers, whom the KMT had historically gripped the tightest, received the harshest treatment.

The KMT had already shown signs of targeted counterattack in 1988, one year prior to the FECF strike. In May 1988, the KMT forcefully put down a farmers' demonstration in Taipei with a twenty-hour street fight that led to 115 injuries and 112 arrests (*United Daily* 1988a). The KMT's Central Executive Committee, the highest decision-making organ of the party, first defined the farmers' protest as "a conspired riot." Some members even suggested that the president should declare martial law again if similar riots should happen in the future (*United Daily* 1988c). Three months later, a transportation workers' strike was put down and 245 union workers were fired (*United Daily* 1988b). As a previous study has shown (Chao 1991, 158–67, 220), from 1988, there was a concerted effort between the state and capital to contain the burgeoning labor movement. It became clear that the repression of the FECF strike was not an isolated event but part of the KMT's purposeful response to the latecomer movement by which the regime felt most threatened. After its fatal blow against the FECF strike, the KMT further revised labor codes so as to impose stricter legal terms on the launching of strikes and to deter the expansion of independent unions and, crucially, prosecuted labor leaders and activists. More than two hundred labor activists and union leaders in the private sector were either fired from their jobs or prosecuted (Wu and Liao 1991, appendix 1). As union leaders got fired, "[the independent] union was basically dead," remarked a union leader in the private sector:

> So far there had been no case in which union cadres in the public sector had got sacked, they had a basic guarantee of job security. They could engage in union activities more freely without much worry. But working at the private sector was completely different. . . . It was extremely rare for an [independent] union not to crumble after union cadres got sacked, *maybe one out of ten cases survived, purely by chance.* (Interview with a private-sector union leader, February 10, 2003, emphasis added)

The impact of early-riser legacy on the labor movement was most pronounced in the latter's participation in institutional politics. Without the environmental movement paving the way into electoral politics, and without the gains, compromises, and political clout that the environmental movement secured through a system of interest representation, it would be difficult to explain the zeal and alacrity of the labor movement in grasping electoral opportunities. Where the environmental movement, because of its lack of an organizational base, had chosen to run for election on the DPP ticket or accepted political appointments from allies, the labor movement pushed one step further. It worked to build its own organ of political articulation in the hope of securing electoral victory through the formation of independent unions and on a rising tide of labor protests between 1987 and 1988.

The labor movement pursued a "triangular" strategy by simultaneously pursuing economic struggles via direct action in the workplace, union reforms within large-scale private and public firms, and the pursuit of political power. It presumed that advances made on one front would inspire and support advances on the other two. The "triangular" strategy, however, ran the risk of losing big. Any setback on one of the three fronts would seriously drag down progress on the other two, and this was ultimately what happened. Taiwanese labor lost the battle on the FECF strike because of state repression before it had consolidated its organizational bases. What immediately followed was the electoral defeat of December 1989—the Workers' Party won no seats in the legislature and even failed to have its incumbent reelected. As strikes and the pursuit of political power lost headway, union reforms could be pursued only under the most precarious conditions, lacking grassroots action and any political shield. Constant threats of legal action from employers and the state were made against union leaders and activists, and many of them paid a high price.

In retrospect, Taiwan's labor movement originated in the labor-intensive (private) sector, whose lesser bargaining power led to a severe crackdown in 1989. This major setback pushed Taiwan's labor movement into scaling back its demands to adjust to a hostile environment. In the following decade, the labor movement worked to reconsolidate its support base and regain ground in electoral politics. After the defeat of the FECF strike and the subsequent witch-hunt against union leaders in the private sector, there was a wave of organizing, targeting large-scale state-enterprise unions. From that point, public-sector unions took definitive control of the movement. Unions at state-owned enterprises—petroleum, telecommunications, railroads, steel, shipbuilding, airlines, water supply, electricity, postal services, tobacco and liquor, and others—were in a more secure position to do union work because of the guarantee of lifelong employment and their enhanced legal recourse. Leaders at these big unions controlled the mobilizing mechanisms, and so the interests and demands of large-scale state-enterprise unions became the core agendas of the movement. As the public sector was threatened by privatization plans in the 1990s, antiprivatization, job security, and the economic well-being of public-sector workers became the main concerns of Taiwan's labor movement.

Since the Workers' and Labor parties only existed nominally,[4] the electoral question became, through which channels can workers' political interests be articulated? The convenient answer was either to run on the opposition party ticket or accept political appointments to take charge of local labor bureaus. Up until then, all of the so-called labor legislators, without exception, had secured their seats through the electoral machinery of the opposition party and not through direct, grassroots support from workers as voters. High-profile labor leaders had joined the race as independent candidates, but the results had always been disappointing.

Flawed involvement in electoral politics and a public-union-centered labor agenda were troubling issues. Much of the strife inside labor movement circles has revolved around these two issues. There was a divide over what was the most effective strategy to advance the movement in terms of its relationship with institutional politics. One side argued that, given the natural disadvantage of being embedded in an SME-dominated economy, the movement should pursue political negotiations and make compromises with major parties on issues such as safety nets and social welfare, to compensate for the rapidly deteriorating labor market conditions caused by the pressure of global competition. From the other side, an oft-heard criticism of this "quick political remedy" was that the labor movement had wasted time engaging in political dealings at the expense of pursuing grassroots organizing, which was the most fundamental task of the movement. This lack of solid grassroots support, it was argued, made unions and their umbrella organization a weak and dispensable partner of major political parties. As a labor activist put it,

> if Taiwan can move in the direction of social democracy, that's fine. But the important point is that Taiwan has different objective conditions. If you want to become a viable center-left force, how can it be possible? For example, if they [the political negotiation camp] want to develop industrial democracy and tripartite negotiation, how do you sustain these? *You want to bargain with others, but how do you get a desirable result if you have no strength?* (interview with a labor activist, November 18, 2002)

Another common complaint skewered the "labor aristocracy." Many argued that workers' leverage could only be built through organizing workers at large, strategic industries. Yet having the public-sector unions lead a labor struggle would maximize the impact while minimizing possible retaliatory action. Furthermore, public-sector unions could also back any political bargaining from their strategic position at the national level. Any positive results coming out of such negotiations, such as unemployment insurance and revisions of outdated labor laws, would benefit the laboring population as a whole. Dissenting activists said that Taiwan's labor movement had merely become a vehicle for advancing the interests of the most secure and comfortable workers. While fighting the government's privatization plans and bargaining for a better deal for public-sector workers, public-sector unions were accused of neglecting the interests and needs of the most disadvantaged workers: those in small, private enterprises; immigrants; and the middle-aged unemployed.

The key point is that these debates must be understood in the context of how a latecomer movement negotiates the early-riser legacy to set its own path. Taiwan's labor movement faltered between two different approaches of movement building. The new and improved electoral politics and the precedents set by the environmental movement pulled the labor movement inside the system. It went along with the early-riser model by relying heavily on political means—accepting political appointments from different parties, locating political alliances, and participating in electoral competition—to compensate for the structural disadvantage of organized labor in an economy consisting of geographically decentralized SMEs. Yet, without bridging various divides inside the working class, the bargaining power of this movement was limited, and negotiations were often at the mercy of major political parties. This movement tried to build solidary, centralized union organizations based in the public sector to realize workers' economic leverage, as labor movements had done elsewhere. Yet this approach reached only a small segment of the laboring population, while those who needed social protection the most were left out.

Korea: A Tango de la Muerte of Political Exclusion and Militancy

When we observe the interactions between the labor movement and the Korean state during the authoritarian period, the most remarkable aspect is a vicious cycle of repression and resurrection that led the movement to develop a self-organization model and foster a culture of militancy.

The Labor Movement and Its Legacy

Korea's labor movement, after emerging in the mid-1970s, progressed by successive waves in confronting heightened repression under both the Park and Chun regimes. The most curious thing is that the subsequent wave of protest became more forceful and sweeping than the previous. Table 5 documents the volume, scope, and level of militancy in the two waves of labor protests (1978–81 and 1986–89). If we look at absolute numbers, the number of disputes, number of workers involved, and total workdays lost in the later wave of labor protests (1986–89) far exceeded the volume and scope of the previous wave (1978–81), showing a twelvefold growth in the number of disputes, a fifteenfold growth in the number of workers involved, and 144 times as many workdays lost as in the previous wave. As far as labor militancy is concerned, the increased level of militancy between 1986 and 1989 can be substantiated by two figures: workdays lost per dispute (eleven times the number in the previous wave) and workdays lost contributed by each worker (nine times).

The secret lay in the model of self-organization that bridged waves of protest and in a culture of militancy that withstood state violence. Here a swimming metaphor is apt. In the butterfly stroke, a swimmer advances by waves, taking effective arm strokes and dolphin kicks under the water so as to have the head and shoulders surface and resurface above the water. What is seen above the water is much like the visible, militant action initiated by the labor movement; what is hidden below the water is all sorts of educational programs, carefully planned small-group meetings, and aggressive organizing work to bring more workers into the movement circle and foster a culture of militancy against constant repression.

The effect of such self-organization showed not only in the scope of protests but also on the unionization front. The number of unions increased dramatically between 1986 and 1989, from 2,658 in 1986, to 4,086 in 1987, 6,142 in 1988, and 7,861 in 1989, an annual growth rate as high as 44 percent. In fewer than two years, the number of labor unions had returned to

Table 5. Two waves of Korean labor protests

	1978–81 (A)	1986–89 (B)	A:B
Number of strikes and lockouts	599	7,514	1:12.5
Number of workers involved	108,412	1,684,534	1:15.5
Total workdays lost	130,107	18,771,171	1:144.3
Number of workers per dispute	181	224	1:1.2
Workdays lost per dispute	217	2,498	1:11.5
Workdays lost contributed by each worker	1.2	11.1	1:9.3

Source: Top three rows from ILO statistics (http://www.ilo.org/ilostat/); bottom three rows from the author's calculations.

their 1979 level, prior to Chun's antilabor campaign. The proliferation of labor unions at the local level further led to the construction of labor federations at the industry level and, eventually, an alternative umbrella organization for all democratic unions. In the late 1980s, blue-collar workers founded multiple Councils of Local Unions, representing 253,540 workers in 630 unions. Similar developments also happened to white-collar workers. Efforts to build interunion solidarity became more pronounced, and federations of labor unions for SMEs and *chaebol* groups also began to form in this period. Korea's labor movement expanded in the late 1980s in both numerical and organizational terms. Eventually, in 1990, the Chunnohyup (Korean Trade Union Council), the forerunner of the current KCTU, was founded (J. K. Kim 2000). Furthermore, another development was "the growing worker solidarity across firms located in the same geographical area. . . . Area-based solidarity struggles . . . by the late 1980s . . . had become a major stream of the democratic labor movement" (Koo 2001, 176).

The origin of the self-organization tradition was, ironically, political exclusion and repression. Throughout the Park and Chun regimes, and even after the democratic transition in the late 1980s, labor was blocked from electoral politics, and its access to political spaces was limited by a variety of legal restrictions. The choice between "organize or die" was an obvious one when all other institutional means for interest mediation were blocked. Aided by the geographical concentration of industrial establishments, the effect of organizing could be amplified if the right strategies were adopted. Since the 1970s, this movement has featured underground organizing, educational campaigns, a strong sense of camaraderie, and dense organizational networks in major industrial cities. State repression, on one hand, supplied the movement with more and more determined labor organizers and, on the other hand, spurred the labor movement into adopting a particular type of organizing model. As to the first point, as labor unions were outlawed and organizers blacklisted, repressive antilabor measures had the opposite effect to what was intended, as they

> produced more determined labor activists with years of union experience who had been expelled from their jobs. Blocked from gainful employment by the government, they had no choice but to become professional labor activists. These outside labor activists played an instrumental role in interconnecting unionists across firms and linking them to dissident political communities. (Koo 2001, 103)

Besides experienced union organizers, there was new blood joining the ranks of labor organizing. The workers' strategic position in countering the military junta and bringing revolutionary change to Korean society was increasingly recognized by other opposition groups, particularly students:

> [College] students have been led to recognize that their role is limited to that of raising the consciousness of the oppressed laboring classes, and that as intellectuals with middle class backgrounds they themselves, however militant their tactics, cannot be the instruments of true revolution. (Brandt 1987, 33)

It is estimated that roughly three thousand students quit college to become factory workers in the 1980s to "raise workers' consciousness" (Koo 2001, 103, 105). Other estimates of the number of students-turned-workers vary from a low of around fifteen hundred to a high of more than five thousand (Brandt 1987, 35). Opinions on the effectiveness of these student activists are rather divided. Some imply that the presence of students-turned-workers in workplaces led to the elevated political and class consciousness of the working class, and "the development of the labor movement in the 1980s was intimately connected to the large number of students who dropped out of college and became students-turned-workers" (Koo 2001, 104). Others explicitly disagree, feeling that the historical significance of students-turned-workers in Korea's labor movement has been exaggerated at the expense of female worker activism since the 1970s (Chun 2003, 196–98). The following quotes from workers are most illuminating:

> The problems with these so-called *hwaldonggas* [student activists] are many. First, they are impatient. They would like to do something very quickly. They feel that they have to do something, so they start a strike that cannot succeed. And then they just leave. No wonder many politically conscious workers despised students and did not want them. Second, they are not good workers. They cannot be since they go to late night meetings and discussions with drinking and smoking. . . . Third, they leave quickly if they feel unwanted. They need to be patient and wait to be accepted by workers. I have seen so many women students leave the factory after three or four months. I wonder why they started to work at all. Factory work should not be a hobby for students. (Kim 1997, 138)

> I hated the way students got involved for a limited period and also hated that the workplace became their experimental ground. For quite a while, I felt betrayed and distrustful. But now I think that everyone has their own location in society. There needs to be a movement that can embrace and consolidate the student movement and the labor movement. (Kim 1997, 139)

I don't think that there are many student activists left in factories now . . . almost all have left to go back to school, so they are now an endangered species. . . . It is natural that they go back where they came from, because they have done their share. But watching them go back to their middle-class life, I feel betrayed. They have their family background and their education, so that they can start at some other place. But we cannot leave our factory work that easily. We are stuck here. (Kim 1997, 140)

Students-turned-workers may or may not have been reckless, but they for sure enlarged the pool of labor organizers. As the number of organizers increased, more workers were exposed to the kind of political education that prepared them to fight the subsequent economic and political battles, inside or outside their workplaces.

Tireless self-organization coordinated through labor activists drove Korea's labor movement forward. Even after Chun Doo-Hwan's merciless killings of existing unions in the early 1980s, "by 1984, workers had regrouped sufficiently to be able to launch a new offensive" (Hart-Landsberg 1993, 272). Between 1984 and 1985, labor activities gradually resumed in major industrial areas, and with the aid of networks of blacklisted labor activists, a few major labor struggles broke out, including the Daewoo Motor strike[5] and the Kuro Industrial Area struggle.[6] What happened between 1986 and 1989, especially the strike wave in 1987, was both the result of previous organizing work and the continuation of the political activation project.

As for the type of organizing model adopted, for the simple reason of survival alone, Korea's labor movement opted for one that could withstand state surveillance and repression. Starting from the 1970s, a method for organizing and recruitment by building networks "of centrally supervised yet largely autonomous 'cells'" was adopted:

> Selected union activists were given the responsibility of supervising small groups of members, between 10 and 15 in each, who worked in their own factory locality; this system became known as the Acacia Meeting. . . . Rather than rely upon the efforts of a few executive committee members to try to visit frequently all those different factories, efforts which could read-ily be frustrated by a determined employer . . . it was so much easier, and a policy much more difficult for owners to counter, for someone within the factory itself, or who perhaps worked in the factory next door or along the corridor, to pop in for a chat with the [workers] during the lunch break. (Chun 2003, 171)

In addition, as thousands of students-turned-workers migrated to factories in the 1980s, the multicentered "spot" system widely used in the student movement circle also migrated with them:

> In the spot system all contacts between . . . groups . . . are carried out by single, designated individuals, who are in turn able to name a back-up if their position is in any way endangered. . . . The designated person knows only his or her contact and no one else in the other group(s). . . . Students say that no one knows the whole structure. (Brandt 1987, 19–20)

The spot system itself was the result of accommodating a repressive political environment. Existing as early as the late 1970s, this form of organization was subsequently refined and expanded. "During the Park years arrests of student leaders and the dismantling of student organizations were effective in disrupting activities, but since 1980 it has been possible to carry on almost without interruption under new leaders and new organizational labels, in spite of continuing repression" (Brandt 1987, 20).

Thus we often hear statements from students-turned-workers about discovering the presence of other disguised workers in the same workplace:

> I went to work [as a disguised worker] at a small electronics factory with 140 employees in Incheon. And guess what? Of those 140 workers, there were about 10 disguised workers. Immediately, I could tell who were activists [*hwaldongga*]. That small factory was overflowing with *hwaldongga*. (Kim 1997, 135)

More importantly, the model of self-organization brought workers in different sectors into the labor movement circle, and Korea's labor movement has been all about infiltrating previously unorganized sectors. This started with female workers in the labor-intensive manufacturing export sector in the 1970s, then moved to semiskilled male workers in large corporations and strategic industries in the 1980s. Between 1987 and 1990, those famous images of industrial workers marching on the streets along with bulldozers, loaders, and other heavy machinery perfectly capture this shift. Male workers in strategic industries entered the labor struggle, replacing the lead role played by female workers in the light manufacturing sector in the 1970s. In the 1990s, the organizing drive began to target workers in the public sector and temporary and immigrant workers.

Intertwined as it is with the self-organization model, the culture of militancy is also worth exploring further. We should take notice that self-organization and militancy were mutually reinforcing in the Korean context. Theoretically speaking, self-organization does not necessarily lead to militant action: it was exclusive institutional arrangements and repressive measures that led workers down the path of militancy. A KCTU staff member remarked,

Many think of us as crazy militants, but this is not in our nature. Government and capital make us turn this way. This is inevitable because we have to fight. The second thing [characteristic of Korea's labor movement] is political. We are trade union organizations yet we have no choice but to be political, because we have to fight against a government which oppresses organized labor. (interview with a KCTU staff member, April 24, 2003)

General strikes, self-immolation, building occupancy, and bodily fighting with riot police were all part of a legitimate action package frequently used during labor struggles. Under this long-standing culture of militancy, negotiations and policy compromises with the political authorities were not encouraged and sometimes led to dreadful fights inside democratic unions and leadership shifts. The best example is that, right after the financial crisis, in 1998, the KCTU joined the Tripartite Commission and, along with government and management, devised a plan that would make layoffs easier in exchange for improving unemployment relief programs, allowing unions a role in politics and enabling teachers to form unions. The rank-and-file workers rejected this layoff accord, and KCTU leaders who had struck the deal were forced to resign and replaced by a more militant group who called for a general strike[7] (*Chosun Ilbo* 1998; *New York Times* 1998a, 1998b). One year later, the KCTU withdrew from the Tripartite Commission completely. Six years after its withdrawal, serious internal strife broke out again just as the KCTU was discussing a return to the Commission in 2005 (*Hankyoreh* 2005; *Korea Times* 2005). Alongside such hesitation over political compromises, the labor movement's formal participation in electoral politics came relatively late. The labor movement initiated a campaign, People's Victory 21, to test the electoral waters in the 1997 presidential election, and it received 1.1 percent of total votes cast. Such experiences eventually led to the formation of the Korean Democratic Labor Party in 2000, almost thirty years after the labor movement took off in Korea.

To sum up the early-riser legacy in Korea, we first observe the formation of a politically excluded minority group that was solidly organized through a series of difficult economic struggles. Since the regime hardly made any compromise with and deployed all kinds of repressive measures and legal restrictions against the labor movement, the long-standing distrust toward the political authorities fostered and sustained a culture of militancy inside the labor movement. This movement, historically speaking, benefited little from positive media coverage or preexisting government-sanctioned unions and relied heavily on its own efforts to haul workers in different sectors into autonomous unions. This added a flavor of self-reliance and self-organization, via channels of communication independent of mainstream media, to the working model of the movement. Situated in a hostile environment and under conditions of political exclusion, Korea's labor movement evolved into a perfect example of overcoming obstacles and achieving goals via self-cultivated strength, and its relationship with political authorities and capital was a showdown of force. Even the process of democratization did not change this dynamic much: labor was still generally blocked from the existing system of political representation, and direct confrontation with the state and capital became the routine.

The Korean State's Responses

The dynamics between Korea's military regimes and its labor movement can best be characterized as follows. The regime adopted a political design that blocked workers from the arena of institutional politics. Without the channel of interest articulation, workers lashed out periodically, and then the regime restored order by force. Workers' militancy and distrust of the political system grew, and the regime had to bet on more tear gas canisters and prison cells. Instead of negotiation and incorporation, repression and further political exclusion seemed to be the instinctive responses of Korea's military regimes to labor challenges.

Historically speaking, under the Park and Chun regimes (1961–87), labor was thoroughly blocked from the electoral route by all sorts of institutional barriers. To strengthen the absolute power of the president, Park Chung Hee put an end to local self-government as soon as he took power in 1961. Under the Yushin regime (1972–79), it was stipulated in the Constitutional Amendments, Supplementary Rules, Article 10 that "local assemblies under the present Constitution shall not be formed until the unification of the fatherland has been achieved" (Hapdong News Agency 1979, 349–65). As a consequence,

> all the local councils were disbanded and heads of local autonomous bodies named by the military government. . . . All the heads of local administrative units including Special Cities, Provinces, cities, *kuns* [county] and *myons* are appointed by the central government while all the local councils remain closed. (Hapdong News Agency 1979, 97)

Chun Doo Hwan continued this practice,[8] and South Korea did not hold one single local election between 1961 and 1991. Without local elections, political elites that might have mediated or alleviated labor grievances at the local level were nonexistent. At the national level, elections and the electoral system were not means of political competition but instruments for securing the regime's power. The government changed the electoral rules whenever it became clear that the electoral system had lost its use, hence the frequent changes of provisions for presidential elections and the electoral system used in legislative elections. (Croissant 2002, 239)

If elections in Taiwan were a game aimed at absorbing dissenting elites, elections in Korea were blatant window dressing intended to limit the participation of existing civil associations and to minimize competition. Article 87 of Korea's Election Law stipulated that "organizations, regardless of their types and names, may not support or oppose any specific political parties or candidates. Nor may they encourage others to support or oppose any specific parties or candidates" (S. Kim 2003, 91n28). Also, on multiple occasions, the military junta banned its opponents from political activities, forbidding them to run for office. Even if opposition members entered the parliamentary system, the president had legal powers to unilaterally dissolve the National Assembly at will. Also, opposition members could easily be expelled from parliament. That Kim Young Sam got expelled in 1979 for hosting the Y. H. Trading female workers at his party headquarters is the best example. Korea's electoral politics prior to the 1990s accommodated only political elites at the very top. As the size of the entire representative organ has never been more than three hundred, this game ran like a high-end country club with a very expensive entrance fee, and the electoral system as a whole was not effective in representing diverse social interests, particularly labor's.

But besides the route of electoral politics, labor can articulate class interests through its own associations. In the case of Korea, however, labor's umbrella organization—the state-sanctioned FKTU—has historically been deprived of playing a role in interest representation. It has even been prohibited from mediating labor disputes and overseeing collective bargaining at the enterprise level since the early 1980s (the "no third-party intervention" clause). Even if workers had formed independent unions at all levels out of dissatisfaction with the FKTU, and even if they had built interfirm solidarity and fought impressive wage battles against employers, the expanding labor movement still confronted great difficulty in translating its strengths into political influence, because of various existing institutional barriers (Y. Lee 2011). The legal codes confined trade unions to the economic arena and were intended to make their advance into politics difficult. Even in the 1997 version of the Trade Union and Labor Relations Adjustment Act, it was strictly stipulated in Article 2 that trade unions were created "for the purpose of maintaining and improving working conditions, or improving the economic and social status of workers." If the aims of the union in question were mainly directed at "political movements," the organization could not be regarded as a trade union—a legal restriction on unions' political activities that had no equivalent in Taiwan's Labor Union Law. Furthermore,

> labor organizations have not been allowed to participate in electoral competition. Electoral laws prohibit labor organizations from donating political funds or forming political organizations. Thus industrial workers have no institutional channel to translate their collective interests into the political system. (Jaung 2000, 49)

All these legal restrictions mean that, even after the June 29 declaration of democratization in 1987 and the subsequent institutional reforms, labor was continuously blocked from the electoral path.[9] Furthermore, the Korean government also responded to militant labor struggles with repression. Figure 15 and Table 6 document the labor repression during different terms of the presidency.

During the term of Chun Doo Hwan, if we exclude those who were sent to "purification camps," the number of arrests was not that high. But the number of workers fired from their jobs because of labor activity hit an all-time record. During Roh's five-year presidency, there were on average 624 workers being fired or arrested each year—almost 2 per day. Right after the peak of labor struggles in 1987, the Roh administration decided to fight the labor offensive by force and with legal measures and began a massive wave of

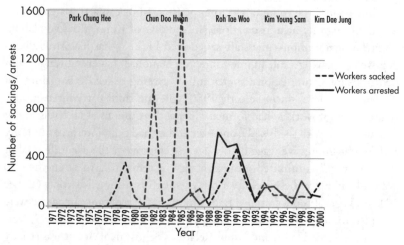

Figure 15. Korea's records of labor repression.

Table 6. Labor repression by presidency

Period	Presidency	Number of workers sacked	Number of workers arrested	Sackings and arrests combined	Sackings and arrests per year
1971–79	Park Chung Hee	514	24	538	60
1980–87	Chun Doo Hwan	2,957	220	3,177	454
1988–92	Roh Tae Woo	1,146	1,974	3,120	624
1993–97	Kim Young Sam	537	514	1,051	210
1998–2000	Kim Dae Jung (first three years)	375	413	788	263

Source: Korean Confederation of Trade Unions (2001, 357–84).

arrests. Thousands of riot police stormed into the Hyundai shipyards in 1989 and 1990 to end the strikes there, and hundreds of workers were arrested (Hart-Landsberg 1993, 296).

> The government is backing up its tough talk by arresting union militants and using the courts to limit labor rights. These tactics are of dubious legality, but they have succeeded in putting labor on the defensive. An embryonic national teachers union was destroyed last year. Chonnohyup's leaders have been jailed and rank-and-file members have been forced to resign or were fired after the federation was declared to be an "illegal group that is leading a vicious conflict with an ideology of class struggle." Chonnohyup was banned on 20 January, two days before its official founding. Its leader [D]an Byung Ho, is still in custody. (Clifford 1990b, 74)

In only five years (1988–92), nearly two thousand workers were arrested, over 80 percent of them in the three years from 1989 to 1991. The level of repression seemed to abate after the inauguration of Kim Young Sam, who led the first civilian government since 1961. Yet the relationship between the labor movement and the government has remained more confrontational and less conciliatory until the present day.

The confrontation between the Korean government and the labor movement was manifested not only through street fights and arrests but also through a well-crafted campaign on the ideological front. An antilabor alliance—the Roh regime, *chaebol*, and conservative media—seized the opportunity of economic recession in the late 1980s to portray the labor movement as the culprit of the downturn (Lim and Kim 1994). Collaborating with major newspapers, in the early 1990s the Federation of Korean Industries—the summit organization of Korean capital—began an aggressive campaign to promote a neoliberal ideology, namely, national competitiveness and a flexible labor market. The media consistently painted the labor movement as a group of greedy, militant labor aristocrats who had enjoyed comparatively high wages but kept wanting more at the expense of national competitiveness. The condition for this ideological counterattack to be effective was that labor's voice was blocked out of mainstream media, as in the case of most developing countries.

While, as usual, suppressing labor from even entering the era of civilian government, the Korean government took a strikingly different approach toward the environmental movement. If the 1980s was an era of militant *minjung* movements consisting of labor, farmers, and urban poor, by the 1990s, they have "seemingly fallen outside of the purview of public discourse" (Abelmann 1997, 251). The 1990s was hailed as an era of moderate *simin* (citizen) movements (Shin 2006) marked by a rapid expansion of the nonprofit sector—of 429 environmental NGOs founded between 1963 and 2005, 76 percent were founded between 1993 and 2002 during the presidencies of Kim Young Sam and Kim Dae Jung (Ju 2011, 137). Owing to the instability of Korea's political parties, consisting of an elite cartel (Choi 2000, 29) that never reflected bottom-up social cleavages or interests (Y. Lee 2011, 83; Shin 2006, 15–16), the NGOs filled the void by performing the role of "a quasi-party" (Choi 2000, 40) or "quasi-legislative organizations" (Shin 2006, 18) and by "providing policy recommendations, bringing lawsuits, or assuming the role of a civil affairs administration" (cf. N. Lee 2011, 51). In response to the growing influence of the nonprofit sector, the Kim Young Sam administration began to provide funding to civil organizations, including environmental NGOs, on a nonregular basis. President Kim Dae Jung embraced NGO advocacy activities and took one step further toward enacting an NGO support law that authorized various government agencies to administer an annual grant of fifteen million U.S. dollars to NGOs (Ju 2011, 141–42). All this institutional legitimation and financial support secured environmental NGOs' role in Korea's institutional politics, in contrast to labor's continued exclusion.

The Succeeding Environmental Movement

Prior to the mid-1980s, Korea's antipollution protests were contained. Environmental conflicts took place disproportionately on the outskirts of a handful of industrial zones, and, as conflicts broke out, the government intervened by relocating pollution victims elsewhere with damage compensation and relocation subsidies. By physically separating polluting facilities and victims, antipollution protests, even with the aid of urban intellectuals, had a hard time sustaining themselves and expanding to a point where the general public and media would have no choice but to take notice.

Against the backdrop of heightened confrontation between labor and the Chun regime, the environmental movement began to take shape with the watershed Onsan incident in 1985. This is the first case in which environmental NGOs launched a large-scale public relations campaign (Eder 1996, 100) and galvanized enough public support to force the government to draft a relocation project for thousands of pollution victims:

> Pollution at the huge Onsan chemical complex south of Ulsan is so bad that the government bought off protesters by offering households Won 15 million each if they were prepared to move. About two-thirds of the 10,000 residents have left. (Clifford 1990a, 72)

It is worth noting that, in the Korean context, environmental organizations comprising professionals and urban intellectuals have from the outset played a key role in shaping the direction of the movement. The Onsan case was publicized by the PRI, a group established by radical clergymen to support victims, research pollution problems, and educate the public (Ku 1996b, 162). In the late 1980s, this movement experienced rapid organizational expansion at both national and local levels. At the national level, the first mass-based environmental organization, the Korean Anti-Pollution Civilian Movement Council, was formed in 1986. One year later, a student-based group, the Korean Anti-Pollution Movement Council, was created. In 1988, these two groups merged to create the Korean Anti-Pollution Movement Association (KAPMA). Five years later, KAPMA merged with regional environmental NGOs to form the Korean Federation of Environmental Movements (KFEM), currently the largest and most influential environmental organization in Korea. The YMCA and the Citizens' Coalition for Economic Justice were also important organizations advocating environmental issues in the early 1990s (Ju 2011, 140–41). At the local level, regional environmental groups came into existence at Mokpo (1987), Pusan (1989), Ulsan (1989), and Kwangju (1989), "largely as a result of local struggles led by farmers, and fishermen" (Hart-Landsberg 1993, 267). On the protest activity front,

> between 1988 and 1991 there were numerous environmental protests and actions in Korea, but they tended to be localized and focused on specific actions or plans of the government or industry. However, they did serve to rally support for environmental concern and highlighted its importance for all of Korea. (Eder 1996, 102)

Opposition to the construction of golf courses was an important concern of environmental activism at that time:

> There were 73 anti-pollution protests in the first seven months of 1990, according to press reports. The National Police Headquarters says that more than 24,000 people took part in environmental demonstrations which were concentrated in the heavily industrial southeastern part of the country. Nearly one-third of the 73 protests were directed at the construction of golf courses, which protesters complain use too much pesticide and fertilizer. (Clifford 1990a, 72)

The first antinuclear protest took place in 1988, local residents being concerned about the issue of nuclear-waste storage. It was reported that a total of one thousand residents near three nuclear power plants—Wolsong, Kori, and Yongkwang—staged separate demonstrations on the same day demanding the removal of radioactive waste or of the plants themselves (*Korea Times* 1988); "they have staged several protests since then demanding that the government move them away from the plant" (Clifford 1989, 55). Antinuclear protest reached its peak in 1990 on a nuclear-waste storage facility sited on Anmyon Island. Anmyon residents held a series of antinuclear protests (*Korea Times* 1990a), and in one of them, as many as ten thousand residents clashed with eleven hundred riot police, and a police car was set ablaze (*Korea Times* 1990c). Students boycotted classes, and residents staged a site occupancy that resulted in more riot police being sent in and sixty arrests (*Korea Times* 1990b). The whole controversy ended with the cancellation of the storage plan (*Korea Herald* 1990).

In 1991, the Naktong river pollution case—some called it a watershed event of Korea's environmental movement (Ku 2011, 213–14)—led to the nationalization of environmental protest. Doosan Chemicals spilled phenol into the river and contaminated the drinking water supply for millions of people. The national boycott against Doosan-related commercial products (including the best-selling OB Beer) signified the rising concerns over environmental degradation.

Much like the Anmyon antinuclear protest described earlier, environmental conflicts throughout the 1980s adopted a militant style of action in direct parallel to the labor and student movements:

> Residents at the southeastern port of Pusan won a government moratorium on the construction of a new industrial dump after 5,000 protesters built barricades, blocked roads and took hostage an Environmental Ministry official in July [1990]. (Clifford 1990a, 72)

As for the anti-golf-course protests, those in Kyungbuk Province evolved from a local petition campaign receiving overwhelming support in 1988 to a site occupancy action and a refusal to send children to school in 1990. Hundreds of people participated in this four-month camp-in campaign, and the whole thing led to clashes with security forces and numerous injuries (Eder 1996, 103).

In short, antipollution protests in the 1980s were part of the "nationalist-democratic movement" and commonly adopted militant strategies to advance the cause. Their ideological inclination was closely akin to other antigovernment movements at that time (Ku 1996b, 162). From the Anti-Pollution Declaration made by the group putting forth the Onsan case, pollution was seen as the product of a repressive regime "which import[ed] the pollution industry on behalf of the multinational corporations and allows the pollution emission of monopoly capital" (cf. Ku 1996b, 167).

If Taiwan's succeeding movement was characterized by immediate defeat and retreat right after its takeoff, Korea's succeeding movement featured a swift transformation of ideology, movement agendas, and the reaching of a truce with the political authorities, private capital, and mass media. To put the transformation very succinctly, in the 1980s, Korea's environmental movement followed an antigovernment, leftist ideology, but in the 1990s, environmental NGOs attempted "to transcend class boundaries" and defined "themselves as speaking from and to the entire national audience" (Eder 1996, 112). As far as movement agendas were concerned, the 1980s was the era of antipollution campaigns in which the state and private capital were beyond doubt the bad guys, but the 1990s was the era of a new environmental movement focusing on ecological issues, conservationism, and international collaborations with financial sponsorship from the government and *chaebol.*

The change of direction took place when Korean NGOs prepared to participate in the 1992 Rio Summit. To make the trip to Rio viable, environmental NGOs accepted both government subsidies and *chaebol* donations. This led to an internal debate over whether the NGO delegation should accept corporate donations to go to Rio. The decision to accept such donations was a controversial one. Given the past opposition to *chaebol* pollution, some activists considered this decision unethical and split from the movement. The Rio experience, however, was transformative in the sense that "the inclination to define the government and big business as the major polluters declined. Among environmental organizations, after the Rio Conference, the recognition that a reformation of the government and enterprise was inevitable gained ground" (Ku 1996b, 172). The change in the position of environmental NGOs was reciprocated by governmental subsidies, invitations to join the advisory council at the Ministry of Environment, and generous business donations.

The reaction from the government and business was quite predictable. After fighting the militant labor movement and other antiestablishment movements for so long, any conciliatory gestures from social movements would be warmly embraced. This new and improved environmental movement also received favorable coverage from major media outlets, which greatly helped the movement organize public support on multiple ecological and conservation issues. Reporters would go so far as to tell environmental NGOs that "your statements aren't fancy enough—make them more newsworthy!" (interview with an environmental activist, April 18, 2003). By mastering "the art of the press release and understand[ing] how to use the media to get their point across to the public and the government" (Eder 1996, 114), the movement received wide public support, which in turn pressured the government and *chaebol* to manage rising environmental concerns. An activist commented on the overall trend,

> There has been a clear change. Now we are focusing on ecological issues. I'm saying this about the movement in general. Things like protecting forests, reservoirs, wildlife habitats, and wetlands. *That kind of issue is much easier to get consensus on.* But now criticizing corporations for pollution is a minor issue. [The change] came about from the middle of the 1990s. (interview with a KFEM staff member, April 18, 2003)

Not a few activists viewed this change of direction with reservation and caution. First there was the issue of overdependence on media to organize public support and the lack of a solid, grassroots base for the movement:

> To organize a few people in the corner of a city is not easy, and it has to be done everywhere. It's too slow, they [activists] could not endure this situation [the level of environmental degradation in contrast to the slow pace of organizing], and they had to do something very quickly. So they chose a way, *they followed the media.* Yes, everywhere we've had to appeal to the media, that's true. *But at the same time we've had to organize.* (interview with a *chaebol* environmental research fellow, March 8, 2004)

In response, environmental NGOs engaged in aggressive membership drives in the mid-1990s. To take just the KFEM as an example, it increased its membership from twenty thousand in 1995, to fifty thousand in 1998, and to one hundred thousand in 2005. Yet even with such an impressive increase in membership, some worried about the low percentage of active members, and others said it was not enough:

Q: Do you think people in the environmental movement agree with you on organizing the grass roots and being less dependent on the media?

A: Yes! Everybody has been saying this for ten years! Yes, they recruited more members, but this is not enough. They still depend on the media and on financing [from *chaebol*]. (interview with a *chaebol* environmental research fellow, March 8, 2004)

Furthermore, an ambiguous relationship with *chaebol* also raised concerns. Some have pointed out that donations from big corporations might not prevent those same corporations from being criticized by environmental NGOs. Nevertheless, the pollution issues of big corporations faded into the background and "most of the criticism focused on the government instead of corporations" (interview with a volunteer of Green Future, March 26, 2003). By sponsoring environmental NGOs and actively expressing a pro-environment stand,

chaebol behaved like they really cared about the environment. Even though it's the corporations that exploited the environment the worst. "We construct highways, and [are] environment-friendly." Geez, how can constructing highways be environment-friendly? But most construction companies advertised like that! (interview with a KFEM staff member, April 18, 2003)

Another activist put it more poignantly:

In the past, environmental NGOs monopolized ecological discourses and environmental issues. But now that it's been democratized, congressmen, conservative political parties talk about environmental issues, business talks about this issue, so the NGOs lose their market. (interview with a *chaebol* environmental research fellow, March 8, 2004)

Even though they were shifting away from anticorporation campaigns in the 1990s, environmental NGOs on occasion still clashed with *chaebol*. But they usually lost:

A: For example, NGOs made strong protests against the LG ship leakage in 1995. But they failed because the media didn't report the protests so much.

Q: Why didn't the media cover anticorporation protests?

A: LG is a very important advertising sponsor, newspapers, broadcasting. . . . Environmental NGOs really relied on media coverage, so they didn't have much leverage to boycott the LG group. (interview with an environmental researcher, March 9, 2004)

Finally, the most troubling issue was the limit of this "cooperation-with-the-establishment" approach. The Korean environmental movement was thoroughly successful at organizing public support on less controversial issues, such as habitat conservation and tougher environmental measures, and put enormous pressure on the state and capital to follow public consensus accordingly. But it found itself lacking media backing when it "tackled very important, major projects that involved huge conflict between the old developmental paradigm and the new ecological paradigm" (interview with an environmental researcher, February 26, 2004). For issues such as nuclear energy, loaded with economic and political significance, the movement was fighting an uphill battle. An activist commented that

> inside [our organization], we had never put down the antinuclear flag. But it's not a generally accepted issue like ecological issues. . . . The antinuclear issue is just not a major issue nowadays. . . . Environmentalists lost the initiative on the nuclear energy issue in general. (interview with a KFEM staff member, April 18, 2003)

Why Does the Early-Riser Legacy Matter?

Protest-cycle scholars have wisely taught us one important lesson: what latecomer movements think and do should not be divorced from what their predecessors have thought and done (McAdam 1995; Tarrow 1994). From the two sets of narratives on Taiwan and Korea, we can highlight the direct and indirect effects of the early-riser movements on the succeeding movements. The direct effect is that both succeeding movements to some extent imitated the early risers' strategies. When an early-riser movement was deeply involved in an open electoral system and achieved a limited degree of success and compromise, the latecomer movement would be lured into this system as well. By contrast, where an early riser was historically excluded from the political arena and developed a strong ethos of self-organization and militancy, the latecomer movement would share this propensity to self-organization and any collaborations with the establishment might result in internal strife. Without early-riser legacies, it would be difficult to understand why Taiwan's labor movement mainly pursued an electoral avenue to advance its cause and used organizing as a supplementary strategy, since "organize or die" has become the universal motto for labor movements elsewhere. It would be equally hard to explain why Korea's environmental movement organized aggressively but postponed its pursuit of electoral politics for almost twenty years after its birth, given its high level of public support and discursive capacities.

This becomes even clearer if we do a simple same-movement, cross-national comparison (Table 7). The idea that an environmental movement should organize aggressively was thoroughly absent in Taiwan's environmental movement, yet the same idea obsessed Korea's environmental activists. While the flagship environmental NGO in Korea has a membership of more than a hundred thousand, the biggest environmental organization in Taiwan has no more than a few thousand.

On the labor front, the two movements have quite different conceptions of electoral politics. The Korean labor movement postponed the pursuit of political power until almost thirty years after its inception and saw the creation of a labor party as the culmination of its organizing power, whereas the Taiwanese movement jumped into the electoral arena immediately and considered electoral victory the means by which to organize. None of these differences can be properly explained without referring back to the early-riser legacy in each national context.

Early-riser movements also had indirect effects on latecomer movements by changing state responses to movements. The ways in which the political authorities deal with latecomer movements are conditioned by experiences learned from encountering early-riser movements. The experience of letting the less politically threatening environmental movement slip out of its hands prepared the KMT to strike out especially hard at a labor movement that it perceived as more threatening. Frustrating the development of the labor movement demonstrated the KMT's strength, and a clear warning sign was

Table 7. Environmental NGO memberships in comparison

Membership	Korea (%) 1997 directory	(%)	Taiwan (%) 1997 survey	(%)
<49	13.5	40	28.4	72.6
50–99	12.2		14.7	
100–199	14.3		29.5	
200–499	17.6	28.3	14.8	19.0
500–999	10.7		4.2	
1,000–9,999	19.3	31.6	8.4	8.4
10,000–99,999	8.9		—	
>100,000	3.4		—	

Source: Taiwan's environmental organizations survey (Hsiao 1997); Korea's data are from the NGO sector at large and are used as a proxy to environmental NGOs (Cho 2000).

sent out to activists in the social movement sector at large to think twice before launching any aggressive assault against the KMT. In the case of Korea, the long and painful confrontation with a militant labor movement made the Korean government welcome any ceasefire agreement with a latecomer movement. Building a conciliatory and cooperative relationship with the new movement neutralized a possible threat on one hand and, on the other, stigmatized the noncooperative, militant stand that the labor movement had taken as blind, senseless, and outdated.

Last but not least, seen through the lens of movement power, latecomer movements' selective appropriation of the early-riser legacy becomes explicable. Korea's environmental movement may have retained the organizing model of the labor movement, but it had no problem dropping its militant culture to build cross-class support bases and not to alienate power holders and the general public. Taiwan's labor movement might have zealously sought political allies, but it could never part from the strategy of union organizing that constituted the source of its power, even though a grassroots-organizing model was thoroughly lacking in Taiwan's environmental movement. All the internal debates taking place inside latecomer movements should redirect us back to the simple fact that latecomer movements would not, and could not, completely imitate early-riser strategies because they were ultimately based on *different* types of movement power. In this sense, the ways that latecomer movements respond to early-riser legacies and to changing state action are by no means random but operate within the constraints of the power base in which the latecomer movements are rooted.

5

Labor and Environmental Trajectories

A strategic comparison of Taiwan's and Korea's labor and environmental movements first renders a series of contrasts between the early-riser and latecomer movements, as presented in the previous chapters. These four movements further entail a dimension of cross-movement comparison that leads to conjectures on possible labor–environmental alliances.

By comparing the four movements, two sharply distinct movement trajectories are noted. For the labor trajectory, both the Taiwanese and Korean labor movements began with a "satanic mill" story in the labor-intensive industries: low wages, hellish working conditions, long hours, pervasive respiratory diseases, and protests in despair. These early spontaneous protests were quickly put down by government repression. Then both movements began to organize in strategic industries such as automobile, petrochemical, postal services, and shipbuilding. Once this strategy bore fruits, accusations of "labor aristocracy" and "union action at the expense of public interest" began to prevail in the media. We also began to see the support base of union movements eroded under capital's counterattack. Alarmed by fits of crisis, both labor movements strove to move beyond the confines of "enterprise unionism" to procure broader social support and to reframe their battles in the light of general interests.

With regard to the environmental trajectory, both environmental movements grew in response to widespread industrial pollution in the wake of industrialization. The early protests were bolstered by a loose coalition of pollution victims and urban intellectuals. This coalition was short-lived owing to different expectations as to protest outcomes and the intervention of new and improved environmental administration. As pollution victims faded out of the coalition, both movements deployed discursive resources in policy research. Most energy was spent on mastering the art of public relations campaigns and on creating newsworthiness. The very success of both environmental movements in pushing through institutional and policy change created new, powerful opponents. The agencies of environmental governance and private capital fought for a commanding position from which to sway public opinion and environmental consciousness. Furthermore, environmental movements in both Taiwan and Korea had a hard time defending the interests of the socially disadvantaged, as at the same time, they were losing battles against corporate power. Pressured and alarmed, the two environmental movements tried to rebuild grassroots linkages and to incorporate diverse economic interests into environmental agendas.

Each social movement strives to maximize its power, and its trajectory depends on which type of power it pursues. To understand movement trajectories as such, we will need to take a departure from the existing literature, which provides general accounts of movement trajectories in terms of "oligarchization," "professionalization," "radicalization," or "institutionalization."[1] This chapter is inspired by Steve Lopez's analysis of the American labor movement, in which the development of a movement is understood as a process of overcoming the obstacles (Lopez 2004, 218). I take the liberty of reformulating Lopez's insight and propose that the difference in movement trajectories results from the fact that labor and environmental movements pursue different types of movement power vis-à-vis their opponents and that their trajectories are conditioned by a process of power maximization and dealing with the consequences of this strategy.

In Taiwan and Korea, labor proceeded by pursuing leverage power in economic struggles while environmental movements maximized their ideological power. Once they had stepped onto the path of power maximization, the composition of the movements changed and their leadership was entrusted to those who were in the best position to exercise these two types of power: semiskilled male workers in strategic industries and urban intellectuals. Power-maximizing strategies resulted in counterattacks from opponents and obstacles that undermined each movement's primary power base. On the labor side, capitalists engaged in plant relocation, withdrawal of lifelong employment guarantees, new managerial strategies, and the deployment of "unorganizable" immigrant and temporary workers. All of these undermined the labor movements' leverage power. On the environmental side, consulting firms and environmental research institutes funded by big corporations began to challenge the movement's monopoly of environmental discourses.

It was only when a crisis point was reached that labor and environmental movements started working toward acquiring the second source of power to compensate for the erosion of their own home advantage. Labor engaged in ideological struggles so as to shed its bad reputation for sectional interest; environmental movements sought to acquire leverage power and consolidate grassroots support to solve the conflict between their ecological vision and the interests of the socially disadvantaged.

The Labor Trajectory: From Leverage to General Social Interest

In contrast to established scholarly opinion on the difference between Taiwan's and Korea's labor movements in terms of militancy, mobilizing capacities, labor dispute structures, and partisan tendencies (Cho and Kim 1998; Chu 1998; Huang 1999; Y. Lee 2006, 2009, 2011; Shieh 1990), this chapter ventures to say something unthinkable: both labor movements are very similar in terms of their pursuit of leverage power, their strategic response to state repression, their shift of movement vanguards, and the obstacles they confronted.

Labor's Pursuit of Leverage

Labor movements in Taiwan and Korea began mainly in the textile industries, which had sustained export-oriented industrialization since the 1960s (Chun 2003; Huang 1999). In the wake of working-class formation, unskilled workers who suffered from low wages and poor working conditions initiated the first wave of labor activism in both countries. This is quite a different starting point from that in France, the United States, and Germany, where artisan culture and craft union traditions played critical roles in the early period of working-class formation (Katznelson 1986, 23). As Koo (2001, 11) has stated, "many of the cultural and institutional factors that are identified as critical facilitating factors for working-class formation in Europe have been absent in South Korea." Much like its Korean counterpart, Taiwan's labor movement evolved without the buttress of artisan culture.

But mobilization in the labor-intensive sector was quickly crushed by state repression, both through physical violence and legal means. Union leaders and activists were fired, blacklisted, arrested, and prosecuted; independent unions were disbanded (Chu 1995; Wu and Liao 1991). In the Taiwanese case, the decisive moment was the defeat of one major strike at Far Eastern Chemical Fibers (FECF) in 1989 (Chao 1991, 1995); in the Korean case, it was the decimation of independent unions between 1980 and 1981 owing to a tightened labor policy under the new military regime (Koo 2001; Ogle 1990).

Such defeats resulted in major strategic reorientations. New strategies were employed to organize workers in strategic industries—crystallized during the industrial deepening strategy of the 1970s—into the labor struggle. These strategic industries included automobile, petrochemical, shipbuilding, heavy metal, and telecommunications. It is also worth noting that the targeted workers happened to be those who were semiskilled, employed in the "protected" sector (Huang 1999), and endowed with better bargaining power vis-à-vis the state and capital. It is at this point that we witness both labor movements' pursuit of leverage power. In the Taiwanese case, even though efforts to reform large unions in both the private and public sectors began when Taiwan's labor movement took off, organizing workers at the state-owned, upstream industries became a conscious, strategic decision of labor organizers only after the decisive defeat in 1989. Given that state enterprises were unionized and put under the patronage of the KMT party machine in the 1950s, organizing state enterprises took the form of fighting for the leadership positions at the unions. The organizer who masterminded the "penetrating state-owned enterprises" strategy remarked,

> After the defeat of the FECF strike, many union cadres were fired and independent unions dared not be as confrontational as they used to be. The movement took a big blow and morale was at its lowest point. My thinking was that, at a time like this, we should focus on organizing and training [for both union cadres and leaders]. . . . The soil of Taiwan's labor movement was barren. Seventy or eighty percent of business establishments belonged to private SMEs hiring fewer than thirty workers. It was impossible to have private-enterprise unions lead this movement. It was difficult to infiltrate state-owned enterprises, but I did have a plan. In each union we began with training fewer than ten workers, and helped them all the way to taking over the union leadership. The most effective way was to take over the state-enterprise unions under the control of the ruling party. . . . Telecommunication, electricity, petroleum, postal services, major big unions were our targets. (interview with a former labor leader and former legislator, November 19, 2002)

Another union leader from a well-organized, militant union echoed the sentiment:

> This was the predicament of Taiwan's labor movement. Our unions were too small . . . one or two hundred people. . . . [The then structure of] enterprise unions restricted horizontal alliances between unions. Alliance-building was a task that big unions in the public sector should carry on,

like telecommunication, railroad, or electricity unions . . . they had more resources. (interview with a transportation union leader, October 20, 2003)

The reason for infiltrating the KMT-controlled public-sector unions was not simply because of their sheer size. That "they had more resources" captures the said unions' privileged position in exercising bargaining power. In contrast to a strike at a textile factory, a halt of production in any of these state enterprises—telecommunications, electricity, petroleum, postal services, railroad, and water supply—would have far-reaching effects on industrial production and ordinary citizens alike. This constituted the greater leverage of state-enterprise unions. The plan was to have these unions spearhead the economic and legal struggles and then turn around to help the structurally disadvantaged unions in the private sector. Similar organizing drives were extended to the financial sector, schoolteachers, and government employees in the 1990s.

Nevertheless, it takes two to tango. The efforts of labor organizers alone would not have succeeded if workers at state enterprises had not become receptive to the idea of self-organization and the exercise of collective power. State-enterprise workers in Taiwan responded well to the organizing drive in the late 1980s because they were greatly troubled by the KMT's policy of privatizing most state enterprises. As a labor scholar has noted, "after the lifting of martial law, the private-sector unions' capacity to protest was weakened, whereas the autonomy and mobilizing capacities of the public-sector unions increased rapidly, which maintained the vitality of Taiwan's labor movement. Ironically, one of the main reasons that led to the increasing mobilization of the public-sector unions was the privatization policy" (Chang 2001, 107–8).

Taiwan's labor movement was not alone in the pursuit of leverage power. After coming to power in the wake of the 1980 Kwangju bloodshed, President Chun Doo Hwan clamped down on labor in the early 1980s, creating a bigger pool of labor organizers—both evicted union cadres and students-turned-workers—who subsequently radicalized the labor movement. From multiple accounts of the development of Korea's labor movement, one major shift in movement configuration took place in the mid-1980s. If throughout the 1970s and the early 1980s it was the heroic deeds of female workers and female union leaders that moved the labor movement forward, in the mid-1980s, male workers in heavy industries became the vanguard of the Korean labor movement, as illustrated by the Daewoo Motor strike (1984–85), the first organized strike to take place in a *chaebol* firm.

The Daewoo Motor case signaled that, in the mid-1980s, "labor activism in South Korea was no longer confined to the light manufacturing sector, but had begun to spread to heavy and chemical industries dominated by large firms" (Koo 2001, 111). If the organizing work at large corporations only started in the early 1980s and "the unionization rate at large manufacturing firms had reached a saturation point by the early 1990s" (196), in fewer than ten years, male workers at strategic industries under the reign of Korea's *chaebol*—automobile, shipbuilding, metal, chemicals, transportation, and others—were either swiftly organized, as in the case of Hyundai, or put under enormous pressure for union reform, as in the case of Daewoo Motor. From the mid-1980s onward, Korea's labor movement had as its bulwark semiskilled, male industrial workers. Major labor struggles between 1987 and 1991 featured the militant actions of male workers on the street, at the shipyard, or even on top of "Goliath," the giant shipbuilding crane. Following the lead of blue-collar workers in the manufacturing sector, white-collar workers—the financial sector, teachers, journalists, and government employees—chimed in during the late 1980s and the early 1990s.[2] The crucial role that female workers had played to sustain the labor movement in the 1970s and the early 1980s was superseded. A female labor leader eloquently articulated the strength differential between female workers and *chaebol* workers:

> In the 1970s and 1980s, in the light manufacturing industry, medium-sized or big companies reduced [the number of] workers, [originally] four hundred, three hundred, now becoming one hundred workers. If you had a strike, it neither had much impact nor raised the concern of [outside] activists. But for *chaebol*, four thousand, five thousand or ten thousand workers were on strike. All the activists were interested [in joining the fight] because, when you fought, they were challenging *chaebol* and multinational companies which were linked to the Korean government. (interview with a labor leader, April 17, 2003)

A comprehensive organizing model backed by a large pool of labor organizers facilitated the leadership shift from female activism in the light manufacturing, labor-intensive sector to male workers in heavy industries. In contrast to the majority of students-turned-workers, who sought employment in small-sized factories requiring few skills and with a very high turnover rate (Lee 2001, 449),[3] some male students-turned-workers took a different approach, infiltrating male-dominated workplaces in the heavy industries near Seoul, starting in the early 1980s. In the historic 1985 Daewoo Motor strike, students-turned-workers played a critical role in organizing and leading the action, in which "[three hundred workers] occupied the factory and threatened to destroy a computer bank if the police attacked. . . . More than two thousand workers expressed support by demonstrating in the factory yards and in the cafeteria. Eight thousand police surrounded the plant. Food and water were cut off from the three hundred inside" (Ogle 1990, 110). Later, the wage negotiation team, led by a student-turned-worker, managed to strike a deal that came very close to the workers' original demands (Koo 2001, 109–11).

Out of this conscious decision to organize strategically, the composition of "vanguards" in both labor movements changed. In Taiwan, state-enterprise unions replaced the private-sector unions, and in Korea, *chaebol* unions occupied center stage. Over time, the leadership of both labor movements was entrusted to those who were in the best position to exercise economic leverage. Along with the leadership shift, movement agendas changed to align with the concerns of the new vanguard groups. The new agenda of Taiwan's labor movement was to fend off a project to privatize state enterprises, which directly affected the interests of state-enterprise workers. Said an interviewee working at the Taiwan Confederation of Trade Unions (TCTU), the organizational culmination of Taiwan's labor movement in the previous two decades,

> Inside the TCTU the really powerful unions that have strong mobilizing capacities are all from state enterprises, they are big unions, and this is the TCTU's power structure. Most of my work deals with labor disputes in state enterprises: year-end bonuses, overtime pay, and many others. By my estimate, more than 60 percent of the TCTU's business is to service state-enterprise unions. (interview with a former TCTU staff member, December 2, 2002)

Another TCTU staff member explained,

> After the TCTU was founded, it was constrained by the demands of state-enterprise unions and had to deal with a lot of issues concerning economic struggles, privatization, plant closure, etc. . . . In the process of privatization, there was much pressure from our member [state-enterprise] unions wanting the TCTU to do something, because "we've paid membership dues [to the TCTU], so you should do this and that for us." (interview with former TCTU chief secretary, November 21, 2002)

On the Korean side, capital deployed a series of managerial strategies to counter labor militancy, such as new working practices, subcontracting, and using temporary workers to get around the problem of high wages and pensions. The Korean labor movement fought back to defend regular employment in its stronghold—heavy industry. In short, labor's agenda shifted from wages and working conditions, which most concerned workers in the labor-intensive sector, to campaigns against privatization and a business offensive that directly undermined the privileged position of workers at state enterprises and in large, private corporations.

Along with the succession of "vanguards," both labor movements redirected their economic battles to the national policy domain. Those battles evolved from conflicts over delayed wages, unpaid overtime, and severance fees in a single workplace to struggles against a far-reaching privatization plan and against a new offensive by business, which included the legalization of hiring temporary workers during strikes and other policy changes in employment relations. The battles moved from the individual workplace to the policy domain at the national level simply because the privatization of state enterprises and the legalization of new employment relations could not be fought at the level of individual plants. For both labor movements to march into the broader policy domain and fight an economic war at a national level, they needed to be backed by increased leverage, supplied by workers from large enterprises and strategic industry.

The Erosion of Labor Power

Very soon after both labor movements set off down the path of maximizing their economic leverage, they were forced to confront the consequences of this strategy. The good news was that, because of their greater leverage, the new leading groups of both movements did secure certain compromises. Taiwan's state-enterprise workers, though unable to stop the privatization plan completely, slowed its process and scored better retirement plans and improved severance packages. On the Korean side, workers from the *chaebol* unions secured wage increases and benefits through annual national wage negotiations.

Yet labor's effort also served to produce a series of reactions from the state and capital. The state interfered in the founding of new labor federations that had the potential to increase labor solidarity and revised labor laws so as to put a leash on collective bargaining and militant action. Capital struck back by relocating production units, increasing the use of irregular and immigrant workers, withdrawing lifetime employment guarantees, and introducing new managerial techniques to control the shop floor (Jung 2000; Yu 1995). In the long run, all of these reactions undercut and weakened labor's leverage. One simple indicator of labor's weakened organizational basis is the constant decrease of union density[4] (i.e., the proportion of workers who belong to unions) after the peak of labor struggle in the late 1980s (see Figure 16). Though Korea's union membership increased slightly in real terms, union density dropped from 18.6 percent in 1989 to 9.88 percent in 2011. Taiwan's industrial unions have lost 160,000 members in the

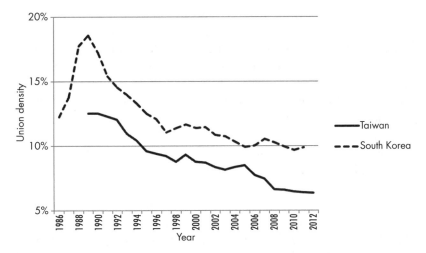

Figure 16. Union density of Korea and Taiwan, 1986–2012. Data for Korea from OECD statistics (http://stats.oecd.org/); data for Taiwan: union membership from the Council of Labor Affairs (http://www.cla.gov.tw/), the number of employed population from the Directorate-General of Budget, Accounting, and Statistics (http://www.dgbas.gov.tw/).

past twenty years, and union density decreased from 12.5 percent in 1989 to 6.3 percent in 2012.

Furthermore, the state and capital collaborated with media outlets and engaged in aggressive ideological campaigns to paint labor struggles as the pursuit of sectional interests at the expense of the wider public. In the case of Taiwan, the antiprivatization drive suffered from the stereotypical impression that state-enterprise workers were inefficient bureaucrats holding "iron rice bowls" and enjoying excellent pension plans paid for out of the taxpayer's pocket, an image that undercut the popularity of the antiprivatization cause among the general public. The Taiwanese government and private capital, interested in taking over state assets, exploited this antilabor public perception to successfully defame the antiprivatization drive. Political elites justified the liquidation of state assets on the grounds of fixing the endemic problems that plagued state enterprise: inefficiency and budget deficits. Labor's antiprivatization campaign was portrayed as the desperate efforts of a group of well-paid workers who were resisting fair market competition. As a result, state-enterprise unions lost the backing of unions from the private sector as well as broad social support (Chang 2001, 215–16).

Another problem was that, as a result of devoting most of its energy and human resources to the fight against privatization, the state-enterprise-dominated labor movement did not pay enough attention to other pressing issues. In Taiwan, the rights of migrant workers and the problem of unemployment among the native working population had loomed large since the 1990s. After Taiwan began to import migrant workers to solve a labor shortage in 1990, the number of foreign workers nearly tripled between 1994 and 2008, accounting for 2.5 percent of the overall labor force. Yet Taiwanese employers frequently abused foreign workers, particularly those from Southeast Asia, and many regulations covering migrant workers were in violation of basic human rights. At the same time, the issue of middle-age unemployment among the native population grew serious as sunset industries such as textiles closed down and relocated to China and Southeast Asia. Both issues reflected a diverse and stratified laboring population whose respective interests did not easily coincide. Yet the mainstream unions did not tackle these issues effectively, and their glaring failure to do so provoked much criticism from within.

On the Korean side, the new wave of economic restructuring—outsourcing, plant relocation, labor market flexibilities—not only put labor on the defensive but also undermined the organizational base of the labor movement by creating divisions between regularly employed and irregular workers and between workers in strategic industries and those who were not. As an observer commented,

> The enterprise unions were quite strong in the Korean labor movement, the *chaebol* especially had strong unions, but their activity was very limited inside the enterprise. They didn't try to go beyond the boundary of the enterprise, extending to social issues, or build solidarity with non-union members or workers in other companies . . . their political and social influence was quite limited. (interview with a KCTU advisor, April 5, 2003)

During each year's "spring struggle" of wage negotiations, the media consistently portrayed labor struggles as senseless actions initiated by a group of greedy, militant labor aristocrats who were gainfully employed but kept demanding more at the expense of national competitiveness. A glimpse at Korean newspapers captures the hostile attitude toward the labor movement:

> How powerful does the confederation [Korean Confederation of Trade Unions] have to be for even the foreign press to have noted how the Korean government and business are at the mercy of hard-line unions and how the unions are the greatest source of instability for the Korean economy? . . . No

foreign capital would be so blind as to want to invest in this country when they see a union that turns the street into a sea of fire. (*Chosun Ilbo* 2003)

Most alarming of all is the dramatic decline in foreign direct investment here, which remained at $2.6 billion during the first half of this year. The annual volume of FDI [foreign direct investment], which peaked in 2000 at $15.2 billion, came down to $9.1 billion in 2002. No wonder if we imagine the impact on a potential foreign investor that a *Financial Times* front-page picture featuring Korean workers on strike, armed with bars and sticks and blocking their plant's entrance, and of CNN footage of unionists marching down the main street on a "general strike" will have. (*Korea Herald* 2003b)

Headlines like "Koreans Less Tolerant of Union Actions" (*Korea Herald* 2003a) and reports of skyrocketing wages putting firms out of business constantly occupied the news pages. "The 'British disease' was frequently quoted to highlight negative consequence of the militant labor movement. Also Thatcherism was mentioned as a cure for the British disease" (Shin 2003, 161). When asked about the social image of the labor movement, a union staff member remarked,

> Q: How do the Korean people perceive labor activists and the labor movement? Is it a good image or a bad one?
> A: [Chuckles] Just my personal opinion. [Long pause] It's not a positive image.
> Q: Why?
> A: [Very long pause] Why? Oh, many people are still conservative and they are afraid of labor movements and the KCTU. Some liberal people and ordinary citizens think the KCTU and labor movements are too radical. They would say, "I support the labor movement." They would say, "I think the labor movement is important in a capitalist society to defend labor rights. But your activities are too radical." They want us to be "moderate." (interview with a KCTU staff member, April 24, 2003)

If an ideological backlash and a lack of public support were new obstacles originating from outside, the power-maximizing strategy also created problems from within, as it increased the level of difficulty in coordinating diverse interests among the working class and led to endless internal strife. Both labor movements acted, and were portrayed, as if they were mainly defending the interests of workers in state enterprises and *chaebol* unions. Struggles for wage increases and job security in this "privileged" sector were often construed as self-interested actions, and both labor movements were accused by radical labor organizers of neglecting the interests of downtrodden female, immigrant, unemployed, and temporary workers.

Korea's KCTU was charged with neglecting the interests of female and temporary or irregular workers. Some argued that women's labor groups had raised the issue of irregular employment in the 1980s but that mainstream unions had brushed aside their concerns. During the International Monetary Fund (IMF) restructuring of the late 1990s, the state, capital, and labor negotiated the terms of legalizing the employment of temporary workers in selected occupations. The mainstream unions fought fiercely against such employment in the one or two categories of occupation in which their members resided but did not object to it in other occupations that were not among their support base. The end result was that the occupations in which temporary employment was "legalized" were principally female dominated and nonunionized. As the problem of irregular employment reached a point where more than 50 percent of the overall labor force were irregular, the KCTU finally picked up on the issue, but by then "it was too late" (interview with a labor scholar, April 8, 2003). Furthermore, on the issue of female workers:

> If we look at the organized sector, among female workers only 5 percent are organized, 95 percent are not unionized. *Chaebol* unions such as subway unions, Hyundai, etc.—if we compare them with female workers, they are the middle class, upper class even. And the KCTU's money is from these big unions. . . . But we [female workers] can't just sit there and complain about the KCTU or FKTU not organizing women, we can't wait, because female workers are growing more marginalized. Now 75 percent of the female labor force are contingent workers or in special hiring. (interview with a labor leader, April 17, 2003)

To sum up, the power-maximizing strategy firmly established both labor movements as legitimate players in national politics, yet their reputations were severely tainted. Pressured and alarmed by all of these internal and external challenges, in the second half of the 1990s, both labor movements began to pursue a variety of strategies to part with their reputation for sectional interest and instead summon broad social support.

Efforts to Represent General Social Interest

To rid themselves of their old "interest group" image, both labor movements pursued policies going beyond the confines of "enterprise unionism" to coordinate the diverse interests within the working class. To summon up broad social support, both labor movements also reframed their battles in the light of general social interests. We should also note that these efforts to "transform" the labor movements were spearheaded by dissenting labor groups inside the movements and that big unions backed the causes only with hesitation.

In the case of Taiwan, mainstream unions and labor rights organizations put pressure on the government to revise immigration policies that forfeited immigrant workers' rights in favor of satisfying business interests (*United Daily* 1996a). Labor organizations also engaged middle-aged unemployed workers in high-risk protests such as occupying railroad tracks and blocking major expressways (*United Daily* 1996b). A few years later, union leaders representing labor at the Economic Development Advisory Conference demanded a cap on the overall number of immigrant workers and the setting up of corresponding measures to alleviate domestic unemployment. Other labor groups also pushed for the passing of a variety of labor protection measures such as the Labor Pension Act 2004, the Protective Act for Mass Redundancy of Employees 2003, and the Protection for Workers Incurring Occupational Accidents Act 2001. All of these efforts to revamp Taiwan's labor laws were backed by the TCTU and other major unions.

State-enterprise unions also reframed their privatization struggle not merely in terms of job security but also in terms of "safeguarding state assets." It was argued that the profit from state enterprises contributed to government revenue that would be used for redistributive purposes—education, welfare expenditure, and other basic infrastructure. The privatization policy was framed as a de facto state-capital collusion, in which the government was selling off state assets cheaply under pressure from private capital and because of the need for short-term cash to deliver on policy promises made during various elections. In the long run, privatizing basic industries like water, electricity, and telecommunications would only benefit private capital; everyone else would lose out (interview with a TCTU staff member, January 14, 2003). The labor movement also began to touch on a variety of issues that concerned general social interests. For example,

> local labor rights activists urged the government not to yield to pressure from major business groups by slashing stock transaction tax and land value increment tax because such tax cuts would only benefit the wealthy and would violate taxation fairness and social justice. (*Central News Agency* 2001)

Union leaders also began to incorporate other social issues into labor education and encouraged members to take part in reform efforts on education, the environment, medical care, community empowerment, and the welfare system (interview with a state-enterprise union leader, July 21, 2003).

On the Korean side, with progressive labor groups leading the way, pressure was placed on the KCTU to address the issues of irregular and female workers. Irregular employment had become a common theme in major labor protests. A KCTU staff member asked,

> How do we deal with irregular workers? Everybody is isolated . . . "Oh, ten million irregular workers are working in South Korea!" But where are they? We can't find them! Not organized, they are scattered and divided. Statistically they are big [in number]; in terms of the labor movement, they are very small. We have to define them in statistical and social movement terms. . . . *Irregular workers' rights are now the most important issue on our agenda.* We've created a new department for irregular workers, we have research teams working on this issue. . . . In every public speech we make, the number one issue is irregular workers. (interview with a KCTU staff member, April 24, 2003)

It was also reported that, during wage negotiations, *chaebol* unions included an item demanding that corporations donate 5 percent of net profits to a special fund to help irregular workers (*Hankyoreh 21* 2004). As for the gender issue, major unions such as the Teachers' Union passed resolutions allotting 30 percent of leadership positions to women. Under the KCTU, a confederation of women's trade unions was organized. The KCTU also began to tackle a variety of "social issues." The KCTU's former policy chief argued that, to deal effectively with the growing disparity in different workers' conditions and to build greater solidarity, the KCTU needed to protect the rights and living conditions of the weaker social classes, of workers at SMEs, and of irregular workers. Furthermore, labor unions not only pursued short-term and direct goals, such as wages or the improvement of working conditions, but also worked toward expanding safety nets and social welfare, reforming the tax system, improving the education system, solving housing and environmental problems, and other issues of general interest (cf. Gray 2008, 80). The labor movement's participation in social reforms started right after the financial crisis and IMF restructuring. In the 1997 general strike, the labor movement featured the best public campaigns through which broad social support had yet been organized. With the founding of the movement's political wing, the Korean Democratic Labor Party, organized labor's ambition to organize and lead public opinion in a broader political arena became even more pronounced. This can be attested by the public relevance of the six main themes of the 2004 Mayday rally:

opposition to the WTO and free trade

work, with health

public participation

withdrawal of troops from Iraq

eradicating differential treatment of regular and irregular workers

labor's three rights

And here we witness a similar evolving pattern of the two labor movements. In the face of weakened economic leverage, both sought to acquire ideological power to fend off the stigma of "sectional interests" imposed by their opponents and to build greater solidarity among workers and forge broader alliances with other social groups. It was a difficult task to coordinate the diverse interests within the labor movement; it was even more taxing to establish a productive relationship with a broader public sphere. This self-transformation project entailed a series of ongoing negotiations to lessen resistance and suspicion from all sides. Many, however, have criticized mainstream unions for only paying lip service to their purported constituency. A KCTU policy advisor summarized the situation aptly:

> Now the KCTU tried to show its "social movement unionism," as many foreign observers explained. It showed very strong solidarity with social movements, like the peace movement, the anti–Iraq War movement. But *this was at the confederation level. At the enterprise level, workers were not interested in these issues.* That was the problem. . . . At the enterprise level, there were conflicts between social movement organizations and labor unions. (interview with KCTU's policy advisor, April 5, 2003)

The difficulty in transcending economic–corporate interests is well recognized. As another KCTU staff member said,

> [The gap between *chaebol* unions and small-enterprise unions] is a big problem, an important problem we have to overcome. *Chaebol* unions have an antiemployer agenda; most issues from small-enterprise and irregular workers concern government policies. So they have different enemies. *On many occasions we can't organize and coordinate them. We haven't succeeded, but we are trying.* (interview with KCTU staff, April 24, 2003)

Even if the tasks ahead for the two labor movements are insurmountable and there is no end in sight, "but we are trying" is a powerful statement that signifies a clear understanding of the difficult situation and a fierce will refusing to surrender.

The Environmental Trajectory:
From Ideology to Reconstituting the Grassroots

The Korean and Taiwanese environmental movements both grew out of the widespread industrial pollution of the 1970s. From the outset they were supported by a loose coalition of pollution victims and urban intellectuals. But the intellectual side quickly came to the ascendancy and pollution victims gradually faded out of the partnership. The dissolution of this coalition was triggered by the disparate expectations of the different parties in the coalition. Urban intellectuals wanted to clear up the pollution mess in its entirety, yet pollution victims were asking simply for financial compensation, a contradiction that undermined social expectations of a movement claiming to defend universal interests. This fragile coalition was destabilized by pollution compensation and relocation subsidies from the outset. In various writings and personal interviews on pollution protests in the 1970s and early 1980s, pollution victims' "material concerns" were often blamed for breaking the urban–rural coalition.

In Pursuit of Ideological Power

In the Taiwanese case, this change of movement composition was triggered by the so-called Lin-Yuan Incident in 1988 and a few similar antipollution disputes in which, brokered by career politicians, pollution victims demanded and received record financial compensation. In the Lin-Yuan case, a petrochemical complex released wastewater into the ocean, causing huge damage to the nearby aquaculture business. One hundred or so fishermen broke into the complex and halted all production. Because this was the major supplier of raw materials for hundreds of downstream factories, the estimated cost of the stoppage was around thirteen million U.S. dollars each day. The KMT immediately intervened, and local politicians managed to raise the compensation from three million dollars to a total of forty million dollars, paid out of taxpayers' pockets, to be distributed among local residents (*United Daily* 1988d, 1988e, 1988f).

What immediately followed was a wave of outcry and public condemnation of pollution victims' "greed" and "selfishness." From then on, Taiwan's environmental movement began to consciously disassociate itself from the "compensation-seeking" action of pollution victims in an attempt to satisfy society's expectations of a universalist environmental movement. The figureheads of the environmental movement often shunned issues like material compensation, the primary concern of pollution victims. On occasion they even went so far as to make a clear distinction between "self-interested" antipollution protests and an "altruistic" environmental movement. One quotation illustrates the growing dissatisfaction on the intellectuals' part over a stigma associated with material compensation that was tainting the name of the environmental movement:

> Self-help [antipollution] protests should not be confused with environmental movements. The head of the New Environmental Foundation . . . pointed out yesterday that it was inappropriate to call those self-interested antipollution protests "environmental movements." He maintained that environmental movements should be altruistic, and that mixing the two would lead the environmental movement astray. (*United Daily* 1990)

Isolated pollution cases like Lin-Yuan most certainly upset the balance between urban intellectuals' concern over "universal interests" and pollution victims' economic needs, but the rift was not beyond repair. A newly instituted environmental administrative system further pulled pollution victims out of coalitional relations. After the Environmental Impact Assessment, monitoring programs, due process of pollution disputes, and the compensation mechanism were firmly installed, pollution victims went directly to the administrative system to address their grievances. The need to collaborate with environmental NGOs greatly diminished. "There was no need to solve their problems through ultra-institutional means like social movements anymore," as an environmental activist remarked (interview, January 8, 2003).

After the dissociation, the movement agenda took an "ecological turn." After a few cases like Lin-Yuan in the late 1980s, in which an astronomical amount of damage compensation provoked public disapproval, environmental campaigns in the 1990s began to bet heavily on conservationism and eco-tourism to fight major development projects. When fighting against a proposed gigantic industrial complex, environmentalists summoned public support to protect endangered species and coastal wetlands; the livelihood of the sea-farming population in the area became a secondary issue. When struggling against dam construction, activists campaigned to protect the way of life of an ethnic minority and to prevent a unique habitat that hosted millions of butterflies from being flooded (see Figure 17).

For the Korean environmental movement too, its delayed emergence mainly resulted from the fragile coalition between pollution victims and urban intellectuals being destabilized by pollution compensation and relocation subsidies. Pollution victims' "material concerns" were repeatedly blamed for breaking the urban–rural coalition. In other words, this intellectual–victim coalition got off to a bad start in Korea.

When the movement finally came into being in the late 1980s, urban intellectuals and pollution victims were united under the banner of *minjung*

Year	Development project in dispute	Major objections
1992	*Binnan* industrial complex (oil refinery, steel)	Protection of endangered species (the black-faced spoonbill) and habitat preservation (Qigu wetlands)
1993	Construction of Meinung Dam	Preservation of Yellow Butterfly Valley, the habitat of yellow butterfly such as *Catopsilia crocale* and *Catopsilia pomona* and other rare wildlife species
1994	Construction of South Expressway	Destruction of the Conservation Zone at Mt. Dawu
1995	Construction of Majia Dam	Flooding of riverine habitat
1996	Siang-Shan industrial complex	Destruction of coastal wetlands and ecodiversity

Figure 17. Taiwan's environmental controversies in the 1990s. McBeath and Leng (2006) and Hou (2001) provide detailed accounts on the Binnan and Meinung cases.

ideology and "nationalist–democratic" movements, but the intellectual wing took the lead from the outset. In the watershed Onsan case, it was the PRI that researched the illness, established the link between cadmium poisoning and public hazard, and led a successful campaign to influence public opinion. The dominance of intellectuals in the Korean environmental movement has continued from that point.

The ideological shift toward conservationism and ecological issues after the Rio Summit firmly marked the declining significance of antipollution issues in Korea's environmental movement. One telling indication of this is that the flagship NGO of Korea's environmental movement changed its name in 1993 from the KAPMA to the KFEM. The fact that "antipollution" was dropped signified a new era in which the movement dwelled on discussions of forests, reservoirs, wildlife habitats, wetlands, and issues with which it was "much easier to reach consensus," as one seasoned KFEM staff member remarked. In addition to pollution issues, the significance of nuclear energy to the movement's agenda also fell:

> Up to the early 1990s . . . antinuclear was one of the main campaign teams, even if there were only two staff on the team, but all the time we had an antinuclear team among others. Ten years later, only one [antinuclear] person was part of the policy-making team. In our organization we don't have an antinuclear team anymore, just one antinuclear campaigner. It means

the antinuclear issue is not the major issue. (interview with a KFEM staff member, April 18, 2003)

What Korea's environmental movement instead took on in the 1990s was a series of ecological and conservation campaigns, including projects on the Nakdong and Han rivers (1994) and Siwha Lake (1996); ski-slope construction on Mt. Dukyu (1995); a golf course in a national park (1996); the illegal trade in whale products (1996); the Dong River dam construction (1998); and the Saemangeum wetlands reclamation (1998).

Though working under different local conditions and with much internal heterogeneity, the two environmental movements successfully fought off many unwanted development projects, preserved ecologically sensitive areas, and repeatedly exposed the public to valuable information on biodiversity and natural habitats. They also showed us an environmental movement trajectory in which the intellectual wing and the ecological stream rose to dominance, two events that I contend profoundly shaped the environmental movements in the 1990s. With the intellectual wing at the helm, discursive capacities were put to use on all fronts. First there was the strengthening of the research wing. Big environmental NGOs set up their own research centers to cover a variety of environmental policies; small environmental NGOs began to specialize in specific policy areas. Second, the movements' spokespersons, press releases, and policy reports relied heavily on scientific language to establish credentials. Finally, as both Taiwan's and Korea's environmental activists acknowledged their reliance on media to "get the message out," more energy and efforts were put into mastering the art of public relations campaigns, writing catchy news releases, and creating newsworthiness.

The ecological turn went hand in hand with intellectual dominance. Focusing on holistic, ecological issues, on one hand, reaffirmed the movements' claims to be working toward universal interests, and the media had been quite receptive to this topic all along. In fact, major media outlets in both countries featured a series of conservation campaigns in the 1990s, either in collaboration with environmental organizations or on their own initiative. On the other hand, the complexity and interconnectedness of the ecosystem justified the need to strengthen research and discursive capacities and to have the "educated" class run the movements. In antipollution struggles, it did not necessarily require highly refined discursive capacities to convince the general public that action was needed (e.g., by spelling out the complex production processes involved, the route of contamination, and the effect of pollution). Damaged crops and ill bodies served as powerful testimonials of human suffering. But to initiate an ecological campaign on behalf of Mother Nature, who in general does not speak for herself and whose workings are so complex that most people understand rather little, such a campaign needs to be backed by extensive research, scientific evidence, lucid explanations—in short, a better command of strategies of discursive persuasion.

From antipollution struggles to ecological campaigns, the two environmental movements continued to fight their battles in the ideological domain. At the antipollution stage, the aim was to introduce to the general public a relatively new phenomenon called "pollution" and to understand it from a perspective very different from the "development first, all else later" viewpoint. As the movements evolved with the dominance of urban intellectuals and ecological issues, the ideological battle grew more sophisticated. The environmental movements, bureaucracy, and corporate-sponsored think tanks were all backed by discursive resources and fought to realize their own vision of environmental management, resource allocation, and sustainable development.

Erosion of Environmental Persuasion

Just like their labor counterparts, both the Korean and Taiwanese environmental movements were forced to confront the consequences of their power-maximizing strategies. On the positive side, both enjoyed overwhelming social support[5] and certainly did not suffer from ideological defamation the way organized labor did. But once the environmental movements proved to everyone the importance of environmental protection, and even private capital began to appropriate environmental symbols to advance its own agendas, problems arose. The difficulty that both environmental movements confronted was twofold: first, the rise of new institutional competitors for discursive power over environmental issues, and second, the inability of environmental movements to organize public consent on issues involving acute conflicts of economic interest.

In terms of institutional competitors, Korean *chaebol* began to set up their own environmental research centers, and in both Taiwan and Korea, large corporations invested in public relations campaigns. In Taiwan, environmental consulting firms were paid by corporations to prepare environmental impact assessment reports for development projects. The state began to set up advisory committees—in Korea, the Presidential Commission of Sustainable Development, in Taiwan, the National Council for Sustainable Development, and various committees under the Environmental Protection Agency as prime examples—comprising experts with varying degrees of commitment to environmental causes. As a consequence, the ideological power of both environmental movements faced serious challenges. This is not to say that the environmental movements had not in the past confronted business and governmental efforts to "explain things away": this had happened all the time in antipollution struggles. The key point is that, come the 1990s, government and business wanted to take back the power to define pollution, natural conservation, and environmental management. Although the building of a comprehensive environmental administrative system was at first a response to the demand from the environmental movements, in the long run it became a powerful tool in gaining the upper hand in ideological warfare with both environmental movements.

Furthermore, both the Taiwanese and Korean governments actively recruited movement activists to sit on the advisory boards and consultation bodies on environmental policies and incorporated the idea of "public participation" in due process. The impact on the environmental movements was "a shift of focus," as one long-term activist commented:

> [Working inside the government agencies] reduces the "movement character" of environmental NGOs. Right now these groups focus on technical problems, like how to implement certain policies. I think this is a natural progression. Originally we encouraged people to do recycling, but the government ignored us. Later on the government decided, "Yeah, let's do recycling, but how do we start?" Then the government said, "Come in, work together, let's find the best way to do recycling." At this stage, movement organizations paid less attention to running a movement, but focused more on policy implementation. (interview with former president of TEPU, November 4, 2004)

With the rise of new institutional competitors, the task of organizing public consent became increasingly difficult. For environmental issues with a high level of consensus, such as an environmental impact assessment and tougher pollution regulations, the government set up new administrative bodies to take over the task. For controversial issues such as nuclear energy, in which new institutional competitors mobilized social support while the environmental movements secured no overwhelming public consent, it was a difficult fight. The movements' ideological power was not based on permanent social relations such as work or kinship but on the persuasiveness of ideas. This rendered the movement powerless when its discursive campaigns failed to sway public opinion, given the movement had no solid mass support through which to pressure its opponents. At the moment of movement downturn, we hear laments like this:

> [Taiwan's environmental movement] did not have power. . . . When you look at labor and peasant movements, the government made concessions to . . . a specific group of people. This is the reason why Taiwan's environmental movement was going downhill all these years, [it] didn't have a specific group of supporters, [it] had issues and an amorphous social base. So you are not going to exert much pressure on the government. (interview with a Green Citizens' Action Alliance [GCAA] staff member, January 8, 2003)

Another Korean activist also remarked, "In reality, if an environmental organization fails to organize people's worries and consciousness, it's a paper tiger. On some issues, we are near to changing the world, but on many other issues, we are just a paper tiger" (interview with a KFEM staff member, April 18, 2003).

After turning attention to ecological issues, the movements in both countries faced the problem of being divorced from their grassroots, a trade-off resulting from the need to increase ideological power by parting company with "sectional interests" represented by pollution victims. As a Korean activist said,

> in the 1980s and until the middle of the 1990s, over half of the staff [in my organization] were working outside [in the field], meeting local people, organizing. But now, most people stick to their desks, writing statements, talking over the phone. This tells us what has changed, and what is the problem, and what is the trend. In that sense we are becoming much more like office workers, not field staff. (interview with a KFEM staff member, April 18, 2003)

A Taiwanese activist further remarked, "These days, there are very few environmental groups organizing at the grassroots, mostly they are conservationist and policy groups" (interview with a Green Formosa Front [GFF] staff member, February 21, 2003).

This dissociation from the grassroots created headaches for environmental NGOs as they handled the conflict between their ecological vision and the interests of disadvantaged groups. The exemplary cases are Taiwan's Magaw Cypress National Park and Korea's Saemangeum wetland conservation. In the national park case, Taiwan's environmental groups sought to preserve a forest of forty-six thousand hectares of cypress trees, "the only homogenous forest of red and yellow cypress trees of its kind in the world . . . [meeting] the standards set by UNESCO to be classed as a World Heritage Site" (*Taipei Times* 2000). But the creation of a national park infringed on the aborigines' rights to live off the land and continue their traditional hunting practices. In the Saemangeum project, the Korean government decided to carry out one of the world's largest land reclamation projects so as to create space for new industrial complexes that promised to bring jobs and prosperity. Whereas Korea's environmental NGOs strongly opposed the reclamation project and initiated one of the country's largest ever protests (Ju 2011, 146), local residents, long suffering from Korea's uneven development, welcomed the project.

On the conflict of sustainability and livelihood, other examples include a city park construction project in Taipei involving the eviction of thousands of slum dwellers and the restoration of an ancient stream, the Cheonggyecheon, in the heart of Seoul by tearing down an elevated highway and uprooting an old flea market and seventy-three thousand street vendors (*Korea Herald* 2004). In both cases, environmental NGOs backed a highly commercialized green vision—building parks and restoring waterways that pushed the already skyrocketing urban land price up even further—but were silent on the needs and interests of slum dwellers and street vendors (Liu and Choi 2004). Even more ironically, Cheonggyecheon was a project that paved the way for Lee Myung Bak's presidential career (Ju 2011, 149). As the then mayor of Seoul, he was named one of *Time* magazine's "Heroes of the Environment" in 2007, along with Al Gore, Mikhail Gorbachev, Prince Charles, Robert Redford, and many others (Walsh 2007). Lee was also described by *Time* as the man most likely to become Korea's next president, a prophecy that came true one year later.

In addition to their inability to address the interests of the economically weak, both environmental movements repeatedly lost battles against corporate interests. As focus shifted to ecological issues, corporate practices generally disappeared from their radar screens.[6] Even when environmental NGOs did occasionally take on the battle against big corporations, they usually lost due either to a lack of media backing or to smear campaigns waged by the corporation-backed media. In addition, some also made an issue of the environmental circle's fuzzy belief in free market, competition, and efficiency. One Taiwanese activist unhesitatingly criticized how mainline environmental groups surrendered to the logic of the liberal market economy:

> Basically they [the mainstream environmental groups] were willing to accept a natural gas–fired power plant at Gongliao [the designated site of the fourth nuclear power plant]. So what did that mean? "Antinuclear" for them literally meant no nuclear power plant, anything else was fine. . . . The rise of nuclear power plants was to provide cheap electricity for manufacturing.

The key question was not just about using an alternative source of electricity to replace nuclear energy but rather *why* do we need so much electricity? If you look closely, [the mainstream environmental groups'] position was to push for private power plants, no more state monopoly of electricity, free and open competition. [They believed that] nuclear energy would be eliminated [under market competition] because it was not the cheapest and the most economical [way to provide electricity]. (interview with a GCAA staff member, February 21, 2003)

There is an ironic contrast in the way that the environmental movements were often in a position to force-feed the economically weak with an ecological vision that threatened the latter's livelihood but were not so effective in imposing the same vision on the economically powerful.

Reconstituting the Grassroots

These new challenges—new institutional competitors, dissociation from the grassroots, and realizing ecological visions in a stratified, unequal society—occurred as a consequence of both environmental movements' successes in realizing their ideological power by persuading society to attend to environmental problems. Like their labor counterparts, both movements attempted to overcome the new challenges by trying a variety of strategies that could be roughly categorized as "professionalization" and "rebuilding grassroots linkages." Professionalization was very clearly directed at new institutional competitors on the terrain of environmental discourse. A Taiwanese environmental activist contended,

An environmental group has to face the government, academia, and capitalists, all of them having more access to information and a better capacity to integrate and analyze data. If you [environmental activists] don't have excellent discursive capacities, and you don't have access to good data, it is impossible to confront those professional, techno-bureaucrats. Never mind fighting them [bureaucrats] as a movement, you don't even have the ability to strike up a conversation with them; this is a very cruel fact. (interview with a GFF staff member, February 21, 2003)

Rebuilding a connection with the grassroots was directed at reincorporating diverse economic interests into environmental agendas. Since the mid-1990s, the Korean environmental movement has strived to enlist a large membership pool, at the urging of activists influenced by the ways the student and labor movements were organized in the 1970s and 1980s. Also, the mind-set of environmental activists began to change as far as the relationship with big corporations was concerned. A Korean activist reflected on the situation:

A: From the early 1990s to the late 1990s, [the movement] always fought against the state very seriously. Many demonstrations, campaigns . . . sometimes we fought with the police, and we shaved our heads. Nowadays people realized that, as globalization went further, corporations had more power. Now we should be careful about big corporations, they have more power over the nation-state.

Q: So in the 1990s the target was the state, and now it has shifted to corporations?

A: Yes, moving to fight corporations. (interview with a Green Future volunteer, March 26, 2003)

Furthermore, environmental groups began to build relationships with labor unions that had the leverage power that the environmental movements lacked:

[In the case of] a Korean power company, there were debates about the privatization of this state-monopoly company. The environmental movement was pro-privatization, but the trade union was against it. Initially there were heated debates between environmental groups and trade unions. But nowadays we have some common ground for discussions. We still keep good relationships with them [unions], we understand most pollution victims are workers, and they also understand environmental issues are very serious even for their union. There are regular meetings between trade unions and environmental groups. For me, if we go further we can find common issues and common interests. Ideological debates are very difficult, but in specific cases we can find common ground, we can make alliances. (interview with a Green Future volunteer, March 26, 2003)

In the Taiwanese case, most environmental groups did not use aggressive membership drives to expand their base. Rather, each of them comprised a small number of committed activists rooted in one community and expanding the breadth of environmental issues in that particular locale. The best example is Meinong People's Association, which started with an antidam campaign and then moved on to address community empowerment, organic farming, and preservation of local culture. Another environmental group— the GCAA—embedded itself in Gongliao, the community at the designated site of the nuclear power plant, and insisted on "let[ting] the grassroots speak [instead of those who have discursive resources]" (interview with a GCAA staff member, January 8, 2003). In recent years, this particular group of activists has made an award-winning documentary film on Gongliao's antinuclear struggle and tracked down former temporary workers in nuclear power plants to observe any long-term health effects from radiation exposure. In this process, the practices of big corporations remained a major concern of environmental groups. In 1998, the GFF, another small environmental NGO, exposed the fact that a leading private enterprise, Formosa Plastics, had illegally exported three thousand tons of toxic mercury waste to Cambodia; the revelation led to international protests. Environmental activists also looked into opportunities to collaborate with the labor movement. One activist said,

> Labor and environment are production costs. When pursuing the highest possible profit, one would want to lower the cost of both. . . . [But labor and environment] are connected in an interesting way. For example, *when a certain natural resource is bordering on being depleted, the working conditions under which workers go in to extract that resource become worse and riskier.* You see all those coal mine accidents in China. This means that they have dug very deep, and the mine is about to be depleted. . . . *These two things* [labor and environment] *are sometimes the same thing.* (interview with a GCAA staff member, January 8, 2003)

Another activist concurred:

> *As labor and environmental movements mature, their goals are eventually the same* . . . . [Taiwan's] labor movement so far hasn't talked about workers' rights from an environmental perspective, and environmental rights [workplace safety, workers' health, occupational hazards] haven't been addressed in the labor movement. This is a point we have been trying to communicate with our friends in the labor movement. (interview with a GFF staff member, February 21, 2003)

At this point, we can observe a convergence in the strategies of the two environmental movements. Confronted with new institutional competitors and the difficulty of organizing public opinion, both movements sought to acquire leverage power through aggressive membership drives and community organizing. They also took on a new round of battles against private capital and even found ways to work with organized labor.

Meeting Each Other Halfway?

The maturation of a movement is constituted by a succession of battles in the economic and ideological domains. Some movements, such as organized labor, start with struggles in the economic domain and then move on to the ideological. Environmental movements fight ideological battles first and only later head toward the economic. Social movements in general start from the domain in which they have comparative advantages. Labor movements are backed by their indispensability in production but are short on discursive resources to fight ideological battles, whereas the environmental movements are resourceful in ideas and discourses but have no inbuilt advantage in the economic domain. The key reason that a movement will move into a different domain of struggle is because the previous gains in its home domain are either eroding or taken away, and only by gaining ground in another domain can its past advantage be recovered. Among the four movements studied, the two labor movements strove to articulate "general interests" only after their leverage power had been truncated. The environmental movements tried out a variety of strategies to consolidate their grassroots only after their ideological supremacy had been challenged. Putting labor and environmental trajectories side by side, we see that they constitute a mirror image of one another (see Figure 18).

Looking through the lens of movement power, our four movements' own initiatives and their opponents' counteractions propose an alternative theory of the long-term development of labor and environmental movements. If we look at labor and environmental movements elsewhere in the world, the trajectories shared by the Taiwanese and Korean cases are not so unfamiliar. The recent struggles of U.S. labor to counter ideological offensives and to win public support are well documented (Chun 2009; Clawson 2003; Fantasia and Voss 2004; Voss and Sherman 2000). These efforts to transform the image and content of the U.S. labor movement took place at a moment of crisis in which the post–World War II social pact between capital and labor was broken and the economic leverage previously exercised by major unions was eroded. Japan's environmental activism, after its antipollution peak in the 1970s, dwindled throughout the 1980s and the early 1990s, suffering from declining public interest in environmental issues and "the Liberal Democratic government's rather swift and apparently thorough legislative and administrative responses to the pollution crisis" (Mason 1999, 189). This is another indication that the environmental movement created new institutional competitors and gradually lost the capacity to sway public opinion effectively. All of these provide fruitful parallels to the Taiwanese and Korean experiences.

For those interested in a red–green alliance, the lesson is that labor and environmental movements have been "traveling toward each other." I implicitly argue that the most favorable timing of alliance making between labor and environmental movements—serious cross-fertilization instead of ad hoc cooperation and opportunistic mutual appropriation—is while labor is at

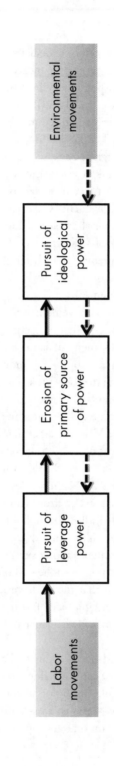

Figure 18. Labor and environmental trajectories juxtaposed.

the stage of pursuing ideological power and the environmental movement is seeking leverage power, that is, when each of them is traveling into the home advantage of the other. By acquiring each other's home advantage and traversing the terrains of economic and ideological struggles, and by engaging in new battles through which their counterpart movements have secured certain victories, activists in the labor and environmental movements might begin to appreciate each other's plight and accumulated skills; the possibility of forging a genuine red–green alliance thereby increases.

Conclusion: What Now?

What does this book—the first to use cross-national protest data to reconstruct the movement histories of two small, East Asian countries that attract relatively little scholarly attention—have to offer to academics, activists, and the wider world? This concluding chapter first puts forward a commentary on the scholarly literature and ends with further reflections on two things: the relationship between democracy, labor, and environment and the prospect of labor and environmental movements in the twenty-first century.

On Social Movement Literature

In most historical narratives of social movements, the story line usually goes something like this. Once upon a time, a group of people was unfairly treated by some or other evil social force. After agonizing over their miserable situation for a long while, they finally decided to act together to voice their discontent and demand the situation be redressed. The powers-that-be were not happy, nor were those who gained most by maintaining the status quo. Some power holders just went ahead and stifled protest activity by force, while others tried to play nice but skirted around the demands, but all of these responses only made the aggrieved group even madder. In the whirlpool of events, many bystanders were dragged in: some sympathized with the suffering; others shrieked out "law and order!" like a mantra. Eventually things quieted down. Either the aggrieved group gained some concessions and retreated, or it got none and the misery continued. The end.

This is a good, though incomplete, story. From a comparative perspective, students of social movements need to ask why, among many aggrieved groups, one of them emerges as a collective actor but others delay in doing so. I tell a story of the reverse sequencing of labor and environmental movements in two rapidly industrializing countries, Taiwan and Korea. Starting from the 1970s, Taiwan's environmental movement and Korea's labor movement emerged from the confines set by authoritarian regimes. Their counterparts—Taiwan's labor and Korea's environmental movements—did not take shape until years later. By juxtaposing the two movement sequences in reverse order, I first use Taiwan as an anomalous case to challenge the assumption that labor movements universally arise earlier than environmental movements, and then attempt to acquire a better understanding of movement emergence, sequences, and trajectories.

If it is the task of a sociologist "to sift through the variance with the hope of identifying regularity" (Esping-Andersen 2000, 75), the contrast of leverage and ideological power offers a theoretical intervention in highlighting how labor and environmental movements develop their bargaining powers and maneuver their courses of action. Workers' leverage rests on their indispensability in the process of production, whereas environmental movements' forte is to use ideas, discourses, and ideology to organize public consent. A movement emerges as the early riser because it takes advantage of a relative lack of structural constraint in the location that corresponds to its specific forms of movement power. So, when labor rises first in Korea, it is because its leverage power is relatively unconstrained vis-à-vis the Korean green movement; Taiwan's environmental movement emerges early because its ideological power is less truncated than that of Taiwan's labor. Then the early risers leave different sets of organizational and cultural legacies that latecomer movements selectively adopt. In addition, labor movements show a tendency to maximize leverage power, whereas environmental movements are driven to optimize ideological power. Subsequently, labor and environmental movements confront new obstacles and limits incurred by the power-maximization strategy. To overcome these obstacles, organized labor and the environmental movements work toward acquiring the second source of movement power that they originally lacked.

By recapitulating the main arguments thus, the conversation with the existing literature may begin. Let me start with the American version of social movement literature. Most works on social movements in the past three decades have stuck to a dominant formula in which explanatory primacy is given to exogenous factors like "political opportunities" (Boudreau 1996; Goodwin 2012; Goodwin and Jasper 1999). This book deviates from this formula and intends to strike a better balance between endogenous (movement-centered) and exogenous (extramovement) explanations. Social

 *interaction*

movements are with no doubt conditioned by their social and institutional ?
surroundings. But these surroundings do not constrain every movement in
the same way. In this sense, the conventional view that political opportunities reign as far as movement dynamics are concerned reveals only a partial
story. Leverage and ideological power as conceptual tools highlight the specific ways in which labor and environmental movements tend to react to their
surroundings, in contrast to traditional interpretations in which the same
conceptual tools—political opportunities, political processes, resource mobilization, and so on—are liberally applied *across* movements without taking
into account that the movements are different in the first place.

Different movements will need different resources to sustain themselves
and will interact with their institutional surroundings in predictably different ways. Workers only means of resisting the forces of capital is by joining ?
together to withhold their labor and thus shutting down the economic
machine. So labor movements will need resources that will support this particular strength—access to workers who can be organized, dedicated labor
organizers, and ideological frames that will convince workers that they are
better off joining together than fighting on their own. By contrast, to fight
polluting facilities and nonchalant government officials, environmental movements define and broadcast an unfamiliar phenomenon called "pollution"
and persuade the public to accept and act on an alternative set of beliefs
based on universal interests and a harmonious human–nature relationship.
So environmental movements will need a different set of resources to sustain
their operations—secured access to mass media, collaborations with academic
disciplines, discursively resourceful staff, and personnel and resources for public relations campaigns.

If leverage and ideological power have proven their merit, the next logical
questions are, what other types of movement power are there besides leverage
and ideology, and to what extent can the concepts of leverage and ideology
be applied to other types of social movement, such as farmers, women,
students, squatters, or civil rights? These are still very much open questions
awaiting empirical investigation. I argue that the maturation and success
of each of the four movements in Taiwan and Korea rely on unique combinations of the two types of power, and if this claim is true, the general principle may apply to other types of social movement as well. The real task is to
explore the social location of each movement to determine what the optimal *From*
structure of its bargaining power is.

Next I need to strike a different tone with the European version of social
movement theory. The post-Marxist efforts to connect social theory and historic episodes (Waters 2008) and to look for "other logics of action (based in

politics, ideology, and culture) and other sources of identity (such as ethnicity, gender, and sexuality) as the sources of collective action" (Buechler 2000, 46) are admirable, but "new social movement" formulations prove to be insufficient. On one hand, the old-to-new social movement sequence is an evolutionary historical interpretation that is challenged by the Taiwanese case. This leads us to inquire, not about the validity of the "deviant" case, but about the suppressed historical alternatives in nineteenth-century Western Europe "obscured or obliterated by the deceptive wisdom of hindsight" (Moore 1978, 376). Engels wrote so eloquently on the wretched conditions of working-class living quarters and the physical conditions of the great towns: "like all other rivers in the service of manufacture, [the Aire] flows into the city at one end clear and transparent, and flows out at the other end thick, black, and foul, smelling of all possible refuse" and "on week-days the town is enveloped in a grey cloud of coal smoke" (Engels 1975, 343). It is no small wonder that popular protests against environmental degradation did *not* occur in the wake of Europe's industrialization and why filthy rivers, polluted air, and high mortality rates were *not* understood in environmental terms.

On the other hand, new social movement theorists prematurely arrive at a verdict that "class actors are dead." The clear-cut distinction between interest and identity also misses the *self-transformative capacities* and the change over time of the "old" and "new" social movements. Labor movements seek to realize class interests but at the same time are compelled to transform themselves to secure the fruits of past struggles. They do so by strengthening discursive capacities and engaging in ideological struggles to present their interests as the interests of all. Environmental movements work to affirm new consciousness and new identity but at the same are vulnerable to the impermanence and instability of consciousness and identity. They devise a variety of strategies to consolidate grassroots support, confront corporate interests, and address the issue of distributive justice. All of these point to the resilience, instead of the rigidity, of labor and environmental movements.

Besides social movement literature, this book also pushes us to think more systematically about the relationships between regime types and vanguard social movements, an undertheorized topic in the literature of democratic transition. Taiwan's incorporationist party state bore some resemblance to Eastern European state socialism, where environmental movements were usually stronger than labor movements. The highly repressive military junta in Korea had parallels in Brazil and South Africa, where labor movements took the leading role. Eventually this might boil down to two variables: (1) the extent to which workers and other popular classes are differentially co-opted and demobilized in different political regimes and (2) whether political

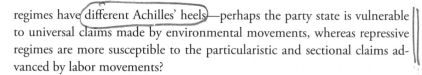

regimes have different Achilles' heels—perhaps the party state is vulnerable to universal claims made by environmental movements, whereas repressive regimes are more susceptible to the particularistic and sectional claims advanced by labor movements?

Reconsidering Polanyi and Gramsci

By returning to Gramsci and Polanyi, this book comes full circle. Careful readers have probably discerned at some point that this project is a Gramscian engagement with Polanyi's "double movement." Polanyi provides a brilliant conception of the tension between economy and society. Self-regulating markets expand to the extent that the integrity of the social fabric is in jeopardy. As a consequence, society is "activated" to defend itself. Polanyi, however, forgoes any concrete analysis of class mobilization and the formation of collective actors so that "social protectionist movements" look almost like an automatic response to market expansion,[1] a formulation on which any trained student of social movements would frown. Furthermore, the protectionist movements, in the Polanyian scheme, were analyzed in isolation from one another as if they were definitively separate entities, and as a consequence we learn relatively little about the interaction and mutual influence between different protectionist movements. For these two conspicuous flaws, Gramsci comes in to fill the void.

In Gramsci's original formulation, it is class actors that undergo the three stages of class formation, from the economic-corporate, to the economic class, to the hegemonic level. Nevertheless, it is by far the best theorization that holistically captures the political, organizational, cultural, and temporal dimensions of the formation of collective actors. It only makes sense to apply it to other collective actors such as social movements. To effectively invoke Gramsci to analyze two "protectionist" movements as different as labor and environment, I make one major theoretical modification: I maintain that the maturation of a movement [collective actor] is constituted by a succession of battles in the economic and ideological domains. Some movements, such as organized labor, start with struggles in the economic domain and then move on to the ideological one. Other movements, such as environmental movements, fight ideological battles first and only later head toward the economic domain. Social movements usually start from the domain in which they have comparative advantages. Labor movements are backed by their indispensability in production but are short on discursive resources to fight ideological battles, whereas the environmental movements are resourceful in ideas and discourses but have no built-in advantage in the economic domain. The key reason that a movement will travel into a different domain of struggle is because the previous gains in its home domain are eroding, and only by gaining ground in another domain can its past advantage be recovered. Among the four movements studied, the two labor movements strove to articulate "general interests" only after their leverage power had been truncated. The environmental movements meanwhile tried on a variety of strategies to consolidate their grassroots only after their ideological supremacy had been challenged.

It is open to debate whether my modification vulgarizes Gramsci. But this modified version might have one point to add to Gramsci's class formation story. Gramsci says outright that the transcendence of one's own corporate interests marks "the decisive passage from the structure to the sphere of the complex superstructures" (Gramsci 1971, 181). Given his obsession with the absence of socialist revolution in the West, it is surprising that he does not specify the conditions under which "the decisive passage" may or may not take place. To say that bourgeois hegemony is at work and that the working class is placated by class compromise is one possible answer. An alternative explanation is that, if the exercise of labor power leads to class compromise, "the decisive passage" would be delayed. But if the exercise of leverage leads to counterattacks that undermine workers' home advantage, the labor movements would be compelled to fight their way into the ideological domain.

Democracy, Labor, and Environment

Mature theoretical considerations shed light on muddied reality and guide one to conduct accurate political analysis. As far as East Asia is concerned, democracy is not a native but an imported concept, and how to live democratically has been a relatively new experience. One thing that people often overlook is that Taiwan and Korea, in contrast to their East Asian peers after World War II, are so far the *only* two countries to have successfully pushed through a fully fledged representative democracy by their people's own initiatives and through waves of popular uprisings and elite compromises.[2] The foundation of Japan's constitutional monarchy was laid down during the U.S. occupation, and twenty-four Americans working at the Supreme Commander of the Allied Powers drafted Japan's new constitution (Huffman 2004, 165), meaning that the Japanese people had no say in how the new political system should be structured and organized. Singapore wore a cloak of "electoral democracy" that did not honor the spirit of party competition—the People's Action Party has been the ruling party since 1963 and has never been defeated in any general election; gerrymandering and libel suits have been employed against opposition leaders; and according to Reporters without Borders data, media censorship has persistently left Singapore in the "unfree" bottom 20 percent of the 170 or so countries listed in the Press Freedom Index. The People's Republic of China is a nondemocratic country by any standard, and whether it will be democratized or run rampant with militaristic ambitions is a question that affects not only the future of East Asia but also geopolitical stability on a global scale. Hong Kong in the past ten-some years has been fighting for the right of self-governance against China's arbitrary encroachment. In addition to the annual vigil for the dead of the Tiananmen Square killings, half a million citizens took to the street in protest of a draconic national security bill pushed by Beijing that aimed to eliminate the opposition in Hong Kong, and community residents protested against the construction of an express rail directly connecting China's coastal city with Hong Kong (Hung and Ip 2012); high school students mobilized ninety thousand pupils, parents, teachers, and activists into a mass demonstration against the imposition of "Chinese patriotism lessons" (Jones 2014, 29–30; *New York Times* 2012); and all of these culminated in a more-than-two-month occupancy action in 2014 fighting to choose freely the city's chief executive without Beijing's meddling (*New York Times* 2014a, 2014b). Despite such waves of protests, the future of Hong Kong remains uncertain.

Taiwan's and Korea's social movements in general, and labor and environmental movements in particular, have contributed to the development of democracy over the past forty years, as many have suggested (Hsiao 2011; Kim 2011; Shin and Chang 2011). Labor and environmental movements helped check arbitrary rulers and worked toward replacing arbitrary rules with just and rational ones; they strove to "obtain a share for the underlying population in the making of rules" (Moore 1966, 414). Early-riser movements clashed with authoritarian regimes prior to democratic transition, while latecomer movements chimed in during the period of democratic consolidation to improve the quality of a young democracy. As a result, labor's economic citizenship became recognized in production sites and in public life, and new environmental governance replaced the unregulated appropriation of limited natural resources. One can now advocate labor rights as much as one likes, as long as others are willing to listen. Forming an environmental NGO has become as ordinary as applying for a bank account or checking out books from a library—all involve getting in line and filling out some papers.

Yet there remain a few inconvenient facts. One is that, democratic transition and consolidation or otherwise, the political delegates of the labor and environmental movements in Taiwan and Korea are yet to celebrate any real electoral victory of their own. Taiwan's Labor Party, launched in 1989, waited twenty years to have one single county councilman elected. Despite securing

policy compromises through their political allies, both environmental movements had great trouble building up their political wings. Taiwan's Green
Party, founded in 1996, and with a membership of three hundred by 2003
and roughly two hundred by 2013, has never (except for one odd case[3]) won
any seat in any national race. Its record was just 1.7 percent of the national
vote in the 2012 legislative election. In the 2014 local election, it finally
scored two seats of township representation with 0.47 percent of the total
votes cast.[4] Korea's Green Party, meanwhile, scored a mere 0.5 percent of the
total vote in the 2012 National Assembly election and, failing to secure 3
percent, was subsequently deregistered in line with Korea's Political Party Act.
Korea's Democratic Labor Party had a promising start, gaining 10 out of 299
seats in the 2004 National Assembly election, but the number dropped to
5 in 2008 owing to a party split one year earlier. After a merger with the
People's Participation Party and a faction from the New Progressive Party
in 2011, it is now called the United Progressive Party and secured thirteen
out of three hundred seats in the 2012 election. To secure 5 percent of seats
in the National Assembly is certainly an achievement, but there is still a long
way to go before that achievement resembles anything like that of Brazil's
Workers' Party or South Africa's ANC/Communist Party ruling alliance.
This serves as a friendly reminder that young democracies are not necessarily
friendly to equally young labor and green parties. On the contrary, the rules
of the electoral game have more often than not protected vested interests and
been biased against young, small, progressive parties.

A failure to build the political wing made the four movements sensitive to a sudden change of political climate. Call it bad karma, but Taiwan
and Korea both experienced a change in their ruling party at the end of the
twentieth century, and both witnessed conservative parties returning to power
in the same year, 2008. Korea's conservative party aggressively pursued neoliberal policies that exacerbated domestic inequality, cut welfare spending
and funding to civil NGOs, manipulated the electoral process through the
state intelligence, and witch-hunted major unions and leading environmental organizations; even the largest left-wing party, the United Progressive Party,
was ordered to dissolve by the court (*Hankyoreh* 2014). Taiwan's KMT
sought closer economic ties through the patronage of the PRC, regardless
of the possible effect on domestic unemployment; turned a blind eye to
dangerous land grabbing, which led to a few suicides and not a few lawsuits;
governed through nontransparency and violated basic democratic procedures; and completely ignored any dissenting voices. The "conservative"
turns of Taiwan and Korea's politics, or of East Asian politics in general if we
throw in Japan, aroused a new wave of civil disobedience to defend the way

of democratic living to which people had been accustomed in the previous two decades. Taiwan's antinuclear rally in 2013 set a new record by attracting 230,000 participants (*Apple Daily* 2013) and Korea's environmental groups worked with Seoul mayor Park Won-soon to initiate the "One Less Nuclear Power Plant" project (*Kyunghyang Shinmun* 2014). Several waves of high-risk labor struggles broke out both in Taiwan and Korea to fight massive layoffs and unfair labor practices (*Hankyoreh* 2011, 2013a, 2013b; *Taipei Times* 2014a, 2014b). Labor and environmental movements stand both at the forefront of the new wave of struggle and at a crossroads. Will they be able to end the current nightmare by steering a democracy-in-form (votes) toward a democracy-in-essence (realization of economic justice)? Or will they fail to retain what they have gained and enter a downward spiral? All depends on what I want to discuss in the next section.

Labor and Environmental Movements in the Twenty-First Century

Wallerstein makes an interesting assertion on 1968, the worldwide year of revolt. The year 1968 was a double revolt, he says, both against U.S. hegemony and Soviet collusion and against the Old Left consisting of vertically organized movements such as social-democratic, communist, or national liberation movements (Wallerstein 2012, 109). The movements of verticalism prior to the 1960s have been replaced by those of horizontalism—feminism, environment, peace, squatters, ethnic groups, sexuality, and so on—in which "there are multiple kinds of justice movements and these movements should speak to each other, deal with each other, without any one movement on top" (Wallerstein 2012, 110).

In the post-1960s era, we witness two parallel developments. On one hand, the neoliberal global force—an ensemble of interwoven networks between profit-seeking capitalist enterprises, think tanks and policy institutes providing ideological backings (Mirowski and Plehwe 2009), and determined government officials—expanded in an unstoppable manner as the "movements of verticalism" declined. Along with the rise of market fundamentalism, various social movements began to "speak to each other," as Wallerstein has suggested. Starting from the 1970s, feminists combined environmental advocacy to coin eco-feminism (Hay 2002, chapter 3); feminists also debated either a healthier marriage to—or a divorce from—Marxism (Hartmann 1981); racial minorities and low-income communities pioneered environmental justice movements (Bullard 1990, 1993; Cole and Foster 2001; McGurty 2000); and waves of cross-border migration also led joint forces of immigrant communities and labor activists to form the modern immigrant rights movement (Johnson and Hing 2007; Koopmans et al. 2005).

By the 1990s, a different partnership was being suggested. Given the economic and environmental devastation under neoliberal globalization through the 1980s, the coming together of "teamsters and turtles" in Seattle as a red–green alliance offered a glimmer of hope (Mitchell 2009). Discussions over labor–environment alliances began to grow, documenting coalitions at the local level (Rose 2000; Susuki 2013), at the national level (Obach 2004), in a single industry (Smith, Sonnenfeld, and Pellow 2006), or for a specific issue such as climate change (Rathzel and Uzzell 2011). Marxism and environmentalism began to converge by reformulating the Marxist framework to accommodate environmental dimensions (Altvater 1993; Benton 1989; Grundmann 1991; O'Connor 1998; Pepper 1993) and by questioning the possibility of "greening" capitalism (Foster 2002; Magdoff and Foster 2011; Tanuro 2013). All is good.

This book is an unashamed advocate of labor–environment alliances for the twenty-first century. We live in a world of unprecedented affluence where, ironically, the issue of necessity grows more pressing than ever. Labor power is sold not only piecemeal but also under a deplorable level of surveillance and subordination. Shared communal resources—rivers, forests, oceans, land, and natural energy—are privatized and commodified to the extent that the poor lose their daily water supply and small-holding farmers and urban residents alike are forced to yield to the forces of land grabbing and speculation. The collusion of global capital and political elites is so overwhelming that neither labor nor environmental movements can fight their own war alone. As Burawoy puts it, the rise of neoliberal global forces since the 1970s, which he calls "third-wave marketization," deepened the commodification of nature—privatizing water and land—and brought with it a series of unnatural disasters that in turn put more pressure on wage labor's survival and intensified its subjugation (Burawoy 2010, 309–10). In other words, labor's plight became closely intertwined with environmental crises. Hence this book is, in truth, a search for the material foundation of labor–environment alliances. To do so, a thorough understanding of both movements' emergences and mutual influences is required. To study the distinct labor and environmental trajectories, furthermore, is intended to reveal the strengths, weaknesses, historical scars, and emotional traumas of each movement in relation to the other.

Hardship alone does not build coalitions. The weak are as likely to cooperate with each other as to pit against one other. To sustain genuine labor–environment alliances, powerful common enemies are not enough either. The powers-that-be can easily break a hard-won alliance by dropping bread crumbs selectively and giving out false promises. By setting out the experiences of Taiwan and Korea, this book differs from past dissections of red–green alliances and pushes Wallerstein's horizontal coalitions one step further by offering new and concrete incentives for both movements to set aside long-standing prejudices and reconsider the possibility of coalition building. Each movement possesses a specific set of skills and natural talents that its counterpart lacks and needs. Labor is strong at grassroots organizing but weak in discursive production, whereas with the environmental movement, it is the other way around. It is this very mutual *complementarity* that makes labor–environment alliances so appealing.

In addition, record-low union density and a lack of public support have demoralized unionists and activists alike and further obstructed labor's pursuit of higher goals. Though environmental crises, such as the Fukushima nuclear disaster, have rekindled a flame of public participation (Hasegawa 2014; Ho 2014), experiences have taught us that such passion will be fleeting and that no fundamental change will occur if the environment movement is not backed by solid grassroots organizing to persist in pressuring the powers-that-be. The making of labor–environment alliances, as advocated by this book, does not stem from romantic sentiments but from objective necessity. For either movement to regain lost strength and to continue flourishing hinges on acquiring each other's home advantage to withstand external assault and overcome internal crisis. Maybe it is time to add three new words to the famous labor slogan: "Organize or die; *collaborate and thrive!*"

historic bloc

Appendix: Notes on Methodology

We compare things all the time. This tree is taller, someone's voice is softer, or a stockbroker enjoys a higher annual income than all assistant professors in the humanities and social sciences. Sociologists are no different than normal folk. Sociologists compare, implicitly or explicitly, though the subject of comparison varies greatly, from consumption patterns, educational attainment, and religious practices to gross domestic products, structures of polity, and social protests. If it is indeed true, as Durkheim says, that all sociological inquiries are comparative in nature, maybe we should try to answer by what standard sociologists choose their cases for comparison, and what these comparisons are for.

This comparative project began when I was nineteen years old. In summer 1987, I was waiting impatiently to become a college sophomore. Out of the blue, the TV news and daily papers began to bombard me with coverage of Korea's social turmoil. It came as a shock that, while my friends and I smoked imported cigarettes at small cafés and fantasized about all the awful scenarios that might come to pass if ever we got arrested for student activism—which did not happen in real life—thousands of Korean students were throwing Molotov cocktails on the streets and many of them indeed were getting arrested, imprisoned, and badly beaten up. It was also bewildering to see that hundreds of thousands of Korean workers, escorted by bulldozers and heavy industrial equipment, were going on strike, while Taiwan's labor movement was in a relatively anemic state. Though I could content myself with simply knowing that this was how things stood on the broad spectrum, a nagging question has planted itself in the back of my mind ever since: why didn't such things happen in Taiwan? I guess the same puzzle might still enter my head while learning of student protests and labor strikes in Poland, Brazil, or India, but the feelings of shock and bewilderment would have been much less intense. After all, different cultural and historical heritages come in handy to explain things away. But South Korea? Aren't we all in the "league of little dragons"?

Years later, I collected data and wrote a book in answer to that nagging question that a nineteen-year-old once had.

Protest Data

The primary data set that this book is based on is a time series of protest events. An event is defined as "a set of 'actions' undertaken by one or more identifiable groups against one or more targets with no break of more than one day between actions" (Markoff 1996, 209). The protest events analyzed in this book exclude collective actions outside of Taiwan and Korea, even if Taiwanese and Koreans took part. They include politically motivated unconventional actions that gathered ten or more participants in the same place and that publicly made a claim on the issues of labor grievance and environmental degradation. Even though the cutoff for collective action is set at ten participants, exceptions are made for dramatic events—such as self-immolation or the murder of one's employers—which often involve less than ten. The approach was to search for sources that mention such actions, with data collection pretty much following the general procedures of protest event analysis pioneered by historians, sociologists, and political scientists in the 1970s (Eisinger 1973; Jenkins and Perrow 1977; Lipsky 1968; Paige 1975; Tilly 1978; Wilson 1961) and further refined by others (Koopmans 1993; Kriesi et al. 1995; McAdam 1999b; Olzak 1989a; Tarrow 1989).

I systematically trawled two national newspapers, the *China Times* and the *Korea Times*, to search for entries that covered such protest events in various action forms (see the next section for a complete list). Once a protest event was identified, we wrote a fifty-word description and coded the "factual" elements of the event, such as the date, the location, the number of participants, their occupations, their demands, the target, the industry to which the target belonged, the form of protest, level of violence, involvement of authority, the duration of the event, and numbers of arrests or prosecutions. Event descriptions and numeric coding were done on Microsoft Excel. While each protest event was assigned a unique ID and a list of protest events over substantial areas and time spans was completed, we sought supplementary information to corroborate the accuracy of the list. Occasionally, after consulting secondary sources, we changed the enumeration, because two events might have been conflated into one or one single event might actually have been two separate events. Once the list of protest events was cleaned up, we proceeded to run a statistical analysis.

Lists of Action Forms

I follow the categorization suggested by Koopmans (1993, 639–40) and Krisei et al. (1995, 267–68) and include the following four types of collective action in the analysis in this book.

> *Demonstrative*: actions permissible under the existing legal and institutional frameworks, such as an administrative/civil/criminal lawsuit; petition letters to politicians, public offices, and the media; presentation of signatures; press conferences; other
>
> *Confrontational*: nonviolent actions seeking to disrupt the routine of public order, such as a public assembly; rally; demonstration; strike; slowdown; walkout; boycott; hunger strike; blockade; symbolic violence (e.g., burning effigies); other
>
> *Light violence*: an event clearly indicating that protesters initiated the violence, such as limited property damage (e.g., throwing stones at government buildings); theft; violent demonstration; seizure of public or private buildings; disruption of assemblies; physical violence against persons (light injury involved); other
>
> *Violence*: severe property damage (e.g., arson, sabotage); physical violence against persons (severe injury or death involved); politically motivated suicide; other

The distributions of different action types are presented in Table 8.

The Choice of Newspapers

Protest event analysis "tends to be time-consuming and costly," and "the coding of large numbers of events can hardly be accomplished by one person in a few months" (Koopmans and Rucht 2002, 241). As Markoff puts it perfectly, the choice of sources in studies of social protests is always that of a compromise between an ideal and the constraints of finite resources (Markoff 1996, 207). This book chooses the *China Times* and the *Korea Times* as the primary news sources. Both newspapers are privately owned, published continuously from the 1950s, and cover news from the entire national territory. Neither is extremely conservative or left wing. Both would most likely be categorized as "liberal-centrist," at least prior to the 1990s.

The analysis of Taiwan's labor and environmental protests covers the years from 1961 through 1987. The main news source used is the *China Times*

Table 8. Distribution of action types

	Taiwan (%)		Korea (%)	
Action type	Environment	Labor	Environment	Labor
Demonstrative	83	72	64	8
Confrontational	12	15	27	78
Light violence	4	5	8	10
Violence	1	8	0	4
Total	100	100	100	100

Source: Taiwan's data are from the *China Times* Fifty-Year Images Databank (http://140.112 .152.45/ttsweb/); Korea's data are from the *Korea Times* and the *Korea Herald* microfilms archived in Harvard-Yenching Library, National Assembly Library of Korea, and National Taiwan University Library.

Fifty-Year Images Database,[1] which digitizes images of entire national, regional, and local papers between 1950 and 1999. For the twenty-seven-year period of 1961–87, we read the daily newspapers for every day and every edition. Besides the *China Times,* we also did keyword searches[2] of two news databanks, the United Daily News[3] and the Taiwan News Search Web,[4] to search for protest events not covered by the *China Times.* A total of 3,079 protest events are recorded, including 1,957 environmental events and 1,121 labor events.

The reason for choosing the *China Times* was its thoroughness. A previous protest-event study comparing five national newspapers confirmed that the *China Times* had a more comprehensive coverage of various social protests in the 1980s (Chang et al. 1992, 9–10, 165). The *China Times* is also the only newspaper containing the full text of local news in the 1970s and 1980s, unlike other news databanks, which only provide either local headlines or local news after the 1990s. Local news editions are important because, in the Taiwanese context, early labor and environmental protests were frequently covered only in the local pages and rarely in the national or regional ones (Liu 2011, 8). Because of its relatively thorough coverage of local news, the *China Times* reported 100 percent of the Taiwanese protest events used in this book.

The primary source for Korea's protest events is the microfilms of the *Korea Times,* one of the three English-language national newspapers in Korea, and the analysis in this book covers the years between 1969 and 1990. Data collection was conducted at three different sites: the Harvard-Yenching Library (Boston), the National Assembly Library of Korea (Seoul), and the

APPENDIX 175

National Taiwan University Library (Taipei). Just like the procedure for recording Taiwanese protest events, we searched through the articles for every edition of the daily newspapers. The *Korea Times* did not have Monday editions, and sometimes the microfilms missed certain dates, and here I used the *Korea Herald* as a substitute. For the twenty-two-year period of 1969–90, we found 494 labor protest events and 60 environmental events, a total of 554 protest events (see Table 9). Eighty-eight percent of protest data come from the *Korea Times* and the rest from the *Korea Herald.* Besides these two English-language newspapers, I also conducted keyword searches of the Korea Integrated News Database System,[5] developed by the Korea Press Foundation, for additional information.

The *Korea Times* was chosen for practical reasons. On top of budget and time constraints, my language skill had not reached the level of reading through Korean-language newspapers both efficiently and accurately, and I went for the next-best option. One likely data bias in using English-language newspapers as the primary source is a systematic underestimation of the overall number of protest events. The Stanford Korea Democracy Project (Shin et al. 2011, 30) reports 748 labor protest events between 1970 and 1992, roughly one and a half times the number of labor protest events analyzed in this book. Yet the Stanford Project uses data compiled through news reports, government documents, organizational archives, personal memoirs, and other manuscripts (Shin et al. 2007, 30) and provides no counting on environmental protest events, which makes it difficult to assess in what way the English-language newspapers underreported the number of labor protest events and also whether the number of environmental protest events was equally underrepresented. Given a lack of other protest event studies on Korea's labor and environmental movements, this English-language newspaper bias waits to be corrected.

Table 9. Numbers of labor and environmental protest events

	Taiwan (1961–87)	Korea (1969–90)	Total
Labor protests	1,121	494	1,615
Environmental protests	1,957	60	2,017
Total	3,078	554	3,632

Source: Taiwan's data are from the *China Times* Fifty-Year Images Databank (http://140.112.152.45/ttsweb/); Korea's data are from the *Korea Times* and the *Korea Herald* microfilms archived in Harvard-Yenching Library, National Assembly Library of Korea, and National Taiwan University Library.

Since the thoroughness of the *Korea Times* is not comparable to that of the *China Times,* I use the two sets of protest data with caution. In fact, I will suggest caution regarding any aggregate number of protest events because "the aggregate number of all incidents identified and counted is in no sense a sample from some clearly defined universe" (Markoff 1996, 216). We simply do not know how many labor and environmental protests out there were reported—or went unreported—in newspapers and government documents. "If we blindly followed the media reports, we might be totally misguided when making inferences to the universe of all protests for a given place and time. Media do not mirror this universe in any representative way" (Koopmans and Rucht 2002, 246). This book does not claim a complete listing of all labor and environmental protests in Taiwan and Korea between the 1960s and the 1980s, but only a portion of them, as collected through two national newspapers, which can be verified or falsified by others. Hence I try my best to avoid direct comparison between the aggregate numbers of Taiwan's protest events and those of Korea. Because it is somehow misleading to directly compare the Taiwanese numbers with those of Korea, I use the variations over time in the percentages of labor and environmental protests while doing cross-national comparisons, as presented in Figures 1 and 2. Even if the *Korea Times* systematically undercounts the aggregate number of protest events, an intra-national comparison is still meaningful, such as the comparison of the number of Korea's environmental and labor protest events in Figure 4. Figure 11, however, is the only one in which I directly compare the Taiwanese numbers with those of Korea. In this unfortunate case, I simply could not find any longitudinal and comparable statistics to indicate the structures of environmental grievance in Taiwan and Korea, and hence the protest event data are used as an imperfect proxy.

Furthermore, as far as the question of identifying early-riser and late-comer movements is concerned, we are more interested in the shift, or the trend lines, of labor and environmental protest over an extensive time span than in the aggregate number of each year's protest events. Assuming the *Korea Times* undercounts the number of labor and environmental protests by 30 percent each year, the aggregate number of protest events would be different, but the curve of the trend lines—where they peak and where they trough—would remain similar.

Data Reliability

Another acute question concerns the impact of media censorship on data reliability. It is well known that the KMT and Korea's military junta exercised strict control over media content during the 1970s and 1980s, and some would go so far as to suggest that newspapers during the authoritarian period are unreliable—if not unusable—sources of protest event analysis (Shin et al. 2011, 271). It comes almost as an obligation to worry about the problem of selection bias for those who use newspapers as the primary source to analyze protest events. Discussions over types of bias, stability of bias, and ways to make reasonable inferences pile up in the literature (Barranco and Wisler 1999; Danzger 1975; Earl et al. 2004; Herkenrath and Knoll 2011; Hug and Wisler 1998; Hutter 2014; Koopmans and Rucht 2002; Mueller 1997; Oliver and Maney 2000; Oliver and Myers 1999; Ortiz et al. 2005; Snyder and Kelly 1977). It is common wisdom among protest event scholars that there is no completely reliable source for social protests, be it newspapers, arrest reports, public statistics of social disturbance, government archives, or personal recollection. All of them tend to undercount social protest and disproportionately collect urban, large, and dramatic protest events, and hence what a researcher needs to do is battle the biases inherent in each type of source and make the best possible use of flawed data.

I learned two particular lessons from using these two newspapers. Taiwan's control over media content was strong in the national news pages but not as strong in the regional and local pages. The first time flipping through the local pages of the *China Times,* I was amazed by the quantity of social conflict reported in regional and local pages. So the first lesson is that the local news pages are a hidden treasure for anyone interested in Taiwan's protest events in the 1960s and 1970s. Korea's media censorship under Park Chung Hee and Chun Doo Hwan was equally bad, and a large number of liberal journalists were fired or unable to find jobs. Yet the *Korea Times* reported, besides major social conflicts, quite a few small and obscure protest cases. Maybe Korea's media control at that time was directed mainly against newspapers in Korean, whereas an English-language newspaper was relatively uncensored or more able to find loopholes. This remains a hypothesis to be tested.

Notes

Introduction

1. In rare cases where an ensemble of social movements in a protest cycle is studied together, the question of why some movements become early risers and others crash the party late is often left unexplained.

2. Polanyi's double movement thesis is backed up by a single case study of nineteenth-century England and his observations of other early industrializers on the European continent, and his cases of protectionist movements include nineteenth-century Owenism, the Chartist movements, and the alliance between landed classes and the peasantry against enclosure and free trade.

3. Taiwan was under Japanese colonial rule for fifty years (1895–1945), and Korea was annexed to the Japanese empire for thirty-five years (1910–45).

4. "If an instance in which the phenomenon under investigation occurs, and an instance in which it does not occur, have every circumstance in common save one, that one occurring only in the former; the circumstance in which alone the two instances differ is the effect, or the cause, or an indispensable part of the cause, of the phenomenon" (Mill 2002, 256).

5. It has been argued that Taiwan and Korea have kept an eye on one another and imitated policy as deemed appropriate, with Korea looking to Taiwan for models of agricultural policy (M. Moore 1988, 119–20). There even existed some anecdotal storytelling on Park Chung Hee's sending delegates to learn how the Kuomintang managed to tame college students (Huang 1999). Thus mutual influences did exist, but so far there has been no compelling evidence to attest that Taiwan and Korea have imitated policies on labor control or environmental governance.

1. The Power Bases of Labor and Environmental Movements

1. Among the discussions of centralized and decentralized forms of association in the movement literature, labor unions and socialist parties are the exemplar of a centralized-bureaucratic model (Michels 1962), but environmental movements stand at the opposite end, an SPR (segmentary, polycentric, and reticulate) model (Gerlach 1999).

2. Objective definitions of *a single movement* and *one location* are not without dispute. In this typology, I try to be faithful to each author's self-definition, and I use McAdam (1999b) and Andrews (2004) as contrasting examples. McAdam studies the civil rights movement from the vantage point of a national phenomenon, and thus in his case, the single location refers to the United States as a whole. Andrews's focus is local, and thus his study is categorized as a single-movement, cross-location study, with "location" in his case referring to various counties of Mississippi.

3. The five examples listed can hardly do justice to the breadth and hetero- geneity of empirical works adopting this research design. Other empirical works of importance include ghetto protests in various American cities (Eisinger 1973), labor movements in Western democracies (Haydu 1988; Western 1997), labor movements in developing contexts (Collier and Collier 1991; Lee 2007; Y. Lee 2011; Seidman 1994; Valenzuela 1989; Webster, Lambert, and Bezuidenhout 2008), labor move- ments across continents (Chun 2009), labor movements around the world (Silver 2003), environmental movements in the West (Bramwell 1989; Jamison, Eyerman, and Cramer 1990), environmental movements in Asia (Lee and So 1999; Weller 2006), peasants' movements around the world (Paige 1975; Wolf 1968), national liberation movements in South Africa and Palestine (Younis 2001), human rights activism (Loveman 1998), guerrilla warfare in Latin America (Wickham-Crowley 1992), and social revolutions around the world (Goodwin 2001; Skocpol 1979).

4. There are a few cases deviating from the dominant positive-sum formula, namely, where early risers have a constraining effect on latecomer movements. Some argue that, when labor politics was still running strong, new social movements had little room to develop, as in the case of France (Kriesi et al. 1995). Another study of Indian women's movements in different political fields (Ray 1998, 1999) also demonstrates that in a homogeneous field where the Communist Party enjoyed a dominant, hegemonic position, autonomous women's groups had little space to maneuver. In contrast, women's groups were relatively unrestrained in a fragmented field without a dominant force. With regard to the constraining effect of latecomers on early risers, there is no explicit empirical work to support this position. Interest- ingly enough, Tarrow also argues that, as multiple movements arise later on, inter- movement competition over resources will replace the earlier positive-sum relations, early-riser movements having established a protected niche that the new entrants cannot challenge or threaten (Tarrow 1994). This assertion is empirically confirmed by Minkoff's (1997, 793–95) study.

5. Early scholars were very fond of making movement typologies. Turner and Killian (1957, 320–30) proposed at least three different ways to classify social movements. Smelser (1963) distinguished norm-oriented movements from value-oriented ones. Tilly differentiated three types of collective action according to the interaction between the group initiating the action and other groups: competitive, reactive, and proactive (Tilly 1978, 144–47). Enthusiasm toward typologies waned considerably among the U.S. scholars, particularly in the 1980s and the early 1990s.

6. Jasper's typology unwittingly bears resemblance to the distinction between movements based on a *beneficiary* constituency and those based on a *conscience* constituency advocated by the resource mobilization school (Zald 1987, 321).

7. It is based on this "resource-poor" argument that we find much discussion of resources poured in from outside. Resources may come from other social groups and classes if a movement is capable of building broader alliances—the sponsorship by the liberal communities of the United Farm Workers is one of the best examples (Jenkins and Perrow 1977). Polanyi (2001, 159) also illuminates this point rather nicely: "the chances of classes in a [protectionist] struggle will depend upon their ability to win support from outside their own membership, which again will depend upon their fulfillment of tasks set by interests wider than their own." Gramsci's (1978) *Southern Question* is another version stressing the importance of class alliance in building a strong Italian labor movement. Or resources may also come from transnational advocacy networks: "when channels between the state and its domestic actors are blocked, the boomerang pattern of influence characteristic of transnational networks may occur: domestic NGOs bypass their state and directly search out international allies to try to bring pressure on their states from outside" (Keck and Sikkink 1998, 12). Though access to resources from outside has more to do with a movement's long-term sustainability than with its genesis, one can still make the case that varying capacities to hook up with other social groups and transnational networks will affect the performance of labor and environmental movements.

8. Tarrow outlines four aspects of political opportunities: (1) the opening up of institutional access to political participation, (2) shifts in ruling alignments, (3) the availability of influential allies, and (4) cleavages within and among elites (Tarrow 1994, 84).

9. The existing resource-centered explanation seems to assume that all movements need the *same* kinds of resources to take off and sustain themselves. For a movement focusing on policy works, we may intuitively assume that a group of able staff specializing in fund-raising, corporate campaigns, and agenda setting is of importance. But the very same group of able staff might be of limited use for a movement based on continuous grassroots mobilization. This simple contrast points to the possibility that different movements may need different kinds of resources and that the importance of one type of resource varies across movements and across stages of a single movement.

10. This formulation of leverage may sound similar to Piven and Cloward's "disruptive power," but in reality disruptive power emphasizes neither incorporation nor indispensability.

11. Eagleton mentions that successful ideologies always involve certain "universalizing" and "naturalizing" strategies. The former is about presenting one's values and interests as the values and interests of all; the latter strives to make ideas and beliefs as natural and self-evident as possible (Eagleton 1991, 56–61). Whether these universalized and naturalized ideas and beliefs are "real" and "true" is not the focus here. We concentrate on analyzing the function of ideas and beliefs in social life—what Eagleton calls the "sociological aspect of ideology."

2. The Tangles of Movement Histories

1. One should not confuse the synchronization thesis with Smelser's generalized beliefs that "activate people for participation in episodes of collective behavior" in a value-added process (Smelser 1963, 13–15, 71–72, 80, 82). Generalized beliefs, for Smelser, are "short-circuited," immature assessments of reality under structural strains, and "collective behavior, then, is the action of the impatient" (72). Thus his cases of generalized beliefs are rumor, superstition, ideology (in its worst sense), hysteria, hostility, and so on. In contrast, my position is that consciousness is bred from both lived experiences and reasoning and contains the possibility of revealing hidden truths of how the social world works.

2. Official documents in Korea used Chinese characters *(hanja)* extensively, and only the well educated were proficient in reading them.

3. Between 1961 and 1971, the number of deaths per year due to coal-mining accidents always exceeded one hundred (Department of Statistics MEA 1995, 227, Table 84). Accidents and casualties as such received wide news coverage. The earliest report can be traced back to 1951, when the *United Daily* covered the news that governmental agencies were concerned about mining accidents and attempting to improve the inspection system (*United Daily* 1951). The first half of the 1980s was similarly littered with mining accidents.

4. This is the first time that a major public hazard—workers and residents near an industrial complex were poisoned by escaped hydride gases—hit the national pages. This event led to one death and hundreds of hospitalizations (*China Times* 1978; *United Daily* 1978). In the past, only government programs on environmental management would be put on the national pages, and pollution news was usually buried in the city/county pages, meaning that people who did not live in the same area would be unaware of such reports.

3. The Emergence of Early-Riser Movements

1. Whether to trace the history of the four movements back to the colonial period is a question of great importance. On the labor side, ample evidence attests to

the vibrant leftist currents and communist organizations intertwined with the anti-colonial national struggles in Taiwan and Korea, and equally ample records show how, during the rule of Syngman Rhee and Chiang Kai-shek, the left was either forced to flee or executed en masse (Chen 1996; Chen 2013; Cumings 2002, 2010; Moore 2007; Scalapino and Lee 1972; Wakabayashi 2007; N.-S. Wang 1989). On the environmental side, colonizers' exploitation of forestry, land, and natural resources from the colonized has been a cause of major environmental conflict, as experiences from Botswana and Java testify (Cliffe and Moorsom 1979; Peluso 1992). As much as I would like to link post–World War II activism back to colonial times, historical evidence of the linkages, both organizational and ideological, between prewar labor–environmental conflicts and postwar activism is yet to be discovered. Work on this subject matter is urgently needed. Without more compelling evidence in place, this book will refrain from discussing the historical continuity of pre– and post–World War II activism and will instead start from the 1970s, when labor and environmental conflicts began to surface.

2. Korea's data for 1972 and 1973 were missing from government and ILO statistics, and I use the two-year averages to estimate the figures for the missing values.

3. "Diversified, huge business conglomerates," a Korean translation of the Japanese *zaibatsu*.

4. Some argue that "Taiwan has had one of the biggest public enterprise sectors outside the communist bloc and Sub-Saharan Africa" (Wade 1990, 176) and that these public enterprises "concentrated on the commanding heights to which European socialists wistfully aspire: petroleum refining, petrochemicals, steel and other basic metals, ship-building, heavy machinery, transport equipment, fertilizer—in addition to standard electricity, gas, water, railway, and telephone utilities" (178–79).

5. Fields also, in his comparative study, points out that "in Korea, huge, horizontally and vertically integrated business conglomerates *(chaebol)* have emerged and flourished. In Taiwan . . . private business groups . . . are much smaller and very different from the Korean counterparts in terms of capital, scale, control of their own trade, and government connections" (Fields 1995, 5).

6. Pollution abatement and control (PAC) expenditures are directly related to the size of an enterprise, and this assertion remains true even decades after the rise of Taiwan's environmental movement. According to 1999 survey data from 2,524 private enterprises in the manufacturing sector, the average PAC expenditure at firms hiring more than one thousand workers was 97.6 times that of those hiring fewer than ten, 30 times that of those hiring between ten and fifty, 8.2 times that of those hiring between fifty and two hundred, and finally, 3.6 times that of those hiring between two hundred and one thousand (Environmental Protection Administration 2000, 4–27, recalculated from Table M-14).

7. In the past few decades, party mergers, renamings, and dissolutions in Korea have been so frequent as to indicate just how thinly the organizational infrastructure of political parties had been stretched.

8. Some have argued that the AFL-CIO and U.S. industries pressed for the enactment of the Labor Standards Law to prevent the dumping of cheap commodities from Taiwan (Ho et al. 1990).

9. *China Times* covered this debate between 1974 and 1975, when the Water Pollution Prevention Act was proposed and discussed inside the cabinet. The Ministry of Economic Affairs held the position that water pollution was a necessary evil in the process of industrialization and that after society had evolved to a higher level, pollution problems would automatically go away. The Department of Health insisted that this Act was necessary to reduce hazards to the general populace.

10. The presence of KMT personnel at antipollution struggles may or may not have sped up the settlement of disputes, but to some extent, they shielded early environmental protests from being labeled as antiregime activities and prevented state-sanctioned witch-hunts.

11. These measures made it illegal to criticize the Yushin constitution (measures 2 and 3) and to join any antiregime organizations (measure 4) and made it possible for the military to occupy universities (measure 7). The most severe of all was the infamous measure 9, barring "any criticism of the constitution, any political activity by students, or any public presentation or statement describing or discussing any act which might violate the decree" (Lee 2001, 75).

12. State intelligence (KCIA) and law enforcement intervened in labor disputes in two ways. Through behind-the-scene maneuvering, including persuasion, threats, and physical torture, they attempted to prevent workers from joining unions. Second, workers' demonstrations and sit-ins were treated as criminal offenses, and harsh measures were invoked that subjected participants to severe penalties. These measures included the Law Regarding Assembly and Demonstration, the Law Concerning Special Measures for Safeguarding National Security (article 7), Emergency Decree 9, and the National Security and the Anti-Communist Law (Choi 1987, 97).

13. As for why postwar Taiwan and Korea adopted different agricultural policies, one obvious reason is that they reflected the immediate needs of the time. Roughly two million mainland immigrants flocked to Taiwan between 1946 and 1952, and this sudden population increase made ensuring agricultural productivity urgent so as to satisfy the corresponding increase in food consumption. In contrast, between 1944 and 1949, Korea's population decreased by five million, and so developing an advanced agricultural sector for food production was not a top priority.

4. Movement Legacy and Latecomer Movements

1. At the national level, the consolidation of environmental affairs to a special agency was completed in 1982, when the EPA was set up as a subsection housed in

the Department of Health. In 1987, this subsection was elevated to the cabinet level. At the county and city level, local EPAs were set up between 1988 and 1991.

2. After the establishment of Taiwan's EPA, formerly a subbranch of the Department of Health, this cabinet-level agency promulgated another 12 sets of environmental laws and 175 regulations and executive orders, on top of the Environmental Impact Assessment Act and the Public Nuisance Dispute Mediation Act (http://www .epa.gov.tw/).

3. The Labor Standards Law, passed in 1984, extended coverage to workers previously unprotected by government standards, and roughly four out of eight million workers in Taiwan were covered after its promulgation (Cohen 1988, 131).

4. The Workers' Party was basically nonexistent after the 1992 legislative election. Its founding chairman resigned and stopped pursuing a political career, and the party has not participated in any electoral races since. The Labor Party joined multiple races, but it was not until 2009 that one of its members secured a seat in the County Council (Wang 2009).

5. This strike "represented three 'firsts'; the first major strike against a *chaebol*; the first time since 1971 that male workers had taken the offensive in a major labor action; and the first time that workers had struck independently of the official company union" (Hart-Landsberg 1993, 272).

6. The Kuro strike has an important place in Korea's labor movement history because it was the first case of a sympathy strike reflecting a broad social alliance. When workers at Daewoo Apparel Textile staged a sit-down strike to protest the arrest of union leaders, the company cut off the water and electricity supply and had the police force surround the plant, when, "much to the surprise of the company and police, more than one thousand workers from nine other factories in the industrial area went out in a sympathy strike. Students, church activists, and progressive political groups also marched in support" (Hart-Landsberg 1993, 272).

7. The KCTU's internal crisis of democracy in 1998 is detailed elsewhere (Gray 2008, 99–104).

8. After Roh Tae Woo made the June 29 declaration subsequently adopted by the National Assembly as the principle to amend the Fifth Republic's Constitution, one of the institutional reforms was "educational autonomy and local self-government through the popular election of local assemblies and executive heads of local governments" (Diamond and Shin 2000, 6).

9. Pro-labor intellectuals did form political parties and joined the 1988 National Assembly election. Both parties—the People's Party and the Hankyoreh Democratic Party—failed to secure 3 percent of the vote and were forced, by law, to dissolve themselves after the defeat. I thank Yoonkyung Lee for providing the historical background on this matter.

5. Labor and Environmental Trajectories

1. At the risk of oversimplification, I outline two existing approaches to the study of movement trajectories, one organization centered and the other institution centered. For the organization-centered approach, scholars dispute whether organizations lead social movements into downward spirals or lift and sustain them. One immediately recalls classic studies on "the iron law of oligarchy" (Michels 1962), the effect of "normalization" (Piven and Cloward 1992), professionalization and formalization (McCarthy and Zald 1987a, 1987b; Staggenborg 1988), and the "revitalization" thesis responding to Michels (Voss and Sherman 2000). The institution-centered approach is led by heavyweight figures such as Charles Tilly and Sidney Tarrow, and their work involves an aggregate of protest events either in a long period of time (Shorter and Tilly 1974; Tilly 1995, 2004; Tilly, Tilly, and Tilly 1975) or within "a phase of heightened conflict and contention across the social system" (Tarrow 1994, 153). Social movements in a Tillyian sense refers to a new form of public politics arising in mid-eighteenth-century Europe. The key question regarding movement trajectory concerns the way social movements establish themselves as legitimate players in the political arena and how their particular form of claim making is standardized and incorporated as part of political decision making. This is an allusion to the institutionalization of social movements. In Tarrow's case (Tarrow 1989, 1994), social movements in each protest cycle end up engaging in strategic interaction with various political players in the arena of institutional politics. Even if social movements initially pursue radical goals, they eventually settle for compromises and reforms, and the end result is hardly an overhaul of the entire system. The subtext of Tarrow's discussions seems to be that, over time, social movements develop sustained interactions with opponents and allies and gradually play the political game according to the set rules. This leads to both institutionalization and a loss of militancy. Other scholars, however, have put forth a "radicalization" thesis in contrast to Tarrow's account of the institutionalization of social movements (Gitlin 1980, 181–82; Kriesi et al. 1995, 122; McAdam 1999b, chapter 8). Both approaches pursue general accounts of movement trajectories and are less inclined to explore the different trajectories that social movements might take.

2. "Except for bank unions, only a few white-collar unions were organized before 1987. Democratic white-collar unions began to emerge after 1987" (Suh 1998, 1–2) and "the growth of white-collar unionism was motivated by the resurgence of the radical blue-collar labor movement on a national and massive scale in 1987" (3–4).

3. Koo also confirms that students-turned-workers "were mostly employed in medium-size manufacturing firms located in major industrial centers around Seoul, Inchon and Pupyong and Anyang. Very few of them went to the heavy industrial belts in the southern part of the country, such as Ulsan, Masan, and Changwon" (Koo 2001, 106).

4. Taiwan's union density is recalculated from labor statistics by dividing the membership of industrial unions by the total of the employed population each year.

5. According to 1991 and 1992 surveys on the support rates for ten different social movements in Taiwan (Hsiao 1994, 49), the environmental movement ranked number one both times with support of up to 87.7 percent. The labor movement ranked seventh and eighth, with support below 50 percent. We lack comparable data on Korea's environmental movement, but from various academic and popular accounts, it is quite clear that the environmental movement is one of the most influential and popular movements in Korea.

6. According to a study on the funding structure of Korea's environmental NGOs, corporate donations accounted for 30 percent of operational budgets, second only to government funding (31 percent) (Ju 2011, 142). Any causality between corporate funding and Korean NGOs' restraint from attacking corporate practices is yet to be established.

Conclusion

1. Many have pointed out the problems of Polanyi's analysis of class formation under Speenhamland. On one hand, the dire consequence on the lives of the poor that Polanyi attributed to Speenhamland is found empirically groundless (Block and Somers 2003). Furthermore, Polanyi's analysis of class formation was based on "an antiquated notion . . . in which disorganization miraculously leads to organization" and "the abolition of Speenhamland did not coincide with the Factory Movement, Chartism, Cooperative Movement, Owenism" (Burawoy 2003, 221).

2. I thank Sheng-Han Chang for loaning me this insight.

3. One local politician, Meng-Ting Kao, ran on a Green Party ticket and got elected as a member of the now defunct National Assembly in 1996. Not long after being elected, he withdrew from the Green Party and wandered between the two main parties, the KMT and the DPP. The Green Party expelled him and lost the only seat that it once held.

4. Data from the Central Election Commission (http://www.cec.gov.tw).

Appendix

1. http://140.112.152.45/ttsweb/.

2. Keywords used included *labor disputes, labor protests, labor movements, strikes, slowdowns, factory occupancy, capital–labor conflicts, environmental disputes, pollution disputes, environmental pollution, ecological conservation, environmental movements, antipollution movements,* and *ecological movements.*

3. http://udndata.com/.

4. http://140.112.113.17:8089/.

5. http://www.kinds.or.kr/.

Bibliography

Abe, Makoto, and Momoko Kawakami. 1997. "A Distributive Comparison of Enterprise Size in Korea and Taiwan." *The Developing Economies* 35, no. 4: 382–400.

Abelmann, Nancy. 1997. "Reorganizing and Recapturing Dissent in 1990s South Korea: The Case of Farmers." In *Between Resistance and Revolution: Cultural Politics and Social Protest*, ed. Richard G. Fox and Orin Starn, 251–76. New Brunswick, N.J.: Rutgers University Press.

Agrawal, Arun. 1996. "Poststructuralist Approaches to Development: Some Critical Reflections." *Peace and Change* 24, no. 4: 464–77.

Alinsky, Saul D. 1989a. *Reveille for Radicals*. New York: Vintage.

——. 1989b. *Rules for Radicals: A Pragmatic Primer for Realistic Radicals*. New York: Vintage.

Altvater, Elmar. 1993. *The Future of the Market: An Essay on the Regulation of Money and Nature after the Collapse of "Actually Existing Socialism."* London: Verso.

Amsden, Alice H. 1985. "The State and Taiwan's Economic Development." In *Bring the State Back In*, ed. Peter Evans, Dietrich Rueschemeyer, and Theda Skocpol, 78–106. Cambridge: Cambridge University Press.

——. 1989. *Asia's Next Giant: South Korea and Late Industrialization*. Oxford: Oxford University Press.

Anbarasan, Ethirajan. 2001. "Choi Yul: The Greening of Korea." *The UNESCO Courier*, February, 47–49. http://unesdoc.unesco.org/.

Andrews, Kenneth T. 2004. *Freedom Is a Constant Struggle: The Mississippi Civil Rights Movement and Its Legacy*. Chicago: University of Chicago Press.

Apple Daily. 2013. "Quantai dayouxing er shi wan ren han feihe, zhe juishi minyi" [Two hundred thousand who attended the anti-nuclear rally shouted No-Nuke, this is public opinion]. March 10.

Barranco, Jose, and Dominique Wisler. 1999. "Validity and Systematicity of Newspaper Data in Event Analysis." *European Sociological Review* 15, no. 3: 301–22.

Barrett, Richard E., and Soomi Chin. 1987. "Export-Oriented Industrializing States in the Capitalist World System: Similarities and Differences." In *The Political Economy of the New Asian Industrialism,* ed. Frederic Deyo, 23–43. Ithaca, N.Y.: Cornell University Press.

Bartley, Tim, and Curtis Child. 2011. "Movements, Markets and Fields: The Effects of Anti-Sweatshop Campaigns on U. S. Firms, 1993–2000." *Social Forces* 90, no. 2: 425–51.

Baviskar, Amita. 1995. *In the Belly of the River: Tribal Conflicts over Development in the Narmada Valley.* Oxford: Oxford University Press.

Benton, Ted. 1989. "Marxism and Natural Limits: An Ecological Critique and Reconstruction." *New Left Review* 178: 51–86.

Bloch, Marc. 1969. "A Contribution towards a Comparative History of European Societies." In *Land and Work in Mediaeval Europe: Selected Papers by Marc Bloch,* 44–81. New York: Harper Torchbooks.

Block, Fred, and Margaret Somers. 2003. "In the Shadow of Speenhamland: Social Policy and the Old Poor Law." *Politics and Society* 31, no. 2: 283–323.

Boudreau, Vincent. 1996. "Northern Theory, Southern Protest: Opportunity Structure Analysis in Cross-National Perspective." *Mobilization: An International Journal* 1, no. 2: 175–89.

Bramwell, Anna. 1989. *Ecology in the 20th Century: A History.* New Haven, Conn.: Yale University Press.

———. 1994. *The Fading of the Green: The Decline of Environmental Politics in the West.* New Haven, Conn.: Yale University Press.

Brandt, Vincent. 1987. "The Student Movement in South Korea." Paper prepared for the Department of State. Released to the Nautilus Institute under the U.S. Freedom of Information Act (FOIA). http://nautilus.org/.

Brenner, Robert. 1985. "Agrarian Class Structure and Economic Development." In *The Brenner Debate,* ed. T. H. Aston and C. H. E. Philpin, 10–63. Cambridge: Cambridge University Press.

Broadbent, Jeffrey. 1998. *Environmental Politics in Japan: Networks of Power and Protest.* Cambridge: Cambridge University Press.

Buchanan, Paul G., and Kate Nicholls. 2003. "Labour Politics and Democratic Transition in South Korea and Taiwan." *Government and Opposition* 38, no. 2: 203–37.

Buechler, Steven E. 2000. *Social Movements in Advanced Capitalism: The Political Economy and Cultural Construction of Social Activism.* New York: Oxford University Press.

Bullard, Robert. 1990. *Dumping in Dixie: Race, Class and Environmental Quality.* Boulder, Colo.: Westview Press.

———. 1993. *Confronting Environmental Racism: Voices from the Grassroots.* Boston: South End Press.

Burawoy, Michael. 1989. "Two Methods in Search of Science: Skocpol versus Trotsky." *Theory and Society* 18: 759–805.

———. 2003. "For a Sociological Marxism: The Complementary Convergence of Antonio Gramsci and Karl Polanyi." *Politics and Society* 31, no. 2: 193–261.

———. 2010. "From Polanyi to Pollyanna: The False Optimism of Global Labor Studies." *Global Labor Journal* 1, no. 2: 301–13.

Calhoun, Craig. 1993. "'New Social Movements' of the Early Nineteenth Century." *Social Science History* 17, no. 3: 385–427.

Central Daily News. 1965. "Xindianxi weihe ranwu" [Why is Hsin-dian Creek Polluted?]. December 6.

Central News Agency. 2001. "Labor, Environmental Groups Protest Outside EDAC Site." August 24.

Chakrabarty, Dipesh. 1988. "Conditions for Knowledge of Working-Class Conditions." In *Selected Subaltern Studies,* ed. Ranajit Guha and Gayatri Chakravorty Spivak, 179–230. Oxford: Oxford University Press.

———. 1989. *Rethinking Working-Class History: Bengal 1890–1940.* Princeton, N.J.: Princeton University Press.

Chang, Chin-fen. 2001. *Taiwan gongying shiye minyinghua: jingji misi de pipan* [The privatization of state-owned enterprises in Taiwan: A critique of the economic myth]. Taipei: Institute of Sociology, Academia Sinica.

Chang, Hsiao-Chuan. 1987. "Gongtou luoxuan le" [KMT-affiliated labor leaders lost the election!]. In *Laoxin laoli ji* [Essays on laboring minds and bodies], 82–88. Taipei: China Tims.

Chang, Mau-Kuei. 1989. *Baling niandai taiwan shehuiyundong fengchao yu zhengzhi zhuanhua* [Social movements and political transformation in the 1980s]. Taipei: Guojia zhengce jikan [Institute of National Policy Research].

Chang, Mau-Kuei, et al. 1992. *Minguo qishi niandai taiwan diqu "zilijiuji" shijian zhi yanjiu* [A study on Taiwan's "self-help" protest events between 1983 and 1988]. Taipei: Research, Development, and Evaluation Commission, Executive Yuan.

Chao, Kang. 1991. "Labor, Community, and Movement: A Case Study of Labor Activism in the Far Eastern Chemical Fiber Plant at Hsinpu, Taiwan, 1977–1989." PhD diss., Department of Sociology, University of Kansas.

———. 1995. "1987 nian de taiwan gonghui, guojia yu gongyun: yi yuanhua gonghui de gean weili" [Taiwan's unions, state, and labor movements in 1987: The case of Far Eastern Chemical Fiber Union]. In *Taiwan de guojia yu shehui* [Taiwan's state and society], ed. Cheng-Kuang Hsu and Hsin-Huang Michael Hsiao, 115–50. Taipei: San min Book.

Chen, Fang-Ming. 1996. *Xie xuehong pingchuan* [Biography of and comments on Xie Xuehong]. Taipei: Cian wei.

Chen, Tsui-Lien. 2013. *Bainian zhuiqiu: Taiwan minzhu yundong de gushi—zizhi de mengxiang* [One hundred years of longing: Stories of Taiwan's democratic movements: Vol. 1. Dreams of self-government]. Taipei: Acropolis.

Chen, Yi-chi, and Monina Wong. 2002. *New Bondage and Old Resistance: Realities and Challenges of the Labour Movement in Taiwan*. Hong Kong: Hong Kong Christian Industrial Committee.

Cheng, Lu-Lin. 1988. "Taiwan laodong tizhi xinggou de jiexi: lishi/jiegou de quxiang" [A dissection of Taiwan's labor regime: A historical/structural approach]. Master's thesis, Department of Sociology, National Taiwan University.

Cheng, Tun-Jen. 1989. "Democratizing the Quasi-Leninist Regime in Taiwan." *World Politics* 41, no. 4: 471–99.

China Times. 1965. "Beishi kongqi wuran chengdu yanzhong yingxiang renti jiankang" [Taipei's air pollution severely harms human health]. December 15.

———. 1970. "Wufeng jifeng shipinchang wushui sunji renchu" [Toxic liquids discharged by Chifong Food Co. harmful to humans and livestock]. July 26.

———. 1978. "Feiqi chenxi nanzi wuchangli: wubaiyu ren zhongdu yi buzhi" [Industrial exhaust hit Nan-zih: Five hundred intoxicated and one death]. November 25.

———. 1982a. "Baiyu zhongmen cunmin beishang chenqing, sanwei xuanjiang zhengxian daifu chezi" [Kaohsiung County Chungmen villagers petitioned to the legislative Yuan, asking to settle the pollution problem caused by Amino Acid Co.]. May 29.

———. 1982b. "Chouqi wushui hai wo duonian, cunmin jifen baofa, chongjin aminuosuan gongsi, po choushui hui jiqi" [Kaohsiung County Chungmen villagers surrounded Amino Acid Co. Ltd, smashing office and machines with clubs and rocks, protesting yearlong pollution and the agreement of factory relocation]. March 29.

———. 1982c. "Cunlizhang dangxuan mingdan" [List of village head-elects]. June 13.

———. 1982d. "Lese fengpo zaiqi: jingfang guanche qiangzhizhixing mingling, dayuan baiyu minzhong shenye dizhi" [Taoyuan County Dayuan town residents blocking roads to resist garbage invasion from Chungli]. August 31.

———. 1982e. "Shelun: paifang yanqi pei yibaiwushi wan—xinjian gonghai peichang chuangxia diyijian anli" [Editorial: Glad to see the first pollution compensation verdict, victims won 1.5 million]. January 4.

———. 1984. "Fandui zai dianzihu she lesechang, longtan jietou xuangua kangyi biaoyu" [Against sanitary landfill, streets in Longtan showed protest banners]. June 3.

———. 1985. "Quanmian changdao fanwuran shizihuiyuan dayouxing" [Lions Club members staged a parade against pollution]. October 9.

Cho, Hee-Yeon. 2000. "Democratic Transition and Changes in Korean NGOs." *Korea Journal* 40, no. 2: 275–304.

Cho, Hee-Yeon, and Eun Mee Kim. 1998. "State Autonomy and Its Social Conditions for Economic Development in South Korea and Taiwan." In *The Four Asian Tigers: Economic Development and the Global Political Economy*, ed. Eun Mee Kim, 125–58. San Diego: Academic Press.

Cho, Soon-Kyoung. 1987. *How Cheap Is "Cheap Labor"? The Dilemmas of Export-Led Industrialization*. PhD diss., Department of Sociology, University of California at Berkeley.

Cho, Young-rae. 2003. *A Single Spark: The Biography of Chun Tae-il*. Seoul: Dolbegae.

Choi, Jang-Jip. 1987. *Labor and the Authoritarian State: Labor Unions in South Korean Manufacturing Industries, 1961–1980*. Seoul: Korea University Press.

———. 2000. "Democratization, Civil Society, and the Civil Social Movement in Korea: The Significance of the Citizens' Alliance for the 2000 General Elections." *Korea Journal* 40, no. 3: 26–57.

Chosun Ilbo. 1998. "KCTU's Reversal." Editorial. February 10.

———. 2003. "Out to Ruin the Country?" November 11.

Chou, Chang-Hung, and Chien Yao. 1980. "Hongshulin de shengtai ji qi jiazhi, Kexue yuekan" [The ecology and value of mangroves]. *Kexue yuekan* [Science monthly], no. 131. http://163.27.3.193/Science/home/index.asp.

Chu, Yin-wah. 1995. *The Struggle for Democracy: A Comparative Study of Taiwan and South Korea*. PhD diss., Department of Sociology, University of California at Davis.

———. 1996. "Democracy and Organized Labor in Taiwan." *Asian Survey* 36, no. 5: 495–510.

———. 1998. "Labor and Democratization in South Korea and Taiwan." *Journal of Contemporary Asia* 28, no. 2: 185–202.

Chu, Yun-han. 1994. "Social Protests and Political Democratization in Taiwan." In *The Other Taiwan: 1945 to the Present,* ed. Murray A. Rubinstein, 99–113. Armonk, N.Y.: M. E. Sharpe.

Chun, Jennifer Jihye. 2009. *Organizing at the Margins: The Symbolic Politics of Labor in South Korea and the United States.* Ithaca, N.Y.: ILR Press.

Chun, Soonok. 2003. *They Are Not Machines: Korean Women Workers and Their Fight for Democratic Trade Unionism in the 1970s.* Burlington, Vt.: Ashgate.

Clawson, Dan. 2003. *The Next Upsurge: Labor and the New Social Movements.* Ithaca, N.Y.: Cornell University Press.

Cliffe, Lionel, and Richard Moorsom. 1979. "Rural Class Formation and Ecological Collapse in Botswana." *Review of African Political Economy* 15/16: 35–52.

Clifford, Mark. 1989. "A Nuclear Falling Out: Opposition Mounts to South Korea's Ambitious Reactor Programme." *Far Eastern Economic Review* 144, no. 20: 55–56.

———. 1990a. "Kicking Up a Stink: South Korean Government Reels from Anti-Pollution Backlash." *Far Eastern Economic Review* 150, no. 44: 72–73.

———. 1990b. "Pre-emptive Strike: Seoul Mobilises Police and Courts to Quell Labour Unions." *Far Eastern Economic Review* 148, no. 16: 74–75.

———. 1998. *Troubled Tiger: Businessmen, Bureaucrats, and Generals in South Korea.* Armonk, N.Y.: M. E. Sharpe.

Cohen, Jean L. 1985. "Strategy or Identity: New Theoretical Paradigm and Contemporary Social Movements." *Social Research* 52, no. 4: 663–716.

Cohen, Marc J. 1988. *Taiwan at the Crossroads: Human Rights, Political Development and Social Change on the Beautiful Island.* Washington, D.C.: Asia Resource Center.

Cole, Luke W., and Sheila R. Foster. 2001. *From the Ground Up: Environmental Racism and the Rise of the Environmental Justice Movement.* New York: New York University Press.

Collier, Ruth Berins, and David Collier. 1991. *Shaping the Political Arena: Critical Junctures, the Labor Movement, and Regime Dynamics in Latin America.* Princeton, N.J.: Princeton University Press.

Council of Labor Affairs. 1996. *Dangqian guonei laozi zhengyi qingshi fenxi baogao* [Report on current situations of labor disputes]. Taipei: Commissions of Labor Affairs, Executive Yuan, ROC.

———. 2003. *Jiushier nian laozi zhengyi qingshi fenxi baogao* [2003 report on current situations of labor disputes]. Taipei: Commissions of Labor Affairs, Executive Yuan, ROC.

Cress, Daniel M., and David A. Snow. 1996. "Mobilization at the Margins: Resources, Benefactors, and the Viability of Homeless Social Movement Organizations." *American Sociological Review* 66: 1088–109.

Croissant, Aurel. 2002. "Electoral Politics in South Korea." In *Electoral Politics in Southeast and East Asia,* ed. Aurel Croissant, 233–76. Bonn: Friedrich-Ebert-Stifung. http://library.fes.de/.

Cumings, Bruce. 2002. *The Origins of the Korean War.* Seoul: Yuksabipyungsa.

———. 2010. *The Korean War: A History.* New York: Random House.

Danzger, M. Herbert. 1975. "Validating Conflict Data." *American Sociological Review* 40, no. 5: 570–84.

della Porta, Donatella, and Dieter Rucht. 1995. "Left-Libertarian Movements in Context: A Comparison of Italy and West Germany, 1965–1990." In *The Politics of Social Protest: Comparative Perspectives on States and Social Movements,* ed. J. Craig Jenkins and Bert Klandermans, 229–72. Minneapolis: University of Minnesota Press.

Department of Statistics MEA. 1995. "Economic Statistics Annual, ROC." Taipei: Ministry of Economic Affairs, Executive Yuan, ROC.

Deyo, Frederic C. 1984. "Export Manufacturing and Labor: The Asian Case." In *Labor in the Capitalist World-Economy: Vol. 7. Political Economy of the World-System Annuals,* ed. Charles Bergquist, 267–88. Beverly Hills, Calif.: Sage.

———. 1989. *Beneath the Miracle: Labor Subordination in the New Asian Industrialism.* Berkeley: University of California Press.

———. 2012. *Reforming Asian Labor Systems: Economic Tensions and Worker Dissent.* Ithaca, N.Y.: Cornell University Press.

Diamond, Larry, and Doh Chull Shin. 2000. "Introduction: Institutional Reform and Democratic Consolidation in Korea." In *Institutional Reform and Democratic Consolidation in Korea,* ed. Larry Diamond and Doh Chull Shin, 1–41. Stanford, Calif.: Hoover Institution Press, Stanford University.

DiChiro, Giovanna. 1998. "Nature as Community: The Convergence of Environment and Social Justice." In *Privatizing Nature: Political Struggles for the Global Commons,* ed. Michael Goldman, 120–43. New Brunswick, N.J.: Rutgers University Press.

Directorate-General of Budget Accounting and Statistics. 2001–3. *Yearbook of Labor Statistics.* Taipei: DGBAS, Executive Yuan, ROC.

Djang, T. K. 1977. *Industry and Labor in Taiwan.* Taipei: The Institute of Economics, Academia Sinica.

Dzeng, Yi-Ren. 1994. "Labor Power and Political Change in Taiwan, 1945–1990." PhD diss., Department of Sociology, Johns Hopkins University.

Eagleton, Terry. 1991. *Ideology.* London: Verso.

Earl, Jennifer, Andrew Martin, John D. McCarthy, and Sarah A. Soule. 2004. "The Use of Newspaper Data in the Study of Collective Action." *Annual Review of Sociology* 30: 65–80.

Eckert, Carter J., Ki-baik Lee, Young Ick Lew, Michael Robinson, and Edward W. Wagner. 1990. *Korea Old and New: A History.* Seoul: Ilchokak.

Economic Daily. 1988. "Taoyuan keyun bagong, laozi jixu xieyi" [Taoyuan public transit workers on strike, negotiations continued]. February 15.

Eder, Norman. 1996. *Poisoned Prosperity: Development, Modernization, and the Environment in South Korea.* Armonk, N.Y.: M. E. Sharpe.

Eisinger, Peter K. 1973. "The Conditions of Protest Behavior in American Cities." *American Political Science Review* 67, no. 1: 11–28.

Engels, Friedrich. 1975. "The Condition of the Working-Class in England." In *Marx and Engels, Collected Works,* vol. 4, 295–583. New York: International.

Environmental Protection Administration. 2000. *Statistics of Environmental Pollution Abatement and Control Expenditures.* Taipei: EPA, Executive Yuan, ROC.

Escobar, Arturo. 1995. *Encountering Development: The Making and Unmaking of the Third World.* Princeton, N.J.: Princeton University Press.

Esping-Andersen, Gosta. 1985. "Power and Distributional Regimes." *Politics and Society* 14, no. 2: 223–56.

———. 2000. "Two Societies, One Sociology, and No Theory." *British Journal of Sociology* 51, no. 1: 59–77.

Esteva, Gustavo. 1992. "Development." In *The Development Dictionary: A Guide to Knowledge as Power,* ed. Wolfgang Sachs, 6–25. London: Zed Books.

Evans, Peter, ed. 2002. *Livable Cities: Urban Struggles for Livelihood and Sustainability.* Berkeley: University of California Press.

———. 2005. "Counterhegemonic Globalization: Transnational Social Movements in the Contemporary Global Political Economy." In *The Handbook of Political Sociology: States, Civil Societies, and Globalization,* ed. Thomas Janoski, Robert Alford, Alexander Hicks, and Mildred Schwartz, 655–70. Cambridge: Cambridge University Press.

Eyerman, Ron, and Andrew Jamison. 1991. *Social Movements: A Cognitive Approach.* University Park: Pennsylvania State University Press.

Fan, Ya-Jiun, ed. 2004. *Zhanhou taiwan laogong yundong shiliao huibian: juanyi, laogong zhengce yu faling* [Documentary collection on labor movement of postwar Taiwan: Vol. 1. Labor policy and laws]. Taipei: Academia Historica.

Fan, Yun. 2000. "Activists in a Changing Political Environment: A Microfoundational Study of Social Movements in Taiwan's Democratic Transition, 1980s–1990s." PhD diss., Department of Sociology, Yale University.

Fantasia, Rick. 1988. *Cultures of Solidarity: Consciousness, Action, and Contemporary American Workers.* Berkeley: University of California Press.

Fantasia, Rick, and Kim Voss. 2004. *Hard Work: Remaking the American Labor Movement.* Berkeley: University of California Press.

Ferguson, James. 1996. *The Anti-Politics Machine: Development, Depoliticization, and Bureaucratic Power in Lesotho.* Minneapolis: University of Minnesota Press.

Fields, Karl J. 1995. *Enterprise and the State in Korea and Taiwan.* Ithaca, N.Y.: Cornell University Press.

Flacks, Richard. 2004. "Knowledge for What? Thoughts on the State of Social Movement Studies." In *Rethinking Social Movements: Structure, Meaning, and*

Emotion, ed. Jeff Goodwin and James M. Jasper, 135–53. Lanham, Md.: Rowman and Littlefield.

Foster, John Bellamy. 2002. *Ecology against Capitalism.* New York: Monthly Review Press.

Freeman, Jo. 1975. *The Politics of Women's Liberation: A Case Study of an Emerging Social Movement and Its Relation to the Policy Process.* New York: Longman.

————. 1999. "On the Origins of Social Movements." In *Waves of Protest: Social Movements since the Sixties,* ed. Jo Freeman and Victoria Johnson, 7–24. Lanham, Md.: Rowman and Littlefield.

Friedmann, John, and Haripriya Rangan, eds. 1993. *In Defense of Livelihood: Comparative Studies on Environmental Action.* West Hartford, Conn.: Kumarian Press.

Gamson, William A. 1975. *The Strategy of Social Protest.* Homewood, Ill.: Dorsey Press.

Gates, Hill. 1979. "Dependence and the Part-Time Proletariat in Taiwan." *Modern China* 5, no. 3: 381–408.

Gerlach, Luther P. 1999. "The Structure of Social Movements: Environmental Activism and Its Opponents." In *Waves of Protest: Social Movements since the Sixties,* ed. Jo Freeman and Victoria Johnson, 85–97. Lanham, Md.: Rowman and Littlefield.

Gerlach, Luther P., and Virginia H. Hine. 1970. *People, Power, Change: Movements of Social Transformation.* Indianapolis, Ind.: Bobbs-Merrill Educational.

Gille, Zsuzsa. 2002. "Social and Spatial Inequalities in Hungarian Environmental Politics: A Historical Perspective." In *Livable Cities? Urban Struggles for Livelihood and Sustainability,* ed. Peter Evans, 132–61. Berkeley: University of California Press.

Gitlin, Todd. 1980. *The Whole World Is Watching: Mass Media in the Making and Unmaking of the New Left.* Berkeley: University of California Press.

Gold, Thomas. 1986. *State and Society in the Taiwan Miracle.* New York: M. E. Sharpe.

Goodwin, Jeff. 2001. *No Other Way Out: States and Revolutionary Movements, 1945–1991.* Cambridge: Cambridge University Press.

————. 2012. "Conclusion: Are Protestors Opportunists? Fifty Tests." In *Contention in Context: Political Opportunities and the Emergence of Protest,* ed. Jeff Goodwin and James M. Jasper, 277–300. Stanford, Calif.: Stanford University Press.

Goodwin, Jeff, and James M. Jasper. 1999. "Caught in a Winding, Snarling Vine: The Structural Bias of Political Process Theory." *Sociological Forum* 14, no. 1: 27–54.

Gouldner, Alvin. 1979. *The Future of Intellectuals and the Rise of the New Class.* New York: Continuum.

Gramsci, Antonio. 1971. *Selections from the Prison Notebooks.* New York: International.

———. 1978. "Some Aspects of the Southern Question." In *Selections from Political Writings 1921–1926,* 441–62. New York: International.

Gray, Kevin. 2008. *Korean Workers and Neoliberal Globalization.* London: Routledge.

Grundmann, Reiner. 1991. "The Ecological Challenge to Marxism." *New Left Review* 187: 103–20.

Guha, Ramachandra. 2000. *The Unquiet Woods: Ecological Change and Peasant Resistance in the Himalaya.* Berkeley: University of California Press.

Habermas, Jurger. 1981. "New Social Movements." *Telos* 49: 33–37.

Haggard, Stephan. 1990. *Pathways from the Periphery: The Politics of Growth in the Newly Industrializing Countries.* Ithaca, N.Y.: Cornell University Press.

Haggard, Stephan, and Chung-in Moon. 1993. "The State, Politics, and Economic Development in Postwar South Korea." In *State and Society in Contemporary Korea,* ed. Hagen Koo, 51–93. Ithaca, N.Y.: Cornell University Press.

Hankyoreh. 2005. "KCTU Must Recover from Aftermath of Violence." Editorial. February 3.

———. 2011. "Kim Jin-suk Returns after a 309-Day Miracle on the Precipice." November 11.

———. 2013a. "Unprecedented Hardline on Striking Railroad Workers." December 11.

———. 2013b. "Workers in Ulsan End 296-Day Aerial Protest at Hyundai Factory." August 9.

———. 2014. "The Constitutional Court's Deadly Blow against South Korean Democracy." December 20.

Hankyoreh 21. 2004. "Imggeumtujaengeul neomeo sahoegaehyeokeuro" [A wage struggle toward social reform]. 507: 32–33.

Hapdong News Agency. 1979. *Korea Annual 1979.* Seoul: Hapdong News Agency.

Hart-Landsberg, Martin. 1993. *The Rush to Development: Economic Change and Political Struggle in South Korea.* New York: Monthly Review Press.

Hartmann, Heidi. 1981. "The Unhappy Marriage of Marxism and Feminism: Toward a More Progressive Union." In *Women and Revolution: A Discussion of the Unhappy Marriage of Marxism and Feminism,* ed. Lydia Sargent, 1–41. Montreal: Black Rose Books.

Hasegawa, Koichi. 2014. "The Fukushima Nuclear Accident and Japan's Civil Society: Context, Reactions, and Policy Impacts." *International Sociology* 29, no. 4: 283–301.

Hay, Peter. 2002. *Main Currents in Western Environmental Thought.* Sydney: University of New South Wales.

Haydu, Jeffrey. 1988. *Between Craft and Class: Skilled Workers and Factory Politics in the United States and Britain, 1890–1922.* Berkeley: University of California Press.

Heirich, Max. 1971. *The Spiral of Conflict: Berkeley, 1964.* New York: Columbia University Press.

Herkenrath, Mark, and Alex Knoll. 2011. "Protest Events in International Press Coverage: An Empirical Critique of Cross-National Conflict Databases." *International Journal of Comparative Sociology* 52, no. 3: 163–80.

Ho, Ming-sho. 2000. "Minzhu zhuanxing guocheng zhong de guojia yu minjian-shehui: yi taiwan de huanjing yundong weili (1986–1998)" [The state and civil society in the process of democratic transition: Taiwan's environmental movement 1986–1998]. PhD diss., Department of Sociology, National Taiwan University.

———. 2001. "Taiwan huanjing yundong de kaiduan: zhuanjia xuezhe, dangwai yu caogen (1980–1986)" [The origin of Taiwan's environmental movement: Experts, opposition, grassroots 1980–1986]. *Taiwan shehueixue* [Taiwanese sociology] 2: 97–162.

———. 2003. "Minjian shehui yu minzhu zhuanxing: huanjing yundong zai taiwan de xingqi yu chixu" [Civil society and democratic transition: The rise and sustainability of the environmental movement in Taiwan]. In *Liangan shehuiyundong fenxi* [Analyses of cross-strait social movements], ed. Mau-Kuei Chang and Yung-Nian Cheng, 29–67. Taipei: New Naturalism.

———. 2014. "The Fukushima Effect: Explaining the Resurgence of the Anti-Nuclear Movement in Taiwan." *Environmental Politics* 23, no. 6: 965–83.

Ho, Samuel P. S. 1979. "Decentralized Industrialization and Rural Development: Evidence from Taiwan." *Economic Development and Cultural Change* 28, no. 1: 77–96.

———. 1982. "Economic Development and Rural Industry in South Korea and Taiwan." *World Development* 10, no. 11: 973–90.

Ho, Shuet-Ying, et al. 1990. *Taiwan, after a Long Silence: The Emerging New Unions of Taiwan.* Hong Kong: Asia Monitor Research Center.

Hobsbawm, Eric. 1962. *The Age of Revolution 1789–1848.* Cleveland, Ohio: World.

———. 1967. *Labouring Men: Studies in the History of Labour.* New York: Anchor Books.

Hong, Sung Woong. 1997. "Seoul: A Global City in a National of Rapid Growth." In *Emerging World Cities in Pacific Asia,* ed. Fu-chen Lo and Yue-man Yeung, 144–78. Tokyo: United Nations University Press.

Hou, Jeffrey. 2001. "Grassroots Practice of Environmental Planning: Enabling Community Actions toward Local Environmental Sustainability in Taiwan." PhD diss., Department of Environmental Planning, University of California at Berkeley.

Hsiao, Hsin-Huang Michael. 1988. *Qiling niandai fanwuran zilijiuji de jiegou yu guocheng fenxi* [Anti-pollution self-help protests in the 1980s: An analysis of structures and processes]. Taipei: Environmental Protection Agency, Executive Yuan.

———. 1992. "The Labor Movement in Taiwan: A Retrospective and Prospective Look." In *Taiwan: Beyond the Economic Miracle,* ed. Denis Fred Simon and Michael Y. M. Kau, 151–67. New York: M. E. Sharpe.

———. 1994. "Taiwan minzhong dui shehuiyundong de lejie yu zhichi: bian yu bubian" [The Taiwanese people's understanding of and support for social movements: Changes and invariance]. In *Taiwan minzhong de shehui yixiang: shehui kexue de fenxi* [The social image of Taiwan: Social science approaches], ed. Chin-Chun Yi, 41–64. Taipei: Sun Yat-Sen Institute for Social Sciences and Philosophy, Academia Sinica.

———. 1997. *Yige jinzhang de gongsheng guanxi: huanbao xingzheng jiguan yu minjian tuanti de hezuo guanxi* [A symbiotic relationship with tension: The relationship between EPA and local environmental groups]. Taipei: Environmental Protection Administration, Republic of China.

———. 1999. "Environmental Movements in Taiwan." In *Asia's Environmental Movements: Comparative Perspectives,* ed. Yok-shiu F. Lee and Alvin Y. So, 31–54. Armonk, N.Y.: M. E. Sharpe.

———. 2002. "Taiwan de difang huanbao yundong (1980–2000): lishi yu kongjian de bijiao fenxi" [Taiwan's local environmental movement (1980–2000): A historical-spatial comparison]. *Yongxu taiwan jianxun* [Sustainable Taiwan] 4, no. 2: 34–68.

———. 2011. "Social Movements in Taiwan: A Typological Analysis." In *Social Movements: Power, Protest, and Change in a Dynamic Region,* ed. Jeffrey Broadbent and Vickie Brockman, 237–54. New York: Springer.

Hsiao, Hsin-Huang Michael, Yo-Ping Cheng, and Joanna Lei. 1982. *Taiwan de xiaofeizhe yundong: lilun yu shiji* [Taiwan's consumer movement: Theory and practice]. Taipei: China Time.

Hsiao, Hsin-Huang Michael, Lester W. Milbrath, and Robert P. Weller. 1995. "Antecedents of an Environmental Movement in Taiwan." *Capitalism, Nature, Socialism* 6, no. 3: 91–104.

Huang, Chang-Ling. 1999. "Labor Militancy and the Neo-mercantilist Development Experience: South Korea and Taiwan in Comparison." PhD diss., Department of Political Science, University of Chicago.

———. 2002. "The Politics of Reregulation: Globalization, Democratization, and the Taiwanese Labor Movement." *Developing Economies* 40, no. 3: 305–26.

———. 2003. "Zhongxin guanzhi de zhengzhi: quanqiuhua yu minzhuhua xia de taiwan laogong yundong" [Re-regulated politics: Taiwan's labor movement under globalization and democratization]. In *Liangan shehuiyundong fenxi*

[Analysis of cross-strait social movements], ed. Mau-Kuei Chang and Yung-Nian Cheng, 69–94. Taipei: New Naturalism.

Huffman, James L. 2004. *Modern Japan: A History in Documents*. New York: Oxford University Press.

Hug, Simon, and Dominique Wisler. 1998. "Correcting for Selection Bias in Social Movement Research." *Mobilization: An International Journal* 3, no. 2: 141–61.

Hung, Ho-fung, and Iam-chong Ip. 2012. "Hong Kong's Democratic Movement and the Making of China's Offshore Civil Society." *Asian Survey* 52, no. 3: 504–27.

Hutter, Swen. 2014. "Protest Event Analysis and Its Offspring." In *Methodological Practices in Social Movement Research*, ed. Donatella Della Porta, 335–67. Oxford: Oxford University Press.

Im, Hyug Baeg. 2011. "The Origins of the Yushin Regimes: Machiavelli Unveiled." In *The Park Chung Hee Era: The Transformation of South Korea*, ed. Byung-Kook Kim and Ezra F. Vogel, 233–61. Cambridge, Mass.: Harvard University Press.

Industrial Development Bureau MEA. 1997. *Gongyequ kaifaquanli: bashiwuniandu nianbao* [1996 annual report of the development and management of industrial parks]. Taipei: Industrial Development Bureau, Ministry of Economic Affairs, ROC.

Isaac, Larry, and Lars Christiansen. 2002. "How the Civil Rights Movement Revitalized Labor Militancy." *American Sociological Review* 67: 722–46.

Jamison, Andrew, Ron Eyerman, and Jacqueline Cramer. 1990. *The Making of the New Environmental Consciousness: A Comparative Study of the Environmental Movements in Sweden, Denmark, and the Netherlands*. Edinburgh: Edinburgh University Press.

Japan Economic Newswire. 1988. "Railway Workers Stage Taiwan's First Strike." May 1.

Jasper, James M. 1997. *The Art of Moral Protest: Culture, Biography, and Creativity in Social Movements*. Chicago: University of Chicago Press.

Jaung, Hoon. 2000. "Electoral Politics and Political Parties." In *Institutional Reform and Democratic Consolidation in Korea*, ed. Larry Diamond and Doh Chull Shin, 43–71. Stanford, Calif.: Hoover Institute Press, Stanford University.

Jenkins, J. Craig, and Charles Perrow. 1977. "Insurgency of the Powerless: Farm Worker Movements (1946–1972)." *American Sociological Review* 42: 249–68.

Jeong, Hoi-Seong, and Deokho Cho. 2002. "From Confrontation to Partnership: Urban Environmental Governance in Korea, the Evolution of Citizen Participation in Metropolitan Ulsan." *International Review of Public Administration* 7, no. 2: 55–69.

Johnson, Kevin R., and Bill Ong Hing. 2007. "The Immigrant Rights Marches of 2006 and the Prospects for a New Civil Rights Movement." *Harvard Civil Rights–Civil Liberties Law Review* 42: 99–138.

Jones, Carol. 2014. "Lost in China? Mainlandisation and Resistance in Post-1997 Hong Kong." *Taiwan in Comparative Perspective* 5: 21–46.

Ju, Chang Bum. 2011. "The Consequences of Government Funding for Environmental NGOs in South Korea." In *South Korean Social Movements: From Democracy to Civil Society,* ed. Gi-Wook Shin and Paul Y. Chang, 135–50. London: Routledge.

Jung, Young-Tae. 2000. "Labor Movement and Democracy in the Age of Global Neoliberalism: The Case of Korea." *Korea Journal* 40, no. 2: 248–74.

Katzenstein, Mary Fainsod. 1987. "Introduction: Comparing the Feminist Movements of the United States and Western Europe: An Overview." In *The Women's Movements of the United States and Western Europe: Consciousness, Political Opportunity, and Public Policy,* ed. Mary Fainsod Katzenstein and Carol McClurg Mueller, 1–20. Philadelphia: Temple University Press.

Katznelson, Ira. 1986. "Working-Class Formation: Constructing Cases and Comparisons." In *Working-Class Formation: Nineteenth-Century Patterns in Western Europe and the United States,* ed. Ira Katznelson and Aristide R. Zolberg, 3–41. Princeton, N.J.: Princeton University Press.

Keck, Margaret. 1995. "Social Equity and Environmental Politics in Brazil: Lessons from the Rubber Tapers of Acre." *Comparative Politics* 27, no. 4: 409–24.

———. 2002. "'Water, Water, Everywhere, nor Any Drop to Drink': Land Use and Water Policy in Sao Paulo, Brazil." In *Livable Cities? Urban Struggles for Livelihood and Sustainability,* ed. Peter Evans, 162–94. Berkeley: University of California Press.

Keck, Margaret, and Kathryn Sikkink. 1998. *Activists beyond Borders: Advocacy Networks in International Politics.* Ithaca, N.Y.: Cornell University Press.

Kim, Eun Mee, and Gil-Sung Park. 2011. "The Chaebol." In *The Park Chung Hee Era: The Transformation of South Korea,* ed. Byung-Kook Kim and Ezra F. Vogel, 265–94. Cambridge, Mass.: Harvard University Press.

Kim, Jin Kyoon. 2000. "Rethinking the New Beginning of the Democratic Union Movement in Korea: From the 1987 Great Workers' Struggle to the Construction of the Korean Trade Union Council (Chunnohyup) and the Korean Confederation of Trade Unions (KCTU)." *Inter-Asia Cultural Studies* 1, no. 3: 491–502.

Kim, Mikyoung. 2003. "South Korean Women Workers' Labor Resistance in the Era of Export-oriented Industrialization." *Development and Society* 32, no. 1: 77–101.

Kim, Se-Kyun. 1994. "Kim Young Same Regime and the Labor Movement." Paper presented at the sixteenth congress of the International Political Science Association, Berlin.

Kim, Seung-Kyung. 1997. *Class Struggle or Family Struggle? The Lives of Women Factory Workers in South Korea.* Cambridge: Cambridge University Press.

Kim, Sunhyuk. 2000. "Democratization and Environmentalism: South Korea and Taiwan in Comparative Perspective." *Journal of Asian and African Studies* 35, no. 3: 287–302.

———. 2003. "Civil Society in Democratizing Korea." In *Korea's Democratization*, ed. Samuel S. Kim, 81–106. Cambridge: Cambridge University Press.

———. 2011. "Democratization and Social Movements in South Korea: A Civil Society Perspective." In *East Asian Social Movements: Power, Protest, and Change in a Dynamic Region*, ed. Jeffrey Broadbent and Vickie Brockman, 141–56. New York: Springer.

Kitschelt, Herbert P. 1986. "Political Opportunity Structures and Political Protest: Anti-Nuclear Movements in Four Democracies." *British Journal of Political Science* 16, no. 1: 57–85.

Koo, Hagen. 1990. "From Farm to Factory: Proletarianization in Korea." *American Sociological Review* 55: 669–81.

———. 1993. "The State, Minjung, and the Working Class in South Korea." In *State and Society in Contemporary Korea*, ed. Hagen Koo, 131–62. Ithaca, N.Y.: Cornell University Press.

———. 2001. *Korean Workers: The Culture and Politics of Class Formation*. Ithaca, N.Y.: Cornell University Press.

Koopmans, Ruud. 1993. "The Dynamics of Protest Waves: West Germany, 1965 to 1989." *American Sociological Review* 58, no. 5: 637–58.

Koopmans, Ruud, and Dieter Rucht. 2002. "Protest Event Analysis." In *Methods of Social Movement Research*, ed. Bert Klandermans and Suzanne Staggenborg, 231–59. Minneapolis: University of Minnesota Press.

Koopmans, Ruud, Paul Statham, Marco Giugni, and Florence Passy. 2005. *Contested Citizenship: Immigration and Cultural Diversity in Europe*. Minneapolis: University of Minnesota Press.

Korea Herald. 1990. "Anmyon Protesters' Fever Quelled as Government Pledges to Cancel Facility." November 10.

———. 2003a. "Koreans Less Tolerant of Union Actions." August 7.

———. 2003b. "Troubled Foreign Firms." September 3.

———. 2004. "Old Flea Market Goes with the Flow: 'Dokkaebi' Finds New Stadium Home." March 19.

Korea Times. 1970. "Sweatshop Worker Tries Fiery Suicide." November 14.

———. 1974. "Arbor Day Observed: Park Plants Trees." April 7.

———. 1977. "Park Asks People Join 'Protect Nature' Drive." November 6.

———. 1978. "President Engages in Forestation Work." November 5.

———. 1981a. "Due to Pollution, 90,000 Ulsan Citizens to Shift Residences." February 24.

———. 1981b. "Police Request Arrest of 11 Sit-in Workers." February 2.

————. 1982. "Compensation for Pollution Demanded." April 25.

————. 1987. "Police Interrogators Will Be Quizzed on Student's Death." January 17.

————. 1988. "Residents Near 3 Nuclear Power Plants Demonstrate." December 6.

————. 1990a. "Anmyon Island Residents Protest Radioactive Waste Storage Plan." November 7.

————. 1990b. "Law Restored in Riot-Hit Anmyon Island, Government Scraps Nuclear Waste Storage Plan." November 10.

————. 1990c. "Protests against N-Waste Storage Get Violent, Score of People Injured in Clash with Police." November 9.

————. 2005. "Internal Strife Rocks Key Labor Group." February 2.

Korean Confederation of Trade Unions. 2001. *1970–2000 Minjunojo tujaeongkwa tanap ui yeoksak* [The history of democratic unions' struggles and repression]. Seoul: Toseochulpan hyeonjongeseo miraeleul.

Kornhauser, William. 1959. *The Politics of Mass Society.* Glencoe, Ill.: Free Press.

Korpi, Walter. 1974. "Conflict, Power and Relative Deprivation." *American Political Science Review* 68, no. 4: 1569–78.

Korpi, Walter, and Michael Shalev. 1979. "Strikes, Industrial Relations and Class Conflict in Capitalist Societies." *British Journal of Sociology* 30, no. 2: 164–87.

Kriesi, Hanspeter. 1989. "New Social Movements and the New Class in the Netherlands." *American Journal of Sociology* 94, no. 5: 1078–116.

Kriesi, Hanspeter, Ruud Koopmans, Jan Willem Duyvendak, and Marco G. Giugni. 1995. *New Social Movements in Western Europe: A Comparative Analysis.* Minneapolis: University of Minnesota Press.

Ku, Dowan. 1996a. *Hanguk Hwankyeong Undong ui Sahoehak* [Sociology of Korea's environmental movement]. Seoul: Munhakkwachisosa.

————. 1996b. "The Structural Change of the Korean Environmental Movement." *Korea Journal of Population and Development* 25, no. 1: 155–80.

————. 2011. "The Korean Environmental Movement: Green Politics through Social Movement." In *East Asian Social Movements: Power, Protest, and Change in a Dynamic Region*, ed. Jeffrey Broadbent and Vickie Brockman, 205–29. New York: Springer.

Kuo, Kuo-Wen. 2003. "Minzhuhua shiqi de guojia yu gongyun (1993–2000)" [The state and labor movements in the era of democratization, 1993–2000]. MA thesis, Graduate Institute of National Development, National Taiwan University.

Kurzman, Charles. 1996. "Structural Opportunity and Perceived Opportunity in Social-Movement Theory: The Iranian Revolution of 1979." *American Sociological Review* 61: 153–70.

Kyunghyang Shinmun. 2014. "What the Results of the 'One Less Nuclear Power Plant' Initiative Signify." Editorial. August 23.

Lang, Kurt, and Gladys Engel Lang. 1961. *Collective Dynamics.* New York: Thomas Y. Crowell.

Lay, Long-Fei. 1992. "Taiwan de xuanju zhidu yu toupiao xingwei" [Taiwan's electoral system and voting behavior]. In *Zhonghuaminguo minzhuhua: guocheng, zhidu yu yingxiang* [Democratization in Republic of China: Process, institutionalization, and impact], ed. Ching-Yu Chang, 225–41. Taipei: National Cheng-Chi University, Institute of International Relations.

Le Bon, Gustave. 1982. *The Crowd: A Study of the Popular Mind.* 2nd ed. Atlanta, Ga.: Cherokee.

Lee, Ching-Kwan. 2007. *Against the Law: Labor Protests in China's Rustbelt and Sunbelt.* Berkeley: University of California Press.

Lee, Jian-Chang. 1991. "80 niandai de taiwan laogong yundong: jiegou yu guocheng de fenxi" [Taiwan's labor movement in the 1980s: An analysis of structure and process]. MA thesis, Department of Sociology, National Taiwan University.

Lee, Namhee. 2001. "Making Minjung Subjectivity: Crisis of Subjectivity and Rewriting History, 1960–1988." PhD diss., Department of History, University of Chicago.

———. 2005. "Representing the Worker: The Worker–Intellectual Alliance of the 1980s in South Korea." *Journal of Asian Studies* 64, no. 4: 911–37.

———. 2011. "From Minjung to Simin: The Discursive Shift in Korean Social Movements." In *South Korean Social Movements: From Democracy to Civil Society,* ed. Gi-Wook Shin and Paul Y. Chang, 41–57. London: Routledge.

Lee, See-jae. 2000. "Environmental Movement in Korea and Its Political Empowerment." *Korea Journal* 40, no. 3: 131–60.

Lee, Su-Hoon. 1999. "Environmental Movements in South Korea." In *Asia's Environmental Movements,* ed. Yok-shiu F. Lee and Alvin Y. So, 90–119. Armonk, N.Y.: M. E. Sharpe.

Lee, Su-Hoon, and David A. Smith. 1999. "The Emergence of South Korean Environmental Movements: A Response (and Challenge?) to Semiperipheral Industrialization." In *Ecology and the World-System,* ed. Walter L. Goldfrank, David Goodman, and Andrew Szasz, 235–55. Westport, Conn.: Greenwood Press.

Lee, Yok-Shiu F., and Alvin Y. So, eds. 1999. *Asia's Environmental Movements.* Armonk, N.Y.: M. E. Sharpe.

Lee, Yoonkyung. 2006. "Varieties of Labor Politics in Northeast Asian Democracies: Political Institutions and Union Activism in Korea and Taiwan." *Asian Survey* 46, no. 5: 721–40.

———. 2009. "Divergent Outcomes of Labor Reform Politics in Democratized Korea and Taiwan." *Studies in Comparative International Development* 44, no. 1: 47–70.

———. 2011. *Militants or Partisans: Labor Unions and Democratic Politics in Korea and Taiwan.* Stanford, Calif.: Stanford University Press.

Li, Yun-Jie. 1992. *Taiwan gonghui zhengce de zhengzhi jingji fenxi* [A political economic analysis of Taiwan's union policies]. Taipei: Ju-Liu.

Lieberson, Stanley. 1985. *Making It Count: The Improvement of Social Research and Theory.* Berkeley: University of California Press.

Lieberson, Stanley, and Arnold R. Silverman. 1965. "The Precipitants and Underlying Conditions of Race Riots." *American Sociological Review* 30, no. 6: 887–98.

Lii, Ding-tzann, and Wen-yuan Lin. 2000. "Shehuili de wenhua genyuan: lun huanjingquan ganshou zai taiwan de lishi xingcheng; 1970–86" [The cultural origins of social forces: The historical formation of perception of environmental rights in Taiwan; 1970–86]. *Taiwan shehui yanjiu jikan* [Taiwan: A radical quarterly in social studies] 38: 133–206.

Lim, Hy-Sop. 2000. "Historical Development of Civil Social Movements in Korea: Trajectories and Issues." *Korea Journal* 40, no. 3: 5–25.

Lim, Hyun-Chin, and Byung-Kook Kim. 1994. "Labor and Democratization in Korea: A Search for a Social Pact." In *Korea in the Global Wave of Democratization,* ed. Doh Chull Shin, Myeong-Han Zoh, and Myung Chey, 205–31. Seoul: Seoul National University Press.

Lin, Li-ying. 2007. "Taoyuan gongyefazhan yu Taoyuan shehuibianqian: yijiuliuliu-nian-yijiujiuliunian" [Taoyuan's industrial development and social change]. Master's thesis, Department of Mechanical Engineering, National Central University.

Lin, Thung-Hong. 2000. *Dapan wei zunyan: datong gonghui fendou shi* [Struggles for dignity: History of Da-Tung Trade Union]. Taipei: Taiwan Labor Front.

Lipset, Seymour Martin. 1959. "Some Social Requisites of Democracy: Economic Development and Political Legitimacy." *American Political Science Review* 53, no. 1: 69–105.

Lipsky, Michael. 1968. "Protest as a Political Resource." *American Political Science Review* 62, no. 4: 1144–58.

Liu, Hwa-Jen. 2010. "Taiwan yijiuqiling niandai de laodong kangzheng chutan" [On Taiwan's labor protests in the 1970s]. *Taiwan minzhu jikan* [Taiwan journal of democracy] 7, no. 1: 31–63.

———. 2011. "Xiaoshi de nongyumin: zhongtan taiwan zaoqi huanjing kangzheng" [Vanishing farmers: Taiwan's early environmental protests revisited]. *Taiwan shehueixue* [Taiwanese sociology] 21: 1–49.

Liu, Hwa-Jen, and Yeyong Choi. 2004. "The role of environmental NGOs in implementing environmental justice: Taiwan and South Korea compared." Paper presented at ISA RC24 Conference on Globalization, Localization, and Environment, Seoul National University.

Lopez, Steven H. 2004. *Reorganizing the Rust Belt: An Inside Study of the American Labor Movement.* Berkeley: University of California Press.

Loveman, Mara. 1998. "High-Risk Collective Action: Defending Human Rights in Chile, Uruguay, and Argentina." *American Journal of Sociology* 104, no. 2: 477–525.

Lukes, Steven. 2005. *Power: A Radical View.* 2nd ed. New York: Palgrave Macmillan.

Ma, Yi-Kung. 1980. "Hongshulin de baohu yu guihua" [Protection and planning of Mangrove Swamp]. *Kexue yuekan* [Science monthly], no. 131. http://163.27.3.193/Science/home/index.asp.

Magdoff, Fred, and John Bellamy Foster. 2011. *What Every Environmentalist Needs to Know about Capitalism: A Citizen's Guide to Capitalism and the Environment.* New York: Monthly Review Press.

Markoff, John. 1996. *The Abolition of Feudalism: Peasants, Lords and Legislators in the French Revolution.* University Park: Pennsylvania State University Press.

Martinez-Alier, Joan. 2002. "The Environmentalism of the Poor." Paper presented at Political Economy of Sustainable Development: Environmental Conflict, Participation, and Movements, United Nations Research Institute for Social Development and University of Witwatersrand, Johannesburg.

Mason, Robert J. 1999. "Whither Japan's Environmental Movement? An Assessment of Problems and Prospects at the National Level." *Pacific Affairs* 72, no. 2: 187–207.

McAdam, Doug. 1988. *Freedom Summer.* New York: Oxford University Press.

———. 1995. "'Initiator' and 'Spin-off' Movements: Diffusion Processes in Protest Cycles." In *Repertoires and Cycles of Collective Action,* ed. Mark Traugott, 217–39. Durham, N.C.: Duke University Press.

———. 1999a. "The Biographical Impact of Activism." In *How Social Movements Matter,* ed. Marco Giugni, Doug McAdam, and Charles Tilly, 117–46. Minneapolis: University of Minnesota Press.

———. 1999b. *Political Process and the Development of Black Insurgency, 1930–1970.* 2nd ed. Chicago: University of Chicago Press.

McBeath, Gerald A., and Tse-Kang Leng. 2006. *Governance of Biodiversity Conservation in China and Taiwan.* Cheltenham, U.K.: Edward Elgar.

McCarthy, John D., and Mayer N. Zald. 1987a. "Resource Mobilization and Social Movements: A Partial Theory." In *Social Movements in an Organizational Society,* ed. Mayer N. Zald and John D. McCarthy, 15–28. New Brunswick, N.J.: Transaction.

———. 1987b. "The Trend of Social Movements in America: Professionalization and Resource Mobilization." In *Social Movements in an Organizational Society,* ed. Mayer N. Zald and John D. McCarthy, 337–91. New Brunswick, N.J.: Transaction.

McGurty, Eileen Maura. 2000. "Warren County, NC and the Emergence of the Environmental Justice Movement: Unlikely Coalitions and Shared Meaning in Local Collective Action." *Society and Natural Resources* 13, no. 4: 373–87.

McKean, Margaret A. 1981. *Environmental Protest and Citizen Politics in Japan.* Berkeley: University of California Press.

Mechanic, David. 1962. "Sources of Power of Lower Participants in Complex Organizations." *Administrative Science Quarterly* 7, no. 3: 349–64.

Melucci, Alberto. 1985. "The Symbolic Challenge of Contemporary Movements." *Social Research* 52, no. 4: 789–816.

———. 1996. *Challenging Codes: Collective Action in the Information Age.* Cambridge: Cambridge University Press.

Meyer, David S., and Nancy Whittier. 1994. "Social Movement Spillover." *Social Problems* 41, no. 2: 277–98.

Michels, Robert. 1962. *Political Parties: A Sociological Study of the Oligarchical Tendencies of Modern Democracy.* New York: Free Press.

Miliband, Ralph. 1989. *Divided Societies: Class Struggle in Contemporary Capitalism.* Oxford: Oxford University Press.

Mill, John Stuart. 2002. *A System of Logic: Ratiocinative and Inductive.* Honolulu: University Press of the Pacific.

Min sheng bao [Min Sheng daily]. 1988. "Huoche tingkai, tielu shi shang touyizao: jiusier ci lieche, zuo jin kaichu liushier ban, jintian qingkuang ruhe, tieluju hai meiyou bawo" [Railways came to a halt, first time ever in history: Only 62 out of 942 trains were on duty yesterday, the Taiwan Railways Administration did not know if it will resume normal today]. May 2.

Minkoff, Debra C. 1997. "The Sequencing of Social Movements." *American Sociological Review* 62: 779–99.

Minns, John, and Robert Tierney. 2003. "The Labour Movement in Taiwan." *Labour History* 80: 103–28.

Mirowski, Philip, and Dieter Plehwe, eds. 2009. *The Role from Mont Pelerin: The Making of the Neoliberal Thought Collective.* Cambridge, Mass.: Harvard University Press.

Mitchell, Dave Oswald. 2009. "Teamsters and Turtles: The Rise of the Planetariat." *Briarpatch,* November/December. http://briarpatchmagazine.com/.

Moon, Chung-in, and Sung-hack Lim. 2003. "Weaving through Paradoxes: Democratization, Globalization, and Environmental Politics in South Korea." *East Asian Review* 15, no. 2: 43–70.

Moore, Barrington, Jr. 1966. *Social Origins of Dictatorship and Democracy.* Boston: Beacon Press.

———. 1978. *Injustice: The Social Bases of Obedience and Revolt.* New York: M. E. Sharpe.

Moore, Jonathan. 1988. "Protests in This Green and Poisoned Land." *Far Eastern Economic Review* 139, no. 8: 44–45.

Moore, Mick. 1988. "Economic Growth and the Rise of Civil Society: Agriculture in Taiwan and South Korea." In *Developmental States in East Asia,* ed. Gordon White, 113–52. London: Macmillan Press.

Moore, Phoebe V. 2007. *Globalisation and Labour Struggle in Asia: A Neo-Gramscian Critique of South Korea's Political Economy.* London: Tauris Academic Studies.

Morris, Aldon. 1984. *The Origins of the Civil Rights Movement: Black Communities Organizing for Change.* New York: Free Press.

Morris, Aldon, and Naomi Braine. 2001. "Social Movements and Oppositional Consciousness." In *Oppositional Consciousness: The Subjective Roots of Social Protest,* ed. Jane Mansbridge and Aldon Morris, 20–37. Chicago: University of Chicago Press.

Mueller, Carol. 1997. "International Press Coverage of East German Protest Events, 1989." *American Sociological Review* 62: 820–32.

Nam, Sang-Woo, and Se-Jong Kim. 1999. "Evaluation of Korea's Exchange Rate Policy." In *Changes in Exchange Rates in Rapidly Developing Countries: Theory, Practice, and Policy Issues,* ed. Takatoshi Ito and Anne O. Krueger, 235–68. Chicago: University of Chicago Press.

Nelson, Richard R. 1995. "Recent Evolutionary Theorizing about Economic Change." *Journal of Economic Literature* 33, no. 1: 48–90.

New York Times. 1998a. "Key South Korean Union Calls Off Strike." February 13.

———. 1998b. "Layoff Pact Rejected." February 10.

———. 2012. "Thousands Protest China's Plans for Hong Kong Schools." July 30.

———. 2014a. "Pro-Democracy Group Shifts to Collaborate with Student Protesters in Hong Kong." September 28.

———. 2014b. "Crackdown on Protests by Hong Kong Police Draws More to the Streets." September 29.

Obach, Brian K. 2004. *Labor and the Environmental Movement: The Quest for Common Ground.* Cambridge, Mass.: MIT Press.

Oberschall, Anthony. 1973. *Social Conflict and Social Movements.* Englewood Cliffs, N.J.: Prentice Hall.

O'Connor, James. 1998. *Natural Causes: Essays in Ecological Marxism.* New York: Guilford Press.

Offe, Claus. 1985. "New Social Movements: Challenging the Boundaries of Institutional Politics." *Social Research* 52, no. 4: 817–68.

Offe, Claus, and Helmut Wiesenthal. 1980. "Two Logics of Collective Action: Theoretical Notes on Social Class and Organizational Form." In *Political Power and Social Theory,* ed. Maurice Zeitlin, 67–115. Greenwich, Conn.: JAI Press.

Ogle, George. 1990. *South Korea: Dissent within the Economic Miracle.* London: Zed Books.

Oliver, Pamela E., and Gregory M. Maney. 2000. "Political Processes and Local Newspaper Coverage of Protest Events: From Selection Bias to Triadic Interactions." *American Journal of Sociology* 106, no. 2: 463–505.

Oliver, Pamela E., and Daniel J. Myers. 1999. "How Events Enter the Public Sphere: Conflict, Location, and Sponsorship in Local Newspaper Coverage of Public Events." *American Journal of Sociology* 105, no. 1: 38–87.

Olzak, Susan. 1989a. "Analysis of Events in the Study of Collective Action." *Annual Review of Sociology* 15: 119–41.

————. 1989b. "Labor Unrest, Immigration, and Ethnic Conflict in Urban America, 1880–1914." *American Journal of Sociology* 94, no. 6: 1033–333.

O'Rourke, Dara. 2002. "Community-Driven Regulation: Toward an Improved Model of Environmental Regulation in Vietnam." In *Livable Cities? Urban Struggles for Livelihood and Sustainability,* ed. Peter Evans, 95–131. Berkeley: University of California Press.

Ortiz, David G., Daniel J. Myers, Eugene N. Walls, and Maria-Elena D. Diza. 2005. "Where Do We Stand with Newspaper Data?" *Mobilization: An International Journal* 10, no. 3: 397–419.

Paige, Jeffery M. 1975. *Agrarian Revolution.* New York: Free Press.

Payne, Charles M. 1995. *I've Got the Light of Freedom: The Organizing Tradition and the Mississippi Freedom Struggle.* Berkeley: University of California Press.

Peluso, Nancy Lee. 1992. *Rich Forests, Poor People: Resource Control and Resistance in Java.* Berkeley: University of California Press.

Pepper, David. 1993. *Eco-socialism: From Deep Ecology to Social Justice.* London: Routledge.

Pichardo, Nelson A. 1997. "New Social Movements: A Critical Review." *Annual Review of Sociology* 23: 411–30.

Pierson, Paul. 2000. "Increasing Returns, Path Dependence, and the Study of Politics." *American Political Science Review* 94, no. 2: 251–67.

Piven, Frances Fox, and Richard A. Cloward. 1979. *Poor People's Movements: Why They Succeed, How They Fail.* New York: Vintage Books.

————. 1992. "Normalizing Collective Protest." In *Frontiers in Social Movement Theory,* ed. Aldon D. Morris and Carol McClurg Mueller, 301–25. New Haven, Conn.: Yale University Press.

Polanyi, Karl. 2001. *The Great Transformation.* 2nd ed. Boston: Beacon Press.

Przeworski, Adam. 1985. *Capitalism and Social Democracy.* Cambridge: Cambridge University Press.

Ragin, Charles. 1987. *The Comparative Method: Moving beyond Qualitative and Quantitative Strategies.* Berkeley: University of California Press.

Rangan, Haripriya. 2004. "From Chipko to Uttaranchal: The Environment of Protest and Development in the Indian Himalaya." In *Liberation Ecologies: Environment,*

Development, Social Movements, ed. Richard Peet and Michael Watts, 371–93. London: Routledge.

Rathzel, Nora, and David Uzzell. 2011. "Trade Unions and Climate Change: The Jobs versus Environmental Dilemma." *Global Environmental Change* 21, no. 4: 1215–23.

———, eds. 2012. *Trade Unions in the Green Economy: Working for the Environment.* London: Routledge.

Ray, Raka. 1998. "Women's Movements and Political Fields: A Comparison of Two Indian Cities." *Social Problems* 45, no. 1: 21–36.

———. 1999. *Fields of Protest: Women's Movements in India.* Minneapolis: University of Minnesota Press.

Reardon-Anderson, James. 1992. *Pollution, Politics, and Foreign Investment in Taiwan: The Lukang Rebellion.* Armonk, N.Y.: M. E. Sharpe.

Reporters without Borders. n.d. "World Press Freedom Index." http://www.rsf.org.

Rose, Fred. 2000. *Coalitions across the Class Divide: Lessons from the Labor, Peace, and Environmental Movements.* Ithaca, N.Y.: Cornell University Press.

Rucht, Dieter. 1996. "The Impact of National Contexts on Social Movement Structures: A Cross-Movement and Cross-National Comparison." In *Comparative Perspectives on Social Movements,* ed. Doug McAdam, John D. McCarthy, and Mayer N. Zald, 185–204. Cambridge: Cambridge University Press.

Scalapino, Robert A., and Chong-Sik Lee. 1972. *Communism in Korea Part I: The Movement.* Berkeley: University of California Press.

Schwartz, Michael. 1976. *Radical Protest and Social Structure: The Southern Farmers' Alliance and Cotton Tenancy, 1888–1890.* Chicago: University of Chicago Press.

Scott, James C. 1985. *Weapons of the Weak: Everyday Forms of Peasant Resistance.* New Haven, Conn.: Yale University Press.

Seidman, Gay W. 1994. *Manufacturing Militance: Workers' Movements in Brazil and South Africa, 1970–1985.* Berkeley: University of California Press.

Sharp, Gene. 1973. *The Politics of Nonviolent Action Part One: Power and Struggle.* Boston: Porter Sargent.

Shieh, Gwo-shyong. 1990. "Manufacturing 'Bosses': Subcontracting Networks under Dependent Capitalism in Taiwan." PhD diss., Department of Sociology, University of California at Berkeley.

———. 1997. *Chun laodong: Taiwan laodong tizhi zhulun* [Labor only: Essays on the labor regime in Taiwan]. Taipei: Institute of Sociology, Academia Sinica.

Shin, Gi-Wook, and Paul Y. Chang, eds. 2011. *South Korean Social Movements: From Democracy to Civil Society.* London: Routledge.

Shin, Gi-Wook, Paul Y. Chang, Jung-eun Lee, and Sookyung Kim. 2007. *South Korea's Democracy Movement (1970–1993): Stanford Korea Democracy Project*

Report. Stanford, Calif.: Shorenstein Asia Pacific Research Center, Stanford University. http://iis-db.stanford.edu/.

———. 2011. "The Korean Democracy Movement: An Empirical Overview." In *South Korean Social Movements: From Democracy to Civil Society,* ed. Gi-Wook Shin and Paul Y. Chang, 21–40. London: Routledge.

Shin, Kwang-Yeong. 2003. "Democratization and the Capitalist Class in South Korea." *Korean Journal of Political Economy* 1, no. 1: 131–75.

———. 2006. "The Citizens' Movement in Korea." *Korea Journal* 46, no. 2: 5–34.

———. 2010. "Globalisation and the Working Class in South Korea: Contestation, Fragmentation and Renewal." *Journal of Contemporary Asia* 40, no. 2: 211–29.

Shorter, Edward, and Charles Tilly. 1974. *Strikes in France 1830–1968.* London: Cambridge University Press.

Silver, Beverly J. 2003. *Forces of Labor: Workers' Movements and Globalization since 1870.* Cambridge: Cambridge University Press.

Skocpol, Theda. 1979. *States and Social Revolutions: A Comparative Analysis of France, Russia, and China.* Cambridge: Cambridge University Press.

Smelser, Neil J. 1963. *Theory of Collective Behavior.* New York: Free Press.

Smith, Ted, David A. Sonnenfeld, and David Naguib Pellow, eds. 2006. *Challenging the Chip: Labor Rights and Environmental Justice in the Global Electronics Industry.* Philadelphia: Temple Univeristy Press.

Snyder, David, and William R. Kelly. 1977. "Conflict Intensity, Media Sensitivity and the Validity of Newspaper Data." *American Sociological Review* 42: 105–23.

Song, Ho-Keun. 1994. "Working-Class Politics in Reform Democracy in South Korea." *Korea Journal of Population and Development* 23, no. 2: 157–77.

———. 1996. "State and Wage Policy: Implications for Corporatism." *Korea Journal of Population and Development* 25, no. 2: 269–86.

———. 2000. "State and Labor under the Park Chung Hee Regime." Paper presented at the Conference on Park Chung Hee Revisited, Korea University, Seoul.

Sonn, Hochul. 1997. "The 'Late Blooming' of the South Korean Labor Movement." *Monthly Review* 49, no. 3: 117–29.

Staggenborg, Suzanne. 1988. "The Consequences of Professionalization and Formalization in the Pro-Choice Movement." *American Sociological Review* 53: 585–606.

Suh, Doowon. 1998. "From Individual Welfare to Social Change: The Expanding Goals of Korean White-Collar Labor Unions, 1987–1995." PhD diss., Department of Sociology, University of Chicago.

Sun, Paul M. H., Ronald D. Knutson, and Yuan-ho Lee. 1998. "Transition and Reform of China's Agricultural System toward a Market-Oriented Economy: Lessons from the Taiwan Experience." Paper presented at Agriculture and Sustainable Development: China and Its Trading Partners, College Station, Tex.

Susuki, Akira. 2013. "Factors Promoting and Constraining the 'Blue-Green Coalition' in the Case of Minamata: Analysis of the Union–Social Movement Coalition in the Struggle against Chisso." Paper presented at the Conference on the Role of Organized Labor in Civil Society in East Asia: Comparisons between Korea, Taiwan, and Japan, Hosei University, Tokyo.

Szasz, Andrew. 1994. *Ecopopulism: Toxic Waste and the Movement for Environmental Justice.* Minneapolis: University of Minnesota Press.

Taipei Times. 2000. "Aborigines Agree to National Park in Cypress Forest." December 21.

———. 2014a. "Ministry, Former Hualon Workers Finally Strike Deal." November 27.

———. 2014b. "Former Toll Workers Block Freeway, Climb Gantries." November 29.

Tang, Shui-Yan, and Ching-Ping Tang. 1997. "Democratization and Environmental Politics in Taiwan." *Asian Survey* 37, no. 3: 281–94.

Tanuro, Daniel. 2013. *Green Capitalism: Why It Can't Work.* London: Merlin Press.

Tarrow, Sidney. 1988. "National Politics and Collective Action: Recent Theory and Research in Western Europe and the United States." *Annual Review of Sociology* 14: 421–40.

———. 1989. *Struggle, Politics, and Reform: Collective Action, Social Movements, and Cycles of Protest.* Ithaca, N.Y.: Cornell University.

———. 1994. *Power in Movement: Social Movements, Collective Action, and Politics.* Cambridge: Cambridge University Press.

———. 1996. "States and Opportunities: The Political Structuring of Social Movements." In *Comparative Perspectives on Social Movements: Political Opportunities, Mobilizing Structures, and Cultural Framings,* ed. Doug McAdam, John D. McCarthy, and Mayer N. Zald, 41–61. Cambridge: Cambridge University Press.

Taylor, Verta. 1989. "Social Movement Continuity: The Women's Movement in Abeyance." *American Sociological Review* 54: 761–75.

Terao, Tadayoshi. 2002. "An Institutional Analysis of Environmental Pollution Disputes in Taiwan: Cases of 'Self-Relief.'" *Developing Economies* 40, no. 3: 284–304.

Therborn, Goran. 1980. *The Ideology of Power and the Power of Ideology.* London: Verso.

Thompson, E. P. 1966. *The Making of the English Working Class.* New York: Vintage Books.

———. 1995. *The Poverty of Theory: Or An Orrery of Errors.* London: Merlin Press.

Tilly, Charles. 1978. *From Mobilization to Revolution.* New York: McGraw-Hill.

———. 1995. *Popular Contention in Great Britain 1758–1834.* Cambridge, Mass.: Harvard University Press.

———. 2004. *Social Movement, 1768–2004.* Boulder, Colo.: Paradigm.

Tilly, Charles, Louise Tilly, and Richard Tilly. 1975. *The Rebellious Century 1830–1930.* London: J. M. Dent.

Touraine, Alain. 1981. *The Voice and the Eye: An Analysis of Social Movements.* Cambridge: Cambridge University Press.

———. 1985. "An Introduction to the Study of Social Movements." *Social Research* 52, no. 4: 749–87.

Tseng, Hua-pi. 2008. "Taiwan de huanjing zhili (1950–2000): jiyu shengtai xiandaihua yu shengtai guojia lilun de fenxi, Taiwanshi yanjiu" [Environmental governance in Taiwan (1950–2000): An analytical study in the light of ecological modernization and eco state theory]. *Taiwanshih yanjiu* [Taiwan historical research] 15, no. 4: 121–48.

Tung, Chuan-Chuan. 1996. "The Rise and Fall of the Labor Movement in Taiwan: A Historical-Structural Approach." PhD diss., Department of Sociology, University of Georgia.

Turner, Ralph H., and Lewis M. Killian. 1957. *Collective Behavior.* Englewood Cliffs, N.J.: Prentice Hall.

United Daily. 1951. "Gongkuang jiancha weiyuanhui shangtao kuangchang anquan" [The Committe of Factory and Mine Inspection convened to discuss workplace safety issues]. October 4.

———. 1964. "Sauchu fanai beishi jinbu de sanda bingliu" [Getting rid of three major tumors against Taipei's progress]. April 20.

———. 1965. "Fei buneng ye shi buwei ye! Women dui jiejue kongqi han heshui wuranwenti de kanfa" [Not because you can't but because you don't do it! Our thoughts on solving air and water pollution]. September 23.

———. 1967. "Gaishan taisheng shuizhi wuran, shiwei zhuanjia tichu jianyi: xu xian cong xindianxi zhuoshou jinxing, zhongshi gongye feiwu jianchu gongzuo" [WHO expert's proposal to lessen water pollution: Starting from Hsindian Creek, pay attention to reduction of industrial pollution]. December 15.

———. 1971a. "Jiaqiang fazhan jingji maoyi, zhengfu yanni gezhong fangan" [To enhance economy and trade, government proposed various action plans]. November 18.

———. 1971b. "Weichi jingji chengzhang, dakai guoji shichang" [Maintain economic growth, explore international market]. November 9.

———. 1978. "Liangbaiyu ren choujin outu: yisheng zhenduan jieguo shi qinghuawu zhongdu" [Over two hundred suffered from cramp and emesis: Doctors' diagnosis, intoxication of hydride]. November 25.

———. 1979. "Shiyou zhong jiaru duolulianben, shiyong hou yinqi pifu guaibing" [Cooking oil added PCBS led to unknown skin diseases]. October 7.

———. 1980a. "Heneng dianchang anquan, zhengfu jiwei zhongshi" [In response to legislator interrogation, the government said it was concerned with the safety issues of nuclear power plants]. May 20.

———. 1980b. "Zhou qingyu de zhuxuanyuan zhizhai heneng fadianchang" [Chow Ching-Yu's staff criticized nuclear power plants]. November 27.

———. 1982a. "Hefeiliao chucun anquan cuoshi, cai zanxiong yaoqiu xiangxi shuoming" [Legislator Cai Zanxiong demands nuclear safety measures]. April 29.

———. 1982b. "Weishengshu jiang jiji yanding huanjing yingxiang pinggu zhidu" [The Department of Health works on establishing the system of environmental impact assessment]. January 7.

———. 1983. "Baohu shengtai fangzhi wuran, jingxuan renshi pubian guanqie" [Ecological conservation and pollution prevention became general concerns of electoral contenders]. November 24.

———. 1984a. "Guangfu yilai zuida kuangzai, yilingyi ren sangsheng: lan zhouquan yu wu aling, yiran xianshen kuangkeng nei" [The worst coal mine accident since 1945: 101 deaths, two workers still trapped in the tunnel]. July 13.

———. 1984b. "Haishan meikuang qiangjiu gao yi duanluo, zuihou yi ming linan kuanggong wachu. Zaibian siwang renshu gongji qishisi (74) ren, aixin juankuan zuo yi yu wuqiansibaiwan (54,000,000) yuan" [Haishan coal mine accident. 74 deaths, charity donation over 54 million new Taiwan dollars]. July 6.

———. 1985. "Fandui xingjian hesichang, liwei shenglang bi de jin" [Opposition to the fourth nuclear power plant from legislators]. April 9.

———. 1988a. "520 shijian 115 ren shoushang: jingfang daibu baishier ming zishi xianfan, jing jianfang zhenxun hou shouya jiushiliu ren" [May 20th incident: 115 hospitalized, 112 arrested, 96 interrogated]. May 22.

———. 1988b. "Bu shangdao? Qing zoulu! Miaoli keyun jiegu ersiwu (245) ren: lianxu kuangzhi san ri yishang tingzhi laobao yifa mianzhi" [Maoli bus fired 245 workers who have not report to work for three days]. August 10.

———. 1988c. "Jiantao 520 shijian: dajia dou tongxin, bixu zhaochu zhumouzhe shengzhiyufa" [Reflecting on the 520 incident: Everyone is sad, must find and prosecute the masterminds]. May 26.

———. 1988d. "Shanwei xieyishu" [Shanwei's compensation agreement signed]. October 16.

———. 1988e. "Shanwei yugang jingjian siyu wushu: huaiyi wuran shuichang paifang feishui budang zhaohuo, baiyu yumin kangyi weiguo, jin xu you xingdong" [Shanwei Port found countless dead fishes: Residents suspected illegal discharge of waste water; hundreds of fishermen protested]. September 23.

———. 1988f. "Yijia buchang jisjiwan bi qian dao liuhele hai shuang" [Each household received hundreds of thousands of new Taiwan dollars as damage compensation, better than winning the lottery]. October 16.

———. 1988g. "Yuanfang xinpu chang xin jian fenghuiluzhuan; ouliwang dianji qian ren daigong kangyi" [FECF controversy, optimistic turn; Oliwon Electronic Engineering, thousands of workers slowed down in protest]. February 11.

———. 1989. "Juzhi yezhe shengyuan yuanfang, xiayue si mian jia bu diaozheng" [Support Far Eastern Textile, no price increase on chemical fiber materials in June]. May 18.

———. 1990. "Zilijiuji bushi huanbao yundong" [Self-help protests are not environmental movements]. February 24.

———. 1996a. "Gongzuo bei wailao qiangguang le! Shei lai tongqing women zhequn oubasang? Zhongnian shiye laogong daochu fanwan beiqing" [Immigrant workers took our jobs! Who pities us middle-aged ladies? Middle-aged unemployed workers voiced their sadness]. April 10.

———. 1996b. "Lianfu yuangong lan huoche, yidu zuduan tielu jiaotong" [Unemployed Lianfu workers occupied rail tracks, traffic was blocked]. December 21.

———. 2000. "Luzhuli nongzuo peichang fangshi jin xietiao" [How to compensate for Luzhuli's crop damage, negotiations begin today]. September 1.

Valenzuela, J. Samuel. 1989. "Labor Movements in Transitions to Democracy: A Framework for Analysis." *Comparative Politics* 21, no. 4: 445–72.

Van Dyke, Nella, and Holly J. McCammon, eds. 2010. *Strategic Alliances: Coalition Building and Social Movements.* Minneapolis: University of Minnesota Press.

Voss, Kim. 1993. *The Making of American Exceptionalism: The Knights of Labor and Class Formation in the Nineteenth Century.* Ithaca, N.Y.: Cornell University Press.

Voss, Kim, and Rachel Sherman. 2000. "Breaking the Iron Law of Oligarchy: Union Revitalization in the American Labor Movement." *American Journal of Sociology* 106, no. 2: 303–49.

Wade, Robert. 1990. *Governing the Market: Economic Theory and the Role of Government in East Asian Industrialization.* Princeton, N.J.: Princeton University Press.

Wakabayashi, Masahiro. 2007. *Taiwan kangri yundongshi yanjiu* [Study on Taiwan's anticolonial movements]. Taipei: Bozhongzhewenhua.

Wallerstein, Immanuel. 2012. "Upsurge in Movements around the Globe." In *We Are Many: Reflections on Movement Strategy from Occupation to Liberation,* ed. Kate Khatib, Margaret Killjoy, and Mike McGuire, 105–12. Oakland, Calif.: AK Press.

Walsh, Bryan. 2007. "Lee Myung Bak: Renouncing Seoul's Polluted Past, He Showed Cities around the World a Greener Path to Development." *Time* 170, no. 17: 41.

Walsh, Edward J. 1981. "Resource Mobilization and Citizen Protest in Communities around Three Mile Island." *Social Problems* 29, no. 1: 1–21.

Wang, Jenn-hwan. 1989. "Taiwan de zhengzhi zhuanxing yu fandui yundong" [Political transition and oppositional movement in Taiwan]. *Taiwan shehui yanjiu jikan* [Taiwan: A radical quarterly in social studies] 2, no. 1: 71–116.

Wang, Jenn-hwan, and Xiau-ding Fang. 1992. "Guojia jiqi, laogong zhengce yu laogong yundong" [State, labor policies, and labor movement]. *Taiwan shehui yanjiu jikan* [Taiwan: A radical quarterly in social studies] 13: 1–29.

Wang, Nei-Sin, ed. 1989. *Taiwan shehuiyundong shi* [History of social movements in Taiwan 1913–1936]. 5 vols. Taipei: Chuang Zao.

Wang, Yi-Fong. 2009. "20 nian lai tou yi zao: laodongdang gao weikai dangxuan xinzhuxian yiyuan, Kulaowang" [First time in twenty years, Gao Wei-Kai of the Labor Party elected Hsinchu County councilman]. *Kulaowang* [Coolloud]. http://www.coolloud.org.tw/.

Waters, Sarah. 2008. "Situating Movements Historically: May 1968, Alain Touraine, and New Social Movement Theory." *Mobilization: An International Journal* 13, no. 1: 63–82.

Weber, Max. 1949. "'Objectivity' in Social Science and Social policy." In *The Methodology of the Social Sciences,* ed. Edward A. Shils and Henry A. Finch, 49–112. New York: Free Press.

Webster, Edward, Rob Lambert, and Andries Bezuidenhout. 2008. *Grounding Globalization: Labour in the Age of Insecurity.* Malden, Mass.: Blackwell.

Wei, Shu-Er. 1987. "Taiwan fangonghai xingdong de shehuixue fenxi" [A sociological analysis of Taiwan's antipollution activism]. MA thesis, Department of Sociology, National Taiwan University.

Weller, Robert P. 2006. *Discovering Nature: Globalization and Environmental Culture in China and Taiwan.* New York: Cambridge University Press.

Weller, Robert P., and Hsin-Huang Michael Hsiao. 1998. "Culture, Gender and Community in Taiwan's Environmental Movement." In *Environmental Movements in Asia,* ed. Arne Kalland and Gerard Persoon, 83–109. Surrey, UK: Cuzon Press.

Western, Bruce. 1997. *Between Class and Market: Postwar Unionization in the Capitalist Democracies.* Princeton, N.J.: Princeton University Press.

Whang, In-Joung. 2001. "Administration of Land Reform in Korea, 1949–1952." In *The Korean Economy: Reflections at the New Millennium,* ed. Korean National Commission for UNESCO, 3–28. Elizabeth, N.J.: Hollym.

Wickham-Crowley, Timothy P. 1992. *Guerrillas and Revolution in Latin America: A Comparative Study of Insurgents and Regimes since 1956.* Princeton, N.J.: Princeton University Press.

Williams, Raymond. 1986. *Marxism and Literature.* Oxford: Oxford University Press.

Willis, Paul. 1977. *Learning to Labour: Why Working Class Kids Get Working Class Jobs.* Farnborough, U.K.: Saxon House.

Wilson, James Q. 1961. "The Strategy of Protest: Problems of Negro Civic Action." *Journal of Conflict Resolution* 5, no. 3: 291–303.

Wolf, Eric R. 1968. *Peasant Wars of the Twentieth Century.* New York: Harper and Row.

World Bank. 1993. *The East Asian Miracle: Economic Growth and Public Policy.* New York: Oxford University Press.

Wright, Erik Olin. 2000. "Working-Class Power, Capitalist-Class Interests, and Class Compromise." *American Sociological Review* 105: 957–1002.

Wu, Jieh-min. 1990. "Zhengti zhuanxingqi de shehui kangyi: Taiwan 1980 niandai" [Social protests in polity transition: Taiwan 1980s]. MA thesis, Department of Political Science, National Taiwan University.

———. 2002. "Jiechu kelaoseweizi de mozhou: fenxi taiwan dangqian shehui gaige yundong de kunjing" [Clausewitzian disenchantment: An analysis of the predicament of current social reform movements]. *Taiwan shehueixue* [Taiwanese sociology] 4: 159–98.

Wu, Naiteh. 1987. "The Politics of a Regime Patronage System: Mobilization and Control within an Authoritarian Regime." PhD diss., Department of Political Science, University of Chicago.

Wu, Naiteh, and Tun-Jen Cheng. 2011. "Democratization as a Legitimacy Formula: The KMT and Political Change in Taiwan." In *Political Legitimacy in Asia: New Leadership Challenges,* ed. John Kane, Hui-Chieh Loy, and Haig Patapan, 239–60. New York: Palgrave.

Wu, Naiteh, and Jin-guei Liao. 1991. "Diguo dafanji: jiegu gongyun ganbu, laozi guanxifa he jieji chongtu" [The empire struck back: Sacking union activists, labor–capital relations laws, and class conflict]. Paper presented at Laodong shichang yu laozi guanxi yantaohui [Symposium of labor market and capital–labor relations], Research Center for Humanities and Social Science, Academia Sinica, Taipei.

Younis, Mona. 2001. *Liberation and Democratization: The South African and Palestinian National Movements.* Minneapolis: University of Minnesota Press.

Yu, Hyunseog. 1995. "Capitalism, the new world economy, and labor relations: Korean labor politics in comparative perspective." PhD diss., Department of Political Science, Northwestern University.

Zald, Mayer N. 1987. "The Future of Social Movements." In *Social Movements in an Organizational Society,* ed. Mayer N. Zald and John D. McCarthy, 319–36. New Brunswick, N.J.: Transaction.

Zhao, Dingxin. 2001. *The Power of Tiananmen: State–Society Relations and the 1989 Beijing Student Movement.* Chicago: University of Chicago Press.

Index

activism, during the Japanese colonial period, 43, 55, 182n1
AFL-CIO, 184n8
agriculture, 2, 7, 63–64, 67, 73–74, 97, 179n5; difference between Taiwanese and Korean, 85, 184n13
Anmyon antinuclear protest, 122
Anti-Communist Law, 184n12
antinuclear movements, 18, 20, 23; in Korea, 122, 126, 146–47; nuclear waste dumping, 52; in Taiwan, 96, 100, 151, 153–54, 167
antipollution movements, 2–3, 54, 94–98, 100–101; farmers and, 26–27, 43–44, 52, 74, 86–88, 95; in Korea, 11, 43–47, 52, 78, 86–88, 120–23, 146–49; local elections and, 94–95, 97–101, 106–7, 165; out-migration of pollution victims and, 86, 88; public opinion and, 16, 52, 76, 97–101, 149, 154; relocation of polluting facilities and, 78; in Taiwan, 2–3, 42, 48, 52, 73–76, 89–91, 94–102, 144–45

Asian-American Free Labor Institute, 80
authoritarian regimes, 6, 41–42, 91, 160, 165, 177; Achilles's heels of, 13, 91, 162–63; exclusionist control and, 11, 76; incorporationist control and, 67, 70, 73, 76, 89, 93–94, 162; Korea's military junta and, 2, 11, 66, 77, 82, 94, 111–12, 117, 176; Taiwan's party-state and, 66, 68–72, 74, 132. *See also* Kuomintang

caogen, 52
chaebol, 59, 64, 183n5; labor protests against, 90–91, 111, 119, 133–36, 138–40, 142–43, 185n5; pollution cases and, 88, 123–25, 148; think tanks funded by, 148
Cheonggyecheon case in Seoul, 151
Cheonggye Garment Workers Union, 81
Chiang, Kai-shek, 67, 182n1
China, 67, 77, 101–2, 138, 154, 165
Chinese Federation of Labor, 103

HWA-JEN LIU is associate professor of sociology at National Taiwan University.

Paul K   o Jim inde
                          o States update   relford v. art
                                                        (colonial)

Vision for   Statewide prwct
Parity for   adjuncts   CFR
        Defined benefit   pensins

Andrea — only other organizer
         in building w/ a spreadsheet

Built network to around 20 engaged
       grad employees + working to
       shift culture   pattern of industrialization
                          econ + ideol always
                          present (33)

Disruption us coersion
        $, coersion, persuasion, position, (wise inaction)

Achilles heal (study targets, interactions)

Mills for my dissertation
(Current labor — idedogical (but historically
                                    true?)
p 80 - No way out   * p 66   FLSA
                          ★ p sales
                             communism

Notes for diss proposal   p 57 ambiguous
        dept regulations   repression
        incorporate Finn notes
           ⊡ Duv's law
           ⊡ clarify 3rd party v. labor party v. Socialism
           ⊡ incorporate JM reading
               ⊡ party identification

Concentric   early riser?
power   movements ∘
circles